SEEKING HUMAN RIGHTS JUSTICE IN LATIN AMERICA

This book studies how victims of human rights violations in Latin America, their families, and their advocates work to overcome entrenched impunity and seek legal justice. Their struggles show that legal justice is a multifaceted process, the overarching purpose of which is to restore human dignity and prevent further violence. Uncovering, revealing, and proving the truth are essential elements of legal justice, and are also powerful tools to activate the process. When faced with stubborn impunity at home, victims, families, and advocates can carry on their work for legal justice by bringing cases in courts in other countries or in the inter-American human rights system. These extra-territorial courts can jump-start the process of legal justice at home. *Seeking Human Rights Justice in Latin America* examines the political and legal struggle through the lens of the human story at the heart of these cases.

Jeffrey Davis is chair and associate professor in the Political Science Department at the University of Maryland Baltimore County (UMBC). He has taught human rights law, international law, constitutional law, and comparative law for more than ten years and has won several teaching awards. He is the author of *Justice across Borders: The Struggle for Human Rights in U.S. Courts* (Cambridge University Press 2008), and has published articles on human rights accountability, the inter-American human rights system, and judicial decision making. Research for this book was conducted in part while serving as a visiting scholar at the University for Peace in San Jose, Costa Rica, site of the Inter-American Court of Human Rights.

Seeking Human Rights Justice in Latin America

TRUTH, EXTRA-TERRITORIAL COURTS, AND THE PROCESS OF JUSTICE

Jeffrey Davis

University of Maryland, Baltimore County

CAMBRIDGE
UNIVERSITY PRESS

CAMBRIDGE
UNIVERSITY PRESS

32 Avenue of the Americas, New York, NY 10013-2473, USA

Cambridge University Press is part of the University of Cambridge.

It furthers the University's mission by disseminating knowledge in the pursuit of education, learning, and research at the highest international levels of excellence.

www.cambridge.org
Information on this title: www.cambridge.org/9780521514361

© Jeffrey Davis 2014

First published 2014

Printed in the United States of America

A catalog record for this publication is available from the British Library.

Library of Congress Cataloging in Publication data
Davis, Jeffrey, 1967–
Seeking human rights justice in Latin America : truth, extra-territorial courts, and the process of justice / Jeffrey Davis, University of Maryland, Baltimore County.
    pages   cm
Includes bibliographical references and index.
ISBN 978-0-521-51436-1 (hardback)
1. International human rights courts – Latin America.   I. Title.
KG574.D38   2013
341.4′8–dc23   2013014272

ISBN 978-0-521-51436-1 Hardback

To my father, Robert W. Davis

CONTENTS

ACKNOWLEDGMENTS

I am extremely grateful to Kate Doyle at the National Security Archive for sharing her expertise, and to her colleagues for making millions of documents available to researchers, advocates, and the public. I am deeply thankful to Wendy Méndez, Oscar Reyes, Cecilia Moran Santos, and Juan Romagoza, who have shared their experiences seeking justice. I also thank Olger González at the Inter-American Court of Human Rights, Almudena Bernabeu at the Center for Justice and Accountability, Roxanna Altholz at the Berkeley School of Law Human Rights Clinic, Soraya Long at the Center for Justice and International Law, and Adrianna Beltran at the Washington Office for Latin America. Without their knowledge, this research would not have been possible. I very much appreciate the help of my current and former students, Edward H. Warner, Micaela Perez Ferrero, and Morgan Vierling. I am grateful to Professor Daniel Whelan for his insightful critiques of an earlier version of this research. Last but certainly not least, I would like to thank my wife, Katie, for her tireless help and support.

1 BUILDING JUSTICE FROM TRUTH – THE PROCESS BEGINS

THE CASE OF THE JESUITS

Justice follows a twisted path from the boiling up of criminal intent, to the act of violence, through a thicket of impunity, emerging into a small clearing of truth, and then venturing off again to more obscure destinations of accountability, deterrence, and reconciliation. On a cool November day in 2009, inside the National Court Building in Madrid, Spain, American researcher Kate Doyle explained to Spanish judge Eloy Velasco how declassified U.S. Central Intelligence Agency (CIA) documents linked former Salvadoran President Alfredo Cristiani and fourteen members of his high command to the murders of six Jesuit priests, their housekeeper, and the housekeeper's sixteen-year-old daughter. Ms. Doyle was an expert witness called by the San Francisco-based Center for Justice and Accountability (CJA) to support its effort to convince Judge Velasco to open a criminal case against Cristiani and his officers for murders committed twenty years earlier in El Salvador.

How U.S. lawyers and witnesses found themselves in Madrid thousands of miles and twenty years removed from the murders in El Salvador is the story of legal justice. This justice must be understood for what it is – a process – and not just a result. It does not stop with the denial, amnesty law, or pardon. It is not encompassed in the guilty verdict, prison sentence, or truth commission report. Legal justice is the *process* that can lead to those results, and it is the *process* that follows them. Revealing the truth, increasingly through original documents like the intelligence communiqués upon which the story of the Jesuits in this chapter is based, catalyzes this process. Justice is the process that can overthrow the cycle of violence and must, if it is to be meaningful, restore at least a measure of human dignity.

"Kill Father Ellacuría and leave no witnesses." Colonel Emilio Ponce gave this order at a secret meeting of military commanders on November 15, 1989.[1] As a prominent Jesuit priest, philosopher, and author and the rector of the Central American University (UCA), Father Ellacuría played a crucial role in El Salvador's peace process. At a peace march just eight months earlier, he had spoken to the crowds, telling them, "We need to work for peace from the perspective of the suffering of the orphans and widows, and the tragedy of the assassinated and disappeared."[2]

Ellacuría formed a link between members of the Farabundo Martí National Liberation Front (FMLN) rebels and the government. According to a secret cable from the CIA in El Salvador obtained by a U.S. nongovernmental organization (NGO) called the National Security Archive, six weeks before November 15 the FMLN had asked Ellacuría to arrange negotiations between its representatives and members of the El Salvadoran military (see Figure 1.1).[3] He had approved of the "five friends" who would represent the FMLN and had contacted military officials seeking representatives. On November 15, the day Colonel Ponce gave the order to have Ellacuría killed, Ellacuría had reported to the FMLN that "arrangements seemed to be going well."[4] Because they were coming days after the FMLN had launched a major offensive on San Salvador, the negotiations were urgent. One of the FMLN demands noted by the CIA cable was the removal from leadership positions of members of the Salvadoran military who were part of the Tandona class in military college. Colonel Ponce had graduated first in the Tandona class.

---

[1] UN Security Council, Annex, *From Madness to Hope: The 12-Year War in El Salvador: Report of the Commission on the Truth for El Salvador*, S/25500, 1993, 5–8. IV, B, 1.

[2] Roger S. Gottlieb, *Liberating Faith: Religious Voices for Justice, Peace, and Ecological Wisdom* (Lanham, MD: Rowman and Littlefield Publishers, Inc.), 229.

[3] Central Intelligence Agency, Secret Cable, Murder of Father Ignacio Ellacuría, document obtained by the National Security Archive, *El Salvador: War, Peace, and Human Rights, 1980–1994*.

[4] Ibid.

Three hours after Colonel Ponce gave the order to kill Father Ellacuría, Colonel Guillermo Alfredo Benavides called his officers together to explain that Ponce had given them special orders to deal with the FMLN offensive. Benavides told them that they were charged with eliminating known subversive elements, including Father Ellacuría. According to a secret cable from the U.S. ambassador in El Salvador, William Walker, to Bernard Aronson at the U.S. State Department, Benavides told his men that Ellacuría "was one of them and he must die" (Figure 1.2).[5] "It's either them or us," Benavides said. He asked his officers if any of them objected to the order.[6] No one spoke up at that time.[7]

Major Hernández Barahona had quickly organized the operation. Lieutenant José Ricardo Espinoza Guerra was selected to command troops from the U.S.-trained Atlacatl Battalion. According to Walker's cable, Espinoza "balked at the command," but Benavides told him, "This is an order and you will do it."[8] "It's either them or us," he explained again. "They have been bleeding our country and we must break them."[9] To make sure, Benavides sent Lieutenant Yusshy René Mendoza Vallecillos, who, according to Walker, Benavides trusted to see the order carried out.[10] Both lieutenants were Tandona graduates. Benavides and his officers planned to blame the FMLN for the murders. They decided not to use their regulation firearms and instead armed Private Mariano Amaya Grimaldi with an AK-47 captured from the FMLN. Amaya remembered being told he was going "to kill some delinquent terrorists." Lieutenant Mendoza told him, "you are the key man."[11]

---

[5] U.S. Department of State, Secret Cable from Ambassador William G. Walker to Bernard Aronson, January 26, 1990, document obtained by the National Security Archive, *El Salvador: War, Peace, and Human Rights, 1980–1994*. http://www.gwu.edu/~nsarchiv/nsa/publications/elsalvador2/.

[6] Lawyers Committee for Human Rights, "The 'Jesuit Case,' The Jury Trial (La Vista Publica)," September 1991, 15.

[7] *From Madness to Hope*. See also Inter-American Commission for Human Rights, *Ellacuría, S. J. y Otros v. El Salvador*, Case 10.488, Report N° 136/99, OEA/Ser.L/V/II.106 Doc. 3 rev. at 608 (1999).

[8] Walker to Baronson, January 26, 1990.

[9] Ibid.

[10] Ibid.

[11] Lawyers Committee for Human Rights, "The 'Jesuit Case,'" 16.

The lieutenants led members of the Atlacatl Battalion to the UCA. After posting a perimeter defense, eight soldiers, including Lieutenants Mendoza and Espinoza, approached the south gate of the university near the Pastoral Centre, the residence of the Jesuit priests. The noise awakened Father Ellacuría and he opened the door and let the soldiers in. They quickly roused four other priests and ordered them into the garden. Father Joaquín López y López hid in one of the adjoining rooms.

Five of the six Jesuit priests at the UCA Pastoral Centre were born in Spain. They were scholars and human rights advocates. Father Segundo Montes founded and directed the UCA Human Rights Institute and he gained international notoriety for his work for refugees in the Americas. For example, he worked closely with Massachusetts congressman Joe Moakley to help Salvadoran refugees in the United States. Father Montes's first teaching job was at a school that served the children of El Salvador's elite classes. One of his students was José Ricardo Espinoza Guerra, who grew up to be Lieutenant Espinoza.[12]

Father Amando López, a philosophy professor, was known for his work with the poor and suffering. In 1975 he was in Managua, Nicaragua, at the Central American University, as President Anastasio Somosa struggled to hold on to power. When President Somosa's forces began bombing civilians, Father López opened the campus to poor families fleeing the violence. In El Salvador he pastored a church in a poor community on the outskirts of San Salvador.[13]

Father Ignacio Martín-Baró was a social psychologist and philosophy professor who became dean of students and chair of the psychology department at UCA. He called his sister, Alicia Martín-Baró, who lived in Spain, the night of November 15. Ms. Martín-Baró asked her brother about the crisis in El Salvador and when it would improve. She remembered her brother telling her, "Oh, many people have to die before that happens."[14]

Like his peers, Father Juan Ramon Moreno was an accomplished academic whose work was inspired by liberation theology. An architect

---

[12] Center for Justice and Accountability, The Jesuits Case, The Victims. http://cja.org/article.php?list=type&type=116 (last accessed June 1, 2010).
[13] Ibid.
[14] Ibid.

of liberation theology, Father Ellacuría often talked about bringing the suffering people of Latin America "down from the cross."[15] The only El Salvadoran-born priest in the Centre that night was Father Joaquín López y López. He founded the Fe y Alegria (Faith and Joy) organization, which opened thirty educational centers in El Salvador. The centers educated marginalized communities across the country, and almost fifty thousand people had received vocational training through Fe y Alegria.

On November 16, Father Ellacuría let the soldiers into the priests' living quarters, the Pastoral Centre, because he recognized the two lieutenants. They had conducted a search of the Centre three nights before, claiming to be looking for FMLN insurgents. It now seems likely that they were conducting reconnaissance for a later attack on the Jesuits. Ellacuría's fellow priests were already awake and partially dressed when the soldiers came in. Father Martín-Baró was angry and protested loudly that "this is unjust," calling the soldiers carrion.[16] Witnesses claimed they heard shouting coming from the Centre. One bystander said she heard voices whispering in unison – as if in prayer.

Once in the garden, the lieutenants ordered the priests to lie face down in the grass. Lieutenant Espinoza ordered his men to shoot and kill the priests, "Apurense. Delen." ("Finish them off. Give it to them.")[17] Private Amaya shot and killed Fathers Ellacuría, Martín-Baró, and Montes.[18] Deputy Sergeant Antonio Ramiro Avalos Vargas shot and killed Fathers López and Moreno.[19] Jolted by the shots, Father López y López, still hiding inside, jerked and gave himself away. Corporal Angel Pérez Vásquez and other soldiers tracked him down and killed him.

The soldiers then searched the other rooms in the residence and found Julia Elva Ramos, who worked at the Centre, and her

---

[15] Jon Sobrino, "Ignacio Ellacuría, The Human Being and the Christian: Taking the Crucified People down from the Cross," in *Love That Produces Hope: The Thought of Ignacio Ellacuría*, María Pilar Aquino, Robert Anthony Lassalle-Klein, eds. (Collegeville, MD: Liturgical Press, 2006), 8.

[16] Walker to Baronson, January 26, 1990.

[17] *From Madness to Hope*; Walker to Baronson, January 26, 1990. The cable quotes Lt. Espinoza as stating "Apurense! Delen."

[18] *From Madness to Hope*.

[19] Ibid.

sixteen-year-old daughter, Celina Mariceth Ramos. Deputy Sergeant
Tomás Zarpate Castillo shot them both, then Private José Alberto
Sierra Ascencio shot them again.[20] Zarpate shot them until he was sure
they were dead because "they no longer groaned."[21] Julia Elva Ramos's
body was found wrapped around her daughter's; she had tried to shield
her from the bullets.[22]

As they left the residence, the troops fired their weapons into the
walls, threw grenades, and launched rockets to give the impression
of an FMLN attack. Father Ellacuría was believed to be in danger of
attack by hard-line FMLN members because of his criticism of its
attacks against civilians. A secret cable from Ambassador Walker to the
U.S. secretary of state on the day of the murders stated:

> It is plausible that extremists on either the right or left may be
> responsible for the murders. Ellacuría, a leading leftist intellectual
> who often sympathized with FMLN positions … would be a target
> for right wing extremists.… However … FMLN extremists may
> have murdered Ellacuría et al. in order to salvage their hoped-for
> popular uprising.[23]

The government troops sought to blame the FMLN for the massacre and thereby turn public opinion against the FMLN during their
offensive. On a piece of cardboard left at the Centre they wrote,
"FMLN executed those who informed on it. Victory or death,
FMLN."[24]

The murder of the Jesuit priests, Julia Elva Ramos, and Celina
Mariceth Ramos was shocking even in the context of the extreme
violence that characterized El Salvador's civil war. Like the assassination of Archbishop Óscar Romero in 1980, the massacre of the Jesuits
attacked the church itself, and, in Father Ellacuría, a prominent voice
for the poor and an indispensible player in the peace process. Like

[20] Ibid.; Walker to Baronson, January 26, 1990.
[21] Lawyers Committee for Human Rights, "The 'Jesuit Case,'" 16.
[22] Center for Justice and Accountability, The Jesuits Case, The Victims.
[23] U.S. Department of State, Secret Cable from Ambassador William G. Walker to George
P. Shultz, November 16, 1989, document obtained by the National Security Archive, *El
Salvador:War, Peace, and Human Rights, 1980–1994.*
[24] *From Madness to Hope*; Documents obtained by the National Security Archive, *El Salvador:
War, Peace, and Human Rights, 1980–1994.*

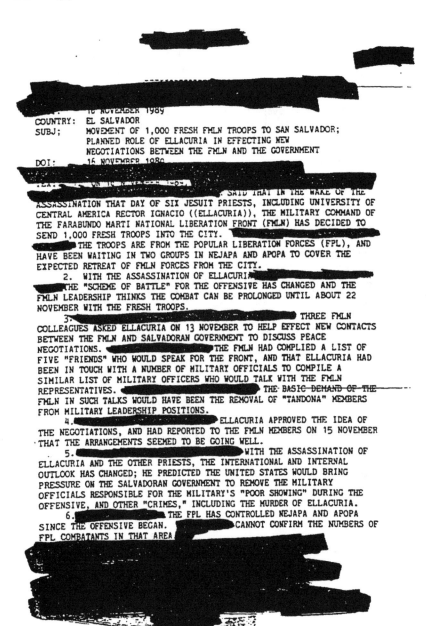

COUNTRY: EL SALVADOR
SUBJ; MOVEMENT OF 1,000 FRESH FMLN TROOPS TO SAN SALVADOR; PLANNED ROLE OF ELLACURIA IN EFFECTING NEW NEGOTIATIONS BETWEEN THE FMLN AND THE GOVERNMENT
DOI: 16 NOVEMBER 1989

... SAID THAT IN THE WAKE OF THE ASSASSINATION THAT DAY OF SIX JESUIT PRIESTS, INCLUDING UNIVERSITY OF CENTRAL AMERICA RECTOR IGNACIO ((ELLACURIA)), THE MILITARY COMMAND OF THE FARABUNDO MARTI NATIONAL LIBERATION FRONT (FMLN) HAS DECIDED TO SEND 1,000 FRESH TROOPS INTO THE CITY. THE TROOPS ARE FROM THE POPULAR LIBERATION FORCES (FPL), AND HAVE BEEN WAITING IN TWO GROUPS IN NEJAPA AND APOPA TO COVER THE EXPECTED RETREAT OF FMLN FORCES FROM THE CITY.
2. WITH THE ASSASSINATION OF ELLACURIA THE "SCHEME OF BATTLE" FOR THE OFFENSIVE HAS CHANGED AND THE FMLN LEADERSHIP THINKS THE COMBAT CAN BE PROLONGED UNTIL ABOUT 22 NOVEMBER WITH THE FRESH TROOPS.
3. THREE FMLN COLLEAGUES ASKED ELLACURIA ON 13 NOVEMBER TO HELP EFFECT NEW CONTACTS BETWEEN THE FMLN AND SALVADORAN GOVERNMENT TO DISCUSS PEACE NEGOTIATIONS. THE FMLN HAD COMPLIED A LIST OF FIVE "FRIENDS" WHO WOULD SPEAK FOR THE FRONT, AND THAT ELLACURIA HAD BEEN IN TOUCH WITH A NUMBER OF MILITARY OFFICIALS TO COMPILE A SIMILAR LIST OF MILITARY OFFICERS WHO WOULD TALK WITH THE FMLN REPRESENTATIVES. THE BASIC DEMAND OF THE FMLN IN SUCH TALKS WOULD HAVE BEEN THE REMOVAL OF "TANDONA" MEMBERS FROM MILITARY LEADERSHIP POSITIONS.
4. ELLACURIA APPROVED THE IDEA OF THE NEGOTIATIONS, AND HAD REPORTED TO THE FMLN MEMBERS ON 15 NOVEMBER THAT THE ARRANGEMENTS SEEMED TO BE GOING WELL.
5. WITH THE ASSASSINATION OF ELLACURIA AND THE OTHER PRIESTS, THE INTERNATIONAL AND INTERNAL OUTLOOK HAS CHANGED; HE PREDICTED THE UNITED STATES WOULD BRING PRESSURE ON THE SALVADORAN GOVERNMENT TO REMOVE THE MILITARY OFFICIALS RESPONSIBLE FOR THE MILITARY'S "POOR SHOWING" DURING THE OFFENSIVE, AND OTHER "CRIMES," INCLUDING THE MURDER OF ELLACURIA.
6. THE FPL HAS CONTROLLED NEJAPA AND APOPA SINCE THE OFFENSIVE BEGAN. CANNOT CONFIRM THE NUMBERS OF FPL COMBATANTS IN THAT AREA

Figure 1.1. Central Intelligence Agency Secret Cable on the Murder of Father Ignacio Ellacuria.

SECRET

Department of State

S/S-O

INCOMING

PAGE 04 OF 08 SAN SA 01107 00 OF 03 280619Z CO4/25 007005 NOD69
GUERRILLAS MOUNTED A CONCERTED EFFORT TO TAKE THE
ILOPANGO AIRBASE AND THERE WAS INTENSE COMBAT IN
SEVERAL OTHER PARTS OF THE CITY. DURING THE DAY ON
THE 15TH. THE NATIONAL POLICE HAD RECEIVED
INFORMATION THAT THE UNTS. THE HEAVILY FMLN
INFILTRATED LABOR FEDERATION. WAS PLANNING A MEETING
AT THE UCA THAT EVENING. THIS INTELLIGENCE WAS
PASSED TO THE MILITARY HIGH COMMAND WHICH IN TURN
PASSED THE INFORMATION TO COL. GUILLERMO BENAVIDES.
COMMANDER OF THE MILITARY SCHOOL AND OF THE ZONE
WHICH INCLUDED THE UCA. BENAVIDES HAD ADDITIONAL
INTELLIGENCE THAT THE GUERRILLAS MIGHT TAKE SOME OF
THEIR WOUNDED TO THE UCA THAT NIGHT   BENAVIDES
ORDERED ELEMENTS OF THE ATLACATL TO PATROL THE AREA
IMMEDIATELY AROUND THE UCA AND CUT OFF ACCESS TO THE
CAMPUS.

7.   SOME TIME AFTER 2000 HRS ON NOVEMBER 15 BENAVIDES
ORDERED LIEUTENANTS ESPINOZA AND CERRITOS TO RETURN
TO THE MILITARY SCHOOL FOR FURTHER ORDERS.   TWO
ATLACATL PATROLS REMAINED NEAR THE UCA WITH
APPROXIMATELY SIXTEEN SOLDIERS.   LIEUTENANTS ESPINOZA
AND CERRITOS MET WITH COL. BENAVIDES AROUND 2300
HRS.   LT. MENDOZA FROM THE MILITARY ACADEMY ALSO WAS
PRESENT.   COL. BENAVIDES TOLD THE LIEUTENANTS THAT
THE TERRORIST LEADERSHIP WAS AT THE UCA. "IT'S EITHER
THEM OR US.   THEY HAVE BEEN BLEEDING OUR COUNTRY AND

WE HAVE TO BREAK THEM.   ELLACURIA IS ONE OF THEM AND
HE MUST DIE.   I DON'T WANT ANY WITNESSES."   LT.
ESPINOZA AND CERRITOS BALKED AT THE COMMAND BUT WERE

TOLD "THIS IS AN ORDER AND YOU WILL DO IT."
BENAVIDES SENT HIS TRUSTED LIEUTENANT MENDOZA ALONG
TO LEAD THE MISSION; MENDOZA WAS THE SENIOR OF THE
THREE LIEUTENANTS.

SECRET

Figure 1.2. Cable from the U.S. Ambassador in El Salvador, William Walker, to Bernard Aronson at the U.S. State Department.

SECRET

Department of State

S/S-0
INCOMING

PAGE #5 OF #8   SAN SA   #1187   ## OF #3   2886192   C#4/25   ##7885   #OD693
1.   AT APPROXIMATELY #188 ON NOVEMBER 16. ABOUT
THIRTY MEN FROM THE ATLACATL. INCLUDING THE THREE
LIEUTENANTS. LEFT THE MILITARY SCHOOL. SOME ON FOOT
AND OTHERS IN VEHICLES.   THEY MET UP WITH THE TWO
PATROLS THAT WERE LEFT NEAR THE UCA AND THE GENERAL
ORDER WAS SHARED THAT AN OPERATION WAS GOING DOWN AT
THE UCA AND THEY WERE GOING TO KILL THE LEADERSHIP OF
THE "TERRORISTS."   THE UNIT APPROACHED THE UCA AND
POSTED PERIMETER SECURITY IN AND AROUND THE CAMPUS.
THEY ENTERED THE UCA GROUNDS BY THE SOUTH GATE AND A
SMALL BAND OF EIGHT. INCLUDING TWO LIEUTENANTS.
ESPINOZA AND MENDOZA. APPROACHED THE LIVING QUARTERS
OF THE PRIESTS.   ELLACURIA; AWAKENED BY THE SOUND OF
THE TROOPS. WENT TO INVESTIGATE.   HE RECOGNIZED THE
LIEUTENANTS FROM THE SEARCH THAT WAS CONDUCTED TWO
DAYS BEFORE AND OPENED THE GATE LEADING TO THE
PRIESTS' QUARTERS.   (THE DOOR WAS FOUND OPEN WITH NO
SIGNS OF HAVING BEEN FORCED.   THE ONLY KEY WAS FOUND
ON THE BODY OF ELLACURIA.)   THE TROOPS ENTERED THE
LIVING AREA. ROUSTED THE PRIESTS WHO WERE AWAKE AND
PARTIALLY DRESSED. AND MANEUVERED THEM INTO THE
GRASSY AREA IN FRONT OF THEIR DORMITORY.   FATHER
JOAQUIN LOPEZ Y LOPEZ INITIALLY AVOIDED DETECTION BY
HIDING IN AN ADJOINING ROOM.   FATHER MARTIN BARO
RESISTED THE SOLDIERS ANGRILY TELLING THEM THAT "THIS
IS UNJUST." AND CALLING THEM CARRION.   THE FIVE
PRIESTS WERE TOLD TO LIE DOWN AND ONE OF THE
LIEUTENANTS ORDERED THEM SHOT "APURENSE. DELEN."

FATHER LOPEZ Y LOPEZ. FRIGHTENED BY THE SHOOTING GAVE
AWAY HIS POSITION BY AN INADVERTENT MOVEMENT.   A
SOLDIER INVESTIGATED. FOUND THE PRIEST AND SHOT HIM.
TWO SOLDIERS SEARCHED OTHER ROOMS. FOUND THE TWO
WOMEN AND KILLED THEM ALSO.   THE TROOPS. AS THEY
DEPARTED. WENT INTO A FRENZY AND STARTED SHOOTING
WILDLY INTO PARKED CARS AND THE CHAPEL.   ONE SOLDIER.
PROVIDING PERIMETER SECURITY AWAY FROM THE SCENE OF

SECRET

Figure 1.2. (*continued*)

SECRET

Department of State

PAGE #6 OF #8   SAN SA   #1187   ## OF #3   2#86192   C#4/25   ##7##5   MOD698
THE MURDER, FIRED HIS M-6# INTO THE OFFICE BUILDING
AND OTHERS FIRED LAWS AND M-79S. SOME TROOPS
RANSACKED THE OFFICES LOCATED BELOW THE LIVING
QUARTERS AND SET THE ROOMS ABLAZE. AROUND #2##, LT.
ESPIMOZA FOUND LT. CERRITOS, WHO HAD BEEN LEFT IN
CHARGE OF PERMITER SECURITY OUTSIDE THE UCA CAMPUS,
AND ORDERED HIM TO FIRE A FLARE INDICATING THE
OPERATION WAS OVER AND THE TROOPS SHOULD WITHDRAW
FROM THE AREA.

9.   UPON RETURNING TO THE MILITARY SCHOOL THE THREE
LIEUTENANTS REPORTED TO COL. BENAVIDES THAT THE
MISSION HAD BEEN ACCOMPLISHED AND THE PRIESTS WERE
DEAD. BENAVIDES ASSURED THE OFFICERS THAT HE WOULD
COVER FOR THEM AND NOT TO WORRY

WHAT KIND OF PEOPLE DID THIS?

1#.   OUR FIRST QUESTION IS WHAT KIND OF MAN IS COL.
BENAVIDES. WE HAVE CONFLICTING REPORTS. ONE SOURCE
HAS CHARACTERIZED HIM AS AN "OLD SCHOOL" OFFICER.
NICKNAMED THE "RAMMER," WHO MAY HAVE BELIEVED THAT
THE JESUITS WERE RESPONSIBLE FOR THE INSURGENCY IN EL
SALVADOR; OTHERS ARE INCREDULOUS THAT A COLONEL WITH
BENAVIDES' REPUTATION AS A POLITICAL MODERATE, AND
VARIOUSLY NICKNAMED THE "SMURFETTE" AND THE "PRINCE"
COULD BE RESPONSIBLE FOR MASTERMINDING THE MURDERS.

11.   IT IS INDISPUTABLE THAT BENAVIDES HAS HELD
VARIOUS FIELD COMMANDS INCLUDING THAT OF THE ELITE
BELLOSO BIRI. BEFORE BEING ASSIGNED TO THE MILITARY
ACADEMY, HE WAS THE C-11, IN CHARGE OF INTELLIGENCE.
HE HAD EXPERIENCED A PERSONAL TRAGEDY ON NOVEMBER 14,
DISCOVERING THAT HIS SON WAS STRICKEN WITH A VIRUS
WHICH LEFT HIM PARALYZED FROM THE NECK DOWN. THE
SMURFETTE MAY HAVE SUCCUMBED TO THE PRESSURES OF HIS

SECRET

Figure 1.2. (*continued*)

the Romero murder, it demonstrated that no one and nothing in El Salvador was safe.

Even the U.S. administration, an unwavering supporter of the El Salvadoran ARENA regime, was emphatic in its condemnation of the massacre of the Jesuits, though it was less emphatic in using its resources to expose the culprits. In a secret communication to Ambassador Walker, Secretary of State James Baker asserted, "there is no alternative to vigorously investigating this heinous crime wherever it may lead and punishing the perpetrators to the fullest extent possible."[25] Baker urged this course of action even if "the extreme right were involved as it appears at this juncture." This cable indicated U.S. officials knew that the El Salvadoran military was responsible almost immediately after the massacre. Baker wanted Walker to strengthen President Cristiani's hand because investigating the massacre would likely "involve moving against elements of his own party and perhaps even divide the army." Even at this early stage Baker knew that the El Salvadoran judiciary would be unable to take on the military: "I doubt that the judicial system is yet up to the strain that this will cause."[26] According to a secret report, the CIA doubted the ability of El Salvador's judiciary system to prosecute and punish the murderers. "Even if the killers are identified, the limitations of El Salvador's legal system, such as restrictions on using certain types of evidence and the vulnerability of judges to bribery or intimidation, probably will hamper a successful prosecution"[27] (see Figure 1.3).

Denial and Institutional Impunity

The investigation of these murders is a case study in institutionalized impunity. Military officials began covering up their involvement in the murders just hours after the attack. Colonel Ponce ordered a suitcase

---

[25] U.S. Department of State, Secret Cable from Secretary of State James Baker to Ambassador William G. Walker, November 22, 1989, document obtained by the National Security Archive, *El Salvador:War, Peace, and Human Rights, 1980–1994.*

[26] Ibid.

[27] U.S. Central Intelligence Agency, Report on Human Rights Concerns, November 21, 1989, document obtained by the National Security Archive, *El Salvador:War, Peace, and Human Rights, 1980–1994.*

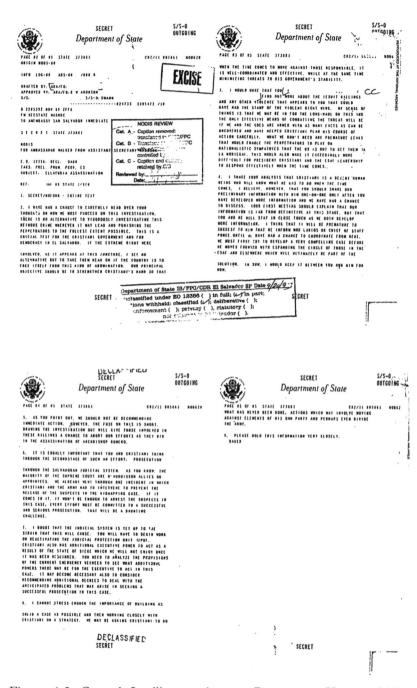

Figure 1.3. Central Intelligence Agency Report on Human Rights Concerns in El Salvador.

stolen from the Jesuit priests in the attack destroyed because it was evidence of military involvement. The witnesses who came forward and accused the military quickly and mysteriously changed their stories. For example, a sergeant in the army and a police officer originally said that they had seen soldiers at the university the night of the killing, but later retracted their statements.

President Cristiani charged the Commission for the Investigation of Criminal Acts (CIHD), an organization led by a military officer, Lieutenant Colonel Manuel Antonio Rivas Mejía, with the task of investigating the murders. When Colonel Benavides told Rivas about the operation to kill the Jesuit priests shortly after the murders, Rivas simply suggested Benavides destroy the barrels on the firearms used in the attack and replace them to prevent identification during ballistic tests.[28] Rivas also suggested Benavides destroy the logbooks of the Military Academy that would have documented the battalion's movements. Benavides ordered them burned.[29]

In a secret communiqué dated December 10, 1989, U.S. deputy mission chief William Dieterich reported receiving intelligence in which a confidential source "pointed an accusing finger at the 'Tandona' … military school graduating class whose members include most of the key colonels in the Salvadoran military."[30] Because the military was running the investigation, however, no one pursued these leads despite mounting evidence that certain officers were culpable. No one investigated military involvement, the role of Tandona, the Atlacatl Battalion, or Colonel Benavides "until confronted with the colonel's role by U.S. diplomats."[31]

On January 5, 1990, U.S. Army Major Eric Buckland admitted that he had information that proved Colonel Benavides ordered the murders. In a sworn statement he reported that Benavides had admitted his role in the murders and that members of the U.S.-trained Atlacatl unit

[28] *From Madness to Hope.*
[29] Lawyers Committee for Human Rights, "The 'Jesuit Case,'" 26.
[30] U.S. Department of State, Secret Cable from Deputy Mission Chief William Dietrich to Ambassador William G. Walker, December 10, 1989, document obtained by the National Security Archive, *El Salvador: War, Peace, and Human Rights, 1980–1994.*
[31] Lawyers Committee for Human Rights, "The 'Jesuit Case,'" 27, citing the *Interim Report of the Speaker's Task Force on El Salvador,* April 30, 1990, at 21.

had actually killed the priests[32] (see Figure 1.4). Buckland also reported that Benavides confessed to Lieutenant Colonel Rivas, the head of the investigation, shortly after Rivas began investigating the murders.

Reacting to these developments, President Cristiani appointed a Special Honor Commission made up of five officers and two civilians to investigate the murders – incredibly still leaving the military in charge of the investigation. The Honor Commission interrogated thirty members of the Atlacatl Battalion before talking to Colonel Benavides despite the fact that he was in command of the zone where the murders took place on the night in question. Finally, on January 11, 1990, the Honor Commission questioned Benavides for the first time. The next day it reported to President Cristiani that nine members of the military had murdered the Jesuits, their housekeeper, and her daughter.[33]

Faced with this result, Salvadoran officials eventually arrested the nine suspects, including Benavides. However, shortly afterward, when Benavides was seen visiting the beach, receiving high-level visitors, and staying in "relative comfort," the case became another example of Salvadoran impunity. President Cristiani assigned the case to Judge Ricardo Zamora, but, like his predecessors, he failed to pursue it with any vigor. He did not meet with the lead investigator, Colonel Rivas, he did not ask for the military's investigation results, and he did not ask for a key piece of evidence – Benavides's notebook. Ambassador Walker observed, "We do not know if it's out of fear, laziness, or ignorance, but the clear impression is that he's not pushing the case."[34] Zamora's reluctance may have been due to his fear that members of the Tandona class in the Salvadoran military would kill him. At this time he asked for visas to send his family to the United States.

The pretrial process took more than eighteen months, during which the military was most uncooperative. Military officials refused to

---

[32] U.S. Department of Defense, Sworn Statement of Major Eric William Buckland to Colonel Milton R. Menjivar, January 5, 1990, document obtained by the National Security Archive, *El Salvador: War, Peace, and Human Rights, 1980–1994*.

[33] Center for Justice and Accountability, The Jesuits Case, Facts of the Case. http://cja.org/article.php?id=471 (Last accessed October 5, 2010).

[34] U.S. Department of State, Secret Cable from Ambassador William G. Walker to Secretary of State, James A. Baker, Regarding Walker's Meeting with President Cristiani, March 3, 1990, document obtained by the National Security Archive, *El Salvador: War, Peace, and Human Rights, 1980–1994*.

... this form, see AR 190-45; the proponent agency is Office of The Deputy Chief of Staff for Personnel.

LOCATION	DATE	TIME	FILE NUMBER
Salvador, El Salvador.	5 Jan 90	0930	-

LAST NAME, FIRST NAME, MIDDLE NAME	SOCIAL SECURITY NUMBER	GRADE/STATUS
[illegible] ERIG WARREN	042-52-1298	MAJ

ORGANIZATION OR ADDRESS
Military Group El Salvador. APO Miami 34023

I, Eric Warren Buckland, WANT TO MAKE THE FOLLOWING STATEMENT UNDER OA...

...am writing this statement of my own will and will present all details, ... I know them, to the best of my ability and as I remember them.

...or about 20 December 1989, I was in the office of the ESAF C-V, COL ...rlos A. Aviles and we were talking about current events, ongoing ...jects for PSYOP - essentially the typical, almost daily conversation we ...d. During the course of our discussion, the case of the Jesuits arose ...d COL Aviles mentioned that he had some new information about the case. ...fore continuing, he repeated several times that I was to use this ...formation for "Break in Case of Emergency." He then began to tell me ... information:

COL Lopez y Lopez had told him (COL Aviles) that LTC Rivas had told him (COL Lopez y Lopez) that when the investigation of the killings had started COL Benavides had approached LTC Rivas and said something to the effect of, "I did it. What can you do to help me?" According to COL Aviles, LTC Rivas was scared and did not know what to do. As a result, the investigation slowed and eventually, COL Lopez y Lopez ... to talk to LTC Rivas. During the conversation LTC Rivas told COL Lopez y Lopez about COL Benavides' comments. COL Lopez y Lopez then passed on the information to COL Aviles and COL Aviles told me. Additionally, he told me that members of the BIRI Atlacatl GOE, lead by a lieutenent had done the actual killing. The GOE had been working out of the Escuela Militar during the offensive.

I asked COL Aviles who else knew and he said no one. I asked if COL Ponce knew and he said he believed that he did, but wasn't sure. He did not feel that it was his place to tell him. I wanted to know why they did not arrest COL Benavides right then and COL Aviles said that nothing could be done until the investigation was completed. We talked about the problem, in general terms and both agreed that the killings made no sense.

In subsequent discussions, I continued to ask about the investigation and COL Aviles told me that it was going well. One lieutenant from the Atlacatl had been questioned a few times and had done poorly with the polygraph - according to COL Aviles, the lieutenant had several excuses for why he had done poorly on the polygraph and that he appeared to be nervous. The Colonel also stated that the troops from the Atlacatl were being questioned and that their stories were starting to conflict. During our last discussion about the issue, COL A... told me that he had seen COL Benavides briefly at the Escuela ...ar and that he looked like he had not eaten, was losing weight and seemed worried. Nothing follows EWB

INITIALS OF PERSON MAKING STATEMENT	PAGE 1 OF 1 PAGES
EWB	

Figure 1.4. Sworn Statement of Major Eric William Buckland.

produce evidence and witnesses and when military witnesses did testify they refused to reveal what they knew. As the Lawyer's Committee for Human Rights reported, "The record is replete with the testimony of soldiers and officers who saw nothing, remember nothing, and whose testimony contradicted themselves, each other, official military documents, military discipline and common sense."[35]

No longer able to ignore military involvement, Salvadoran military officials tried to cover up the role of high-level officers and paint Colonel Benavides as the sole conspirator. The U.S. embassy relayed information from a military informant claiming that those looking beyond Benavides "were now embarked on a senseless, damaging witch-hunt that is extremely damaging to the ESAF [El Salvadoran Armed Forces] and totally helpful to the FMLN."[36] The U.S. embassy official passing on the intelligence saw this as another failure of the Salvadoran justice system. "They're throwing Benavides to the wolves," he commented, "and at the current pace of Salvadoran justice and military accountability the wolves will go hungry for a good while longer."[37]

Some U.S. officials initially believed the Salvadoran military's story. "The Embassy is inclined to the conclusion that he acted alone and not as part of a conspiracy," wrote Ambassador Walker about Benavides's role in the murders. "A thoughtful conspiracy would have come up with a better plan, this operation was a blunder."[38] One embassy source described Benavides as "old school," nicknamed "the rammer," and said Benavides blamed the Jesuits for the insurgency. However, another source claimed Benavides was a moderate nicknamed "Smurfette" or the "Prince" who was incapable of planning the murders.[39]

In addition to the involvement of the U.S. executive branch, Congressman Joe Moakley led the Congressional Task Force on El Salvador and directed an investigation into the Jesuits murders and the Salvadoran investigation. In April 1990, when Judge Zamora's pretrial investigation seemed to be going nowhere, the task force released its

---

[35] Lawyers Committee for Human Rights, "The 'Jesuit Case,'" 30.
[36] U.S. Department of State, Confidential, Cable, 13828, From the U.S. Embassy Defense Attaché to the U.S. Defense Intelligence Agency, October 12, 1990, document obtained by the National Security Archive, *El Salvador: War, Peace, and Human Rights, 1980–1994.*
[37] Ibid.
[38] Walker to Baronson, January 26, 1990.
[39] Ibid.

interim report criticizing the Salvadoran military and the investigation. This was the first foreign investigation of the Jesuits' murders to expose Salvadoran failings, and it sparked movement in El Salvador. The military increased its cooperation, although only marginally. Then, in August 1990, Congressman Moakley accused the El Salvadoran high command of being "engaged in a conspiracy to obstruct justice" and of having "withheld evidence [and] destroyed evidence."[40] Five days after this statement, President Cristiani agreed to appear personally to testify in Judge Zamora's investigation. Top military officials met with President Cristiani, the Supreme Court president, and Judge Zamora and promised to cooperate with Zamora's case.

In November 1990, Judge Zamora charged the defendants with murder and terrorist acts, charges never before brought against a military official. One month later, when Judge Zamora tried to begin the jury trial of the defendants, they appealed his decision to charge them with murder and terrorism. The appeal not only delayed the start of the trial, but procedural rules prohibited the admission of new evidence while the case was on appeal. After the court denied this appeal, the defendants filed habeas corpus petitions and tried other delay tactics, but finally, in September 1991, the jury trial began.

Just like the pretrial investigation, the trial itself was riddled with improprieties. The Salvadoran military and government ignored Judge Zamora's requests to produce witnesses and evidence. Zamora and the jury found only Colonel Benavides and Lieutenant Mendoza guilty of murder and acts of terrorism, and sentenced them to the maximum sentence of thirty years in prison. The court convicted Espinoza Guerra and Guevara Cerritos of acts of terrorism and sentenced them to three years. Zamora convicted one other soldier, Hernández Barahona, as an accessory to murder and sentenced him to three years. Only Mendoza and Benavides ever spent a day in prison, and they served less than three years of their thirty-year sentences.

Though this was a step in the right direction for Salvadoran justice – two military officers were sent to prison for the murder of the Jesuits – any thought that El Salvador was finally embracing the rule of law was quickly quashed. Barely two years later, El Salvador passed an amnesty law forbidding prosecution or punishment for crimes committed during

---

[40] Statement of Congressman Moakley, August 15, 1990.

the civil war. When the law was challenged in the Supreme Court of Justice, it ruled that it was incompetent to rule on the constitutionality of the law because it was an "eminently political" act.[41] Benavides and Mendoza walked out of prison. They were free.

The case had finally stumbled through a Salvadoran system clogged with military influence, professional incompetence, and lack of resources, but the result was wiped away with Cristiani's signature on the amnesty law. If perceived as a result, legal justice in the Jesuits' case was imperfect – with only partial convictions – and then obliterated by the amnesty law, but the process continued. This case demonstrates that victims and their advocates can keep the process of legal justice moving – even against Salvadoran-style impunity – by exposing evidence of truth, by bringing that evidence before courts in other countries, and by coordinating their international litigation with their accountability efforts at home. As I demonstrated with the documents used to recount this story, advocates are basing their efforts increasingly on exposing the truth through secret government documents.

SEEKING JUSTICE FOR HUMAN RIGHTS VIOLATIONS

Frequently, justice for human rights violations is perceived simply in terms of legal outcomes. However, as Eric Stover revealed in his analysis of the experiences of victims and witnesses before the International Tribunal for the Former Yugoslavia:

> [Justice] means returning stolen property; locating and identifying the bodies of the missing; capturing and trying all war criminals, from the garden variety killers in their communities all the way up to the nationalist ideologues who had poisoned their neighbors with ethnic hatred; securing reparations and apologies; leading lives devoid of fear; securing meaningful jobs; providing their children with good schools and teachers; and helping those traumatized by atrocities to recover.[42]

Legal remedies alone cannot repair the damage inflicted by widespread violent human rights violations. They are merely part of the

---

[41] *Ellacuría et al. v. El Salvador*, Case 10.488 Inter-Am. Comm'n H.R. Report No. 136/99 (1999).

[42] Eric Stover, *The Witnesses: War Crimes and the Promise of Justice in The Hague* (College Station: University of Pennsylvania Press, 2007), 16.

solution – one path to healing part of the wound inflicted. Legal remedies correct the often-expressed assertion that the violations were just by proclaiming their unjustness. They rebut state denials by creating records of truth supported by evidence, and they overturn the belief that vengeance is the only mechanism with which to punish the offender. Even in these three areas, the results are imperfect. The goal of proclaiming the unjustness of violations and overcoming impunity can be misinterpreted in cases in which the defendants are exonerated. The truth recognized by courts of law is based only on discoverable evidence – which is mostly in the control of the oppressor – and the testimony of witnesses whose version of the truth "often lies not in the facts but in their moral interpretation."[43] In this book, I clarify the contribution to justice made by the legal process. As Stover observed, "Hannah Arendt's admonition that a trial should never promise more than it can deliver ought to become the mantra of our ongoing experiment in international criminal justice."[44]

Observers frequently cite the importance of trials in the aftermath of widespread violent human rights violations. Prosecutions are necessary, according to these scholars, to demonstrate society's rejection of the violation, to deter, to avoid collective guilt, to facilitate reconciliation, and to aid democratic consolidation. Some argue that the failure to punish human rights crimes of the past fosters "contempt for the law and encourage[s] future violations."[45] Diane Orentlicher queried, "If law is unavailable to punish widespread brutality of the recent past, what lesson can be offered for the future?"[46] She argued that, "failure of enforcement vitiates the authority of the law itself, sapping its power to deter proscribed conduct, especially for large scale violations."[47] Herbert Fingarette agreed, holding that if a state fails to punish transgressions, the law "becomes functionally a mere appeal" and "the concept of law as a requirement becomes unintelligible."[48] Advocates and scholars also argue that legal accountability

---

[43] Ibid., 15.
[44] Ibid., 14.
[45] *Supra*, note 95, at 512.
[46] *Supra*, note 120.
[47] Ibid.
[48] Herbert Fingarette, "Rethinking Criminal Law Excuses," *Yale L.J.* 89(1002): 1014.

"strengthens fragile democracies since the rule of law is integral to democracy itself."[49] Orentlicher echoed William Pitt's assertion that "tyranny begins where law ends."[50] Jamie Mayerfeld argued that punishment "communicates society's condemnation of [the] violation, and helps actual and potential aggressors to absorb the lesson that such violation is morally wrong."[51] He asserted that "the obligation to deter constitutes the core rationale for punishing human rights violations."[52] Jennifer Widner pointed out that by punishing violators, courts can provide a credible threat that future violations will be punished as well.[53] To guarantee human rights in the present, past threats to punish must be carried out.[54] According to Mayerfeld, effective judicial dispute resolution systems "encourage social reconciliation by modeling a fair procedure for the just disposition of violent conflicts fueled by bitter political and ideological divisions."[55] Even truth commission scholars often describe justice as resulting from a criminal trial. "The pursuit of justice does not presuppose a retributive view of punishment," Amy Gutman and Dennis Thompson argued. "It means only bringing individuals to trial who are credibly alleged to have committed crimes and are seeking a legal verdict and an appropriate punishment if they are found guilty."[56]

Courts absorb victims' desire for revenge by punishing individual defendants, and in so doing, may also serve to protect against future violations.[57] Brian Grodsky observed that, "by individualizing blame, accountability policies can end the 'dangerous culture of collective

---

[49] Ibid., 2543.

[50] *Supra*, note 120.

[51] Jamie Mayerfeld, "Who Shall Be Judge?: The United States, the International Criminal Court, and the Global Enforcement of Human Rights," *Human Rights Quarterly* 25: 93–129, 100.

[52] Ibid., supra note 16 at 99..

[53] Jennifer Widner, "Courts and Democracy in Post-Conflict Transitions: A Social Scientist's Perspective on the Africa Case," *American Journal of International Law* 95(1): 64–75.

[54] See ibid. and Mayerfeld, "Who Shall be Judge?".

[55] Mayerfeld, supra note 16 at 100.

[56] Amy Gutmann and Dennis Thompson, "The Moral Foundation of Truth Commissions," in *Truth v. Justice: The Morality of Truth Commissions*, Robert I. Rotberg and Dennis Thompson, eds. (Princeton, NJ: Princeton University Press, 2000), 22.

[57] Julie Mertus, "Only a War Crimes Tribunal: Triumph of the International Community, Pain of the Survivors," in *War Crimes: The Legacy of Nuremberg*, Belinda Cooper ed. (New York : TV Books, 1999).

guilt' that contributes to long-term instability."[58] Judicial action against human rights violators may also prevent future abuses by reestablishing norms such as respect for the rule of law and basic human rights.[59] Ruti Teitel stated that "when criminal justice denounces these crimes, such prosecutions have a systemic impact transcending the implicated individual ... [and to] society, such trials express the normative value of equality under the law, a threshold value in the transformation to liberal democratic systems."[60] Martha Minow agreed with this assertion: "To respond to mass atrocity with legal prosecutions is to embrace the rule of law."[61] Human rights trials, according to Minow, transfer individual desires for vengeance to the state and this "transfer cools vengeance into retribution, slows judgment with procedure and interrupts, with documents, cross-examinations and the presumption of innocence, the vicious cycle of blame and feud."[62] Legal justice helps the nation to reach "consensus on the historical wrongs" and helps form a "new societal bond," according to Grodsky.[63]

In this book, I examine how justice is shaped by the pursuit of historical truth and legal accountability. I reveal how victims and advocates try to overcome the obstacles to justice and the limits of legal accountability. As Minow advocated, this study will "combine honest modesty about the promise of trials with the willingness to be inspired" as it reveals "the hard, grubby work of gathering evidence and weaving legal sources into judgments."[64] In the Jesuits' case, the victims' families and their advocates continue to do this "hard, grubby work."

[58] Brian Grodsky, "Re-Ordering Justice: Towards a New Methodological Approach to Studying Transitional Justice," *Journal of Peace Research* (46)6: 820, quoting Neil J. Kritz, "Coming to Terms with Atrocities: A Review of Accountability Mechanisms for Mass Violations of Human Rights," *Law and Contemporary Problems* 59(4): 127–52.

[59] Naomi Roht-Arriaza. "Punishment, Redress, and Pardon: Theoretical and Psychological Approaches," in *Impunity and Human Rights: International Law Practice*, Naomi Roht-Arriaza ed. (New York: Oxford University Press, 1995); Jaime Malamud-goti, "Transitional Governments in the Breach: Why Punish State Criminals?" *Human Rights Quarterly* 12(1): 11–13.

[60] Ruti Teitel, "Transitional Jurisprudence: The Role of Law in Political Transformation," 106 *Yale L.J.* 106(2009): 2047–48.

[61] Martha Minow, *Between Vengeance and Forgiveness* (Boston, MA: Beacon Press, 1998), supra note 15 at 25.

[62] Ibid., 26; see also Widner supra note 19.

[63] Grodsky, "Re-Ordering Justice,' 820.

[64] Minow, *Between Vengeance and Forgiveness*, 51.

THE JESUITS CASE – REACHING BEYOND THE STATE

Just hours after Salvadoran soldiers gunned down the six Jesuit priests, Mrs. Julia Elba Ramos, and Celina Mariceth Ramos, Americas Watch filed a complaint with the Inter-American Commission for Human Rights. In its complaint, Americas Watch claimed that El Salvador had violated the American Convention on Human Rights by extrajudicially executing the eight victims. As the case developed, Americas Watch filed supplemental complaints alleging that members of El Salvador's military had committed the murders, that the state had failed to adequately investigate the crime, that it had failed to investigate high-ranking intellectual authors, and that by passing the amnesty law the state had imposed "absolute impunity" for the crime.[65]

The commission agreed. After receiving evidence from El Salvador and Americas Watch and holding a hearing on the case, in November 1999 the commission ruled that officials in the Salvadoran military had planned, committed, and covered up the assassinations. It held "Colonel René Emilio Ponce, in the presence of and in collusion with General Juan Rafael Bustillo, then Colonel Juan Orlando Zepeda, Colonel Inocente Orlando Montano and Colonel Francisco Elena Fuentes, gave Colonel Guillermo Alfredo Benavides the order to kill Father Ignacio Ellacuría and to leave no witnesses."[66] Furthermore, "all these officers and others, knowing what had happened, took steps to conceal the truth."[67] The commission found substantial evidence that Colonel Rivas, the officer charged with investigating the murders, "learned the facts and concealed the truth and also recommended to Colonel Benavides measures for the destruction of incriminating evidence."[68] More important perhaps, the commission ruled that the Salvadoran amnesty law violated the American Convention by denying victims and their families their right to an investigation, to know the truth, and to justice.

---

[65] *Ellacuría et al. v. El Salvador*, Case 10.488 Inter-Am. Comm'n H.R. Report No. 136/99 (1999).
[66] Ibid.
[67] Ibid.
[68] Ibid.

IMPUNITY UNDER THE MASK OF FORGIVENESS

Despite this ruling, El Salvador refused to comply with commission demands that it reopen the case. In March 2000, the rector of the University of Central America, José Maria Tojeira, formally asked the ministerio publico (public prosecutor) to charge the six intellectual authors of the murders.[69] The ruling ARENA party "called the university's demands 'political.'"[70] It issued a statement that "ARENA wishes to express its public support and recognition to the former president [Cristiani] and to the distinguished generals who were members of the high command of our armed forces."[71]

The failure of justice in El Salvador allowed the ARENA party to not only reject the immorality of the murders, but to glorify the actions of those responsible for the crimes. This confirms the arguments from scholars like Mayerfeld, Teitel, and Minow that legal justice is necessary to communicate society's moral condemnation of the crimes committed by the regime. In El Salvador, impunity allowed the assassins and the architects of the attack to laud themselves as the saviors of Salvadoran democracy. The government's story that the Jesuits supported the rebels and needed to die – or that they even deserved execution – remained officially unchecked, at least in El Salvador. With impunity the perpetrators silenced the victims and achieved the ultimate goal of the rights violation.

Not only has this impunity allowed the government to claim the moral high ground, to the extent any wrongdoing is alleged, the government claimed it had been forgiven. In response to calls for lifting the amnesty law, President Francisco Flores argued "amnesty carried with it the concept of forgiveness, which ... made national reconciliation possible after the conflict ended."[72] "Reconciliation produced a new country in El Salvador."[73] The reconciliation claimed by the state

---

[69] "El Salvador: Government Balks at Reopening 1989 Jesuit Murder Case," NotiCen: Central American & Caribbean Affairs, May 4, 2000. http://www.allbusiness.com/noticen-central-american-caribbean-affairs/41081–1.html (Last accessed January 29, 2011).
[70] Ibid.
[71] Ibid.
[72] Ibid.
[73] Ibid.

was illusory. Gregorio Rosa Chavez, the archbishop of San Salvador, rejected President Flores's claim that the amnesty facilitated reconciliation. "We are a country that signed the peace but is not reconciled in truth and justice," Rosa argued. "Many are afraid of the past and want to build the future on pardons and forgetting." However, according to Archbishop Rosa, "truth and justice are prerequisites for pardons."[74]

Flores's claims to forgiveness also fundamentally misinterpreted the role of forgiveness in the aftermath of widespread violence. Forgiveness can have a powerful impact in confronting atrocities. It is, perhaps, the only path over which the victim has complete control. Forgiveness rejects vengeance, releases the offender, and can end the cycle of violence. As Minow pointed out, forgiveness reaches out to the common humanity of the perpetrator and avoids the destructive qualities of victimhood. It allows the victim to reestablish his or her own dignity. However, as powerful as forgiveness can be, it "does not and should not take the place of justice and punishment."[75] Forgiveness only changes the victim's view of the offender. It does not diminish the state's obligation to enforce the rule of law. By imposing an amnesty to protect themselves from legal accountability, Salvadoran officials stole the victims' sole right to forgive. They merely hid impunity beneath the mask of forgiveness. In the thirteen years since the Inter-American Commission ruled El Salvador's amnesty law was void, no one has faced trial for the Jesuits massacre.

That is why the victims' families turned to CJA, and that is why, with CJA's help, they filed criminal charges in the Spanish National Court against President Cristiani and fourteen former officers and soldiers of the Salvadoran army. Filing the case in Spain allowed victims to pursue justice under Spain's universal jurisdiction law, and it is an effort to inspire renewed action in El Salvador. Upon filing the case, CJA's executive director, Pamela Merchant, commented, "We hope that the filing of this important case will jumpstart justice efforts in El Salvador on a grander scale."[76] The families of the victims issued

---

[74] Ibid.
[75] Minow, *Between Vengeance and Forgiveness*, 15.
[76] Center for Justice and Accountability (CJA), "Criminal Charges Filed before the Spanish National Court for 1989 Massacre of Jesuit Priests in El Salvador," Press Release (November 13, 2008).

a statement in which they expressed their hope that through the case "people around the world and future generations will come to know the human qualities and life work" of the Jesuit priests, Mrs. Ramos, and her daughter, Celina.[77] This hope, to reverse the efforts by the Salvadoran government to silence the victims and erase their contributions from their nation's collective memory, is an essential element of legal justice. The family members of the victims are fighting to restore the truth that the victims were "extraordinary people that dedicated their lives to fight injustice and sought to improve the lives of the less fortunate."[78]

CJA sees this case as a crucial part of a global struggle for justice for human rights violations. "This is yet another sign that the movement for international justice is gaining momentum," Merchant argued. "Like al-Bashir, Fujimori, Pinochet and others, the architects of the Jesuit Massacre and other abuses committed during the 12-year Salvadoran civil war cannot escape justice."[79] U.S. congressman Jim McGovern, who was the lead investigator for Congress's investigation of the assassinations in 1989, also expressed his hopes for the Spanish case: "The world awaits a transparent and open investigation into the killings of these peaceful men of God, their housekeeper and her daughter."[80]

Former ambassador for El Salvador Robert White saw the case as carrying a broader message. "By giving uncritical support to the counter revolutionary forces in Central America, the United States moved away from its long-established respect for international legal norms of state behavior." White asserted that "by prosecuting those former Salvadoran military leaders guilty of atrocities ... the Center for Justice and Accountability reminds our elected leaders of their obligation to restore to United States foreign policy 'a decent respect for the opinions of mankind' urged on us by [the] founding fathers."[81]

---

[77] CJA, "Statement of the Families of the Victims on the Filing of the Jesuits Massacre Case" (November 13, 2008).
[78] Ibid.
[79] CJA, "Criminal Charges Filed before Spanish National Court."
[80] CJA, "Quotes on the Significance of the Jesuits Massacre Case" (November 13, 2008).
[81] Ibid.

After reviewing the case, Judge Eloy Velasco Nuñez of the Spanish National Court charged fourteen former Salvadoran officers, including General Ponce and General Larios, with crimes against humanity and state terrorism. While President Cristiani was not indicted, Judge Velasco reserved the right to do so during the investigation of the case. In May 2009, the first witnesses testified, including two Spanish special counsels who investigated the Jesuits murder and subsequent investigation and trial for a parliamentary commission. In addition, the former Spanish ambassador to El Salvador, Fernando Alvarez de Miranda, testified. These witnesses were not only called to give evidence in the case but also to testify to the connections between the case and Spain. This was deemed a necessary condition for jurisdiction under Spanish law. Given the fact that five of the Jesuit priests were born and ordained in Spain, CJA would have no trouble meeting this standard.

QUESTIONS ASKED BY THE JESUITS CASE – METHODS, RESEARCH QUESTIONS, AND OUTLINE OF THE BOOK

The case of the Jesuits exposes the many-headed monster that obstructs the search for justice. During the assassination, Salvadoran troops painted a sign that purported to claim responsibility for the murders on behalf of the FMLN rebels. It stated the FMLN had killed the Jesuits for their complicity with the government. State denials persisted throughout the investigation, and continue despite guilty verdicts and acceptances of international responsibility. Even more shocking is the state's continued justification of the killings as an acceptable act of self-defense in protecting democratic El Salvador. Because of entrenched impunity legislated in the amnesty provision, the state's claims that the Jesuits supported terrorist FMLN factions remain unchallenged in the courts. The state continues to refuse calls to reopen the investigation even in the face of the Inter-American Commission's demands. President Francisco Flores said that if the state opens one case, "we would have to begin investigations of the thousands and thousands of people who perished violently during the war."[82] The result is that

[82] Ibid.

the guilty walk free, the truth remains hidden, and the stories of the victims' lives remain untold.

In this book, I examine how victims and advocates from a handful of Latin American countries have built the process of legal justice in cases blocked by their own governments. I address the following research questions:

1. How should legal justice for widespread human rights violations be conceptualized?
2. What are the goals of legal justice and what is its overarching purpose when addressing widespread human rights violations?
3. What are the elements of the process of legal justice?
4. What is the effect of uncovering and revealing the truth in the process of legal justice?
5. How do human rights advocacy groups move the process of justice?
6. Is there a right to truth?
7. Is there a right to government information?
8. What are the role and effect of extra-territorial courts in the process of legal justice?

To address these research questions, I gather data by interviewing participants in human rights cases and by analyzing court transcripts, human rights reports, and judicial decisions. I use case studies to conduct my analysis, focusing on several Latin American countries and on a set of legal cases arising from those countries. I pay particular attention to Guatemala because that nation has suffered widespread human rights violations, its government has been particularly diligent in preserving impunity, and advocates have looked to advance justice in Guatemalan cases in U.S., Spanish, and the Inter-American courts. The cases I study represent a small sample of the shamefully enormous population of victims of atrocities committed on every continent on the planet.

These cases are our teachers. Through them I uncover how victims overcome deeply entrenched impunity by turning to foreign and regional forums and how they use these extra-territorial efforts to awaken the dormant machinery of legal justice at home. These are the stories of mothers, fathers, brothers, and sisters living in villages hours from the nearest courthouse working for legal justice for murdered family members in the capitals of foreign states and then bringing the power of their work back home.

For these victims and their advocates, proving the factual truth is a crucial element of legal justice and a monumentally difficult task when they are faced with repeated state denials, cover-ups, and obfuscation. Advocates are revolutionizing the concept of justice by convincing jurists that *truth* is an essential component of human rights, and they are revolutionizing the pursuit of justice by uncovering and analyzing documentary evidence that often contradicts decades of state denial. I show how secret dossiers, moldy police files, and clandestine communiqués are being pieced together to elevate truth over the din of impunity.

My approach facilitates an analysis of justice that takes into account the meaning of the concept to those participating in the process. It enriches the definition of legal justice by including subjective as well as objective elements. Through my analysis, the book is also a vehicle for revealing the truth regarding the human rights violations that are the subject of my study.

In Chapter 2, I argue that legal justice for human rights violations is best understood as a process rather than a result, and that it is not a universal absolute but a continuum with subjective and objective elements. Conceptualizing legal justice simply as a conviction or punishment underspecifies the full meaning of the term and ignores the importance of other aspects of the process. Many transitional justice scholars and practitioners accept that postconflict transitions are complex processes with diverse elements, of which legal accountability is one. I argue that legal justice should be conceptualized as a process as well. I demonstrate this in Chapter 2 through the experiences of victims, advocates, and activists working for justice for human rights violations. The process does not end when the truth is revealed, nor when the judgment is issued, nor when the convicted are punished. It returns home with the victims to become part of the domestic legal, economic, and political struggle. It crosses borders and oceans to inspire others who seek to overcome their own barriers of impunity. It is the struggle for justice that teaches us its meaning. My analysis reveals that the purpose of the process of justice must be at least in part to restore the equilibrium of human dignity. The precondition to egregious human rights violations is the destruction of the victims' human dignity. As long as that dignity remains unrestored, the risk of more violence exists. The case studies I discuss in Chapter 2 also reveal the absolute importance of exposing the truth in the process of justice.

In this book, I argue that truth is the foundational precondition for legal justice and a fundamental element in the process. Chapter 3 explains the crucial importance of truth in the process of legal justice. Often the goal of oppression is to erase the victims from the history – the collective memory – of a society. Truth repairs this wrong. It fights back the years of repeated state denials, of blame for the victims, and of obfuscation. Truth cracks open the dam and lets the currents of justice seep through. Again, in this chapter I conduct my analysis through the experiences of participants in the process. In several examples victims see finding the truth as the ultimate goal of the process.

In Chapter 4, I demonstrate that there is a right to truth in international law. I show that this right is expressed in several treaties and that it has developed into a customary rule of international law. I also explain what the right is. As the right to truth has been enforced, a corollary right to government information has also developed. In Chapter 5, I examine innovative techniques advocates use to uncover the truth and to use that truth to foster legal accountability. One such technique is using original contemporaneous documents – such as the CIA documents I used to tell the story of the Jesuits case – to prove a case. This is a global phenomenon in which advocates have obtained secret government documents to overcome decades of denials. The right to government information has been an important part of this story. In some cases this right has facilitated the release of documents, and in others the right has grown out of the unauthorized release of secret documents.

In Chapter 6, I demonstrate the importance of extra-territorial legal action in exposing the truth and activating the process of justice. El Salvador's legal system was incapable of properly investigating the Jesuits' murders – and of investigating crimes by powerful members of the military. The military controlled the investigation from the outset, with the principal investigator, Lieutenant Colonel Rivas, advising Colonel Benavides on how to destroy evidence of the military's guilt. Judge Zamora was unable to get the military to cooperate with the pretrial investigation or with the trial itself. The guilty verdicts fell short of reaching Colonel Ponce or President Cristiani. This is a fundamental obstacle in achieving justice after widespread human rights violations – an ineffective, weak, and corrupt judiciary. In Chapter 6, I examine how victims and advocates circumvent their ineffective legal systems by seeking justice abroad. I analyze the paths along the process of justice taken by these victims and advocates in national courts in Spain and the United States as well as in the inter-American human rights system. Finally, in Chapter 7, I analyze the effects of these extra-territorial legal actions on the participants in the cases and on the efforts to move the process of justice at home. Frequently extra-territorial legal rulings can restart legal processes at home, and in this chapter, I examine this phenomenon and the other effects of taking cases beyond the state.

THE ACCOMARCA MASSACRE – THE PROCESS BEGINS

When twelve-year-old Teófila Ochoa Lizarbe went outside her home in the Peruvian village of Lloccllapampa early in the morning she saw them: black-booted soldiers encircling her village armed with machine guns and hiding behind ski masks. "They had surrounded us already and I was scared and trembling," Teófila recalled.[83] Soldiers from Peru's Lince (lance) Company marched into the Andean village of Lloccllapampa near the town of Accomarca.[84] It was August 14, 1985, and Peru's military was pursuing elements of the Sendero Luminoso (Shining Path) rebel group.

Sendero Luminoso had begun its violent insurgency in 1980 as Peru transitioned to democracy. In the twenty years of conflict that followed, both Sendero Luminoso and Peruvian security forces committed widespread atrocities, including disappearances, torture, rape, and massacres.[85] Together Sendero Luminoso and Peru's security

---

[83] Transcript of Trial at 44, *Ochoa Lizarbe v. Hurtado*, No. 07–21783-CIV-JORDAN, 2008 U.S. Dist. LEXIS 109517 (S.D. Fla. March 4, 2008).
[84] Complaint at 12–13, *Ochoa Lizarbe v. Rondón*, No. 8:07-cv-01809-PJM (S.D. Md. July 11, 2007).
[85] Report of the Commission on Truth and Reconciliation, Peru, General Conclusions, Part II(A)(12–13).

forces killed approximately 69,280 people, and more than 40 percent of the deaths and disappearances took place among the Andean communities in the department of Ayacucho.[86] The government of Peru declared most of Ayucucho an "emergency zone" in October 1981, and suspended all constitutional protections.[87] The military began its "counter-subversive" campaign in the department in December 1982, eventually concentrating on Quebrada de Huancayoc, including the town of Accomarca. Patrols marched through villages looking for insurgents, often killing and raping civilians regardless of their affiliation with the rebel group.[88]

In August 1985, General Wilfredo Mori Orzo, the commander of the emergency zone of Ayucucho, ordered his staff to "capture and/or destroy terrorist elements in Quebrada de Huancayoc."[89] Lieutenant Colonel Carlos Medina Delgado called a meeting to discuss "Operation Huancayoc." Four patrols were sent into the area, two of which were from an intelligence and counter-subversive unit called Lince Company. Lieutenant Rivera Rondón commanded Lince's Unit 6 and Lieutenant Telmo Ricardo Hurtado commanded Unit 7. These units entered the area around Accomarca on August 13, 1985, and the next morning Lieutenant Hurtado ordered his unit into Teófila's village of Lloccllapampa.[90]

Two soldiers entered Teófila's home while her mother cooked the morning meal. They ordered the family to walk down to the open field, but Teófila's mother invited them to stay and offered them soup. The soldiers ate there as Mrs. Ochoa cried with fear, and when they left, they still insisted that the family gather in the field below. Mrs. Ochoa told Teófila to stay behind because she was the eldest. "Take me with you," Teófila begged her mother. "I didn't want to stay there by myself," she later testified, "so she left me there with my brother, Gerardo, hugging me."[91]

Teófila's mother, sister, and three brothers went down to the field. Teófila and Gerardo watched as soldiers beat her family and neighbors

---

[86] Peru Truth and Reconciliation Commission Report, Part I(2–4).
[87] Peru Truth and Reconciliation Commission Report, vol. 7, p. 40.
[88] Ibid., vol. 7, pp. 155–57.
[89] Ibid., vol. 7, p. 157; Ochoa Complaint at 12.
[90] Ibid., vol. 7, pp. 158–59.
[91] Hurtado Transcript at 45.

with their weapons. They dragged young girls into houses, and she listened to the girls scream only to be silenced by the sound of shots. The soldiers separated the men and women in the field, and many of the women were pulled away and raped.[92] Then they forced the villagers into a single-file line and marched them into three different buildings: a nearby house, a straw hut, and a freestanding kitchen. "Just as the last ones were going into the house, that's when the firing began," Teófila remembered. "All of the soldiers started shooting. And then there was a tremendous cry – children, little girls, little boys."[93] Lieutenant Hurtado ordered his troops to fire on the houses, and then threw a grenade into one of the buildings.[94]

When twelve-year-old Cirila Pulido saw the soldiers coming, she and two of her siblings hid in their house. Like Teófila, she watched as soldiers beat her family and her neighbors, dragged women off, and forced them into single-file lines in the field. She saw her mother forced down to the field with Cirila's nine-month-old brother, Edgar, on her back. Then she saw the soldiers force the villagers into the three buildings. "Into the straw hut, they put all of the men. Into the adobe hut, they put all of the women and then in the small little kitchen, a few of the women and the children," recalled Cirila.[95] "After putting them into those houses, the soldiers stood in a line and they began to fire. And then one of the soldiers threw something, and then there was an explosion." "That's the way it was," she remembered, "there were three explosions, and then all three houses caught fire and then you could hear the people screaming and the children screaming."[96]

As the buildings burned, the soldiers poured back into the village to root out witnesses. "Then the soldiers began to come towards us," Teófila recalled, "and I ran up the hill and my ... brother, Gerardo, ran down. He was followed ... they shot him."[97] Gerardo was just ten

---

[92] Rondón Complaint at 12.
[93] Hurtado Transcript at 47.
[94] Peru Truth and Reconciliation Commission Report, vol. 7, pp. 159–60.
[95] Hurtado Transcript at 72.
[96] Ibid. at 72.
[97] Ibid. at 47.

years old when soldiers gunned him down. "Bullets would fly by my neck, bullets would fly by my feet … and then I tripped and fell on a rock." Teófila managed to hide and watch the soldiers search for her. "Where I had fallen, that's where they were looking for me, looking like as if they were looking for gold."[98] She was certain they would find her right away, but somehow they did not. "And I spent the whole night there trembling.… I had no one.… I had lost what I had loved the most."[99]

After hiding for almost three weeks, Teófila, Cirila, and others started returning to their homes, believing that it was finally safe to do so. They were wrong. Upon hearing allegations that several massacres had occurred in the department, Peru's senate ordered an investigation. Soldiers swept in to kill witnesses just days before a senate commission was scheduled to visit the village to investigate. "They came in a helicopter," Cirila remembered, "to look for the people." Once again Cirila ran. "I escaped with my father up … into the brush, and two soldiers followed me. I hid under a rock. And bullets were flying above me and bullets were kicking up all of the dirt."[100] Cirila survived by hiding behind a waterfall.[101]

Search for the Truth

Teófila and Cirila eventually moved to Lima and established an association for the victims of the Accomarca Massacre. The state continually denied the victims' stories and claimed that the village was indeed harboring Sendero Luminoso terrorists. The Peruvian Senate Commission investigated the allegations and in October 1985 determined that sixty-nine villagers had been murdered. The commission held that these were civilian crimes not subject to the exclusive jurisdiction of the military justice system. Civilian authorities opened an investigation, but the Peruvian Supreme Court overruled the Senate Commission and held the crimes to be military in nature. The court based this decision on the fact that the

---

[98] Ibid. at 48.
[99] Ibid. at 49.
[100] Ibid. at 83.
[101] Ibid. at 83–84.

killings took place in an area designated to be an emergency zone and thus within the exclusive authority of the military. Peru's military does not allow victims to seek reparations.

In 1987, the military justice system ruled that military defendants could not be charged with homicide for killing civilians. It therefore exonerated Hurtado, Rondón, and other defendants of murdering villagers in the Accomarca Massacre. Hurtado alone was convicted of anything, and he was only convicted of abuse of authority. He was sentenced to four years in prison, but later that year the Supreme Council for Military Justice voided Hurtado's conviction. In 1992, after five years and two additional trials, Hurtado was once again convicted of abuse of authority and this time sentenced to six years in prison. Despite these accusations, trials, convictions, and prison sentences, Hurtado remained active in the military and was promoted three times, attaining the rank of major. A secret memorandum from the U.S. embassy in Lima in 1993 reported that despite being convicted and sentenced, Hurtado "is still on active duty and is not incarcerated" (see Figure 1.5).[102] Several years later the U.S. State Department Human Rights Report stated that Hurtado continued his military career. "In May, published photographs appeared to show former Second Lieutenant Ricardo Telmo Hurtado presiding at a public function in uniform with the rank of major."[103]

The secret embassy memo pointed out that the Hurtado conviction was only the second conviction in a human rights case in thirteen years, yet the government of Peru used it as proof of "its willingness to discipline those responsible for human rights cases that involved the military."[104] However, the embassy discovered Commander General Pedro Villanueva Valdivia ordered Hurtado's release immediately after his conviction by the military court. Embassy officials understated the implications: "This information would negate the positive results

---

[102] Secret memo from the American Embassy in Lima, Peru to Secretary of State Warren Christopher, December 1993, document obtained by the National Security Archive, "The Search for Truth: The Declassified Record on Human Rights Abuses in Peru." Tamara Feinstein, ed., August 28, 2003. http://www.gwu.edu/~nsarchiv/NSAEBB/NSAEBB96 (last accessed February 27, 2013).

[103] U.S. Department of State, Human Rights Report, Peru, 1999.

[104] American Embassy to Secretary Christopher, December 1993.

UNCLASSIFIED   *E27*

Current Class: ▓▓▓   Page: 1
Current Handling: n/a
Document Number: 1993LIMA12846   Channel: n/a

                                              RELEASED IN PART
PAGE 01   LIMA 12846 032114Z   B1, 1.5(B), 1.5(D)
ACTION ARA-01

INFO   LOG-00   ACDA-17 AID-01   AMAD-01 C-01   OASY-00 EB-01
       HA-09   H-01   INM-02   TEDE-00 INR-00   IO-16   JUSE-00
       L-03   ADS-00   NSAE-00 NSCE-00 OIC-02   PA-01   PM-02
       PRS-01   P-01   RPCS-01 SIL-00   -SP-00   SR-00   SS-00
       STR-16   TRSE-00 USIE-00 RPE-01   /078W
       ------------------0C57D0   032114Z /38
O 032115Z DEC 93
FM AMEMBASSY LIMA
TO SECSTATE WASHDC IMMEDIATE 3249
INFO AMEMBASSY QUITO
AMEMBASSY BOGOTA
AMEMBASSY LA PAZ
DIA WASHDC
CIA WASHDC ,
USCINCSO QUARRY HEIGHTS PM

▓▓▓▓LIMA 12846

SOUTHCOM ALSO FOR POLAD

E.O. 12356: DECL: OADR
TAGS: PHUM, PREL, PGOV, KJUS, PE
SUBJECT: ARMY OFFICER CONVICTED IN ACCOMARCA
-            CASE REPORTEDLY NOT JAILED

REFS: (A) LIMA 2302
             (B) LIMA 1798 ▓▓▓

▓▓▓▓

PAGE 02   LIMA 12846 032114Z

1. ▓▓▓/NOFORN - ENTIRE TEXT.

2. [   ] REPORT THAT ARMY   B1
CAPT. TELMO HURTADO, WHO HAD BEEN CONVICTED FOR
THE 1985 ACCOMARCA MASSACRE, IS STILL ON ACTIVE
DUTY AND IS NOT INCARCERATED. IN FEBRUARY 1993,
THE REVIEW PANEL OF PERU'S SUPREME COUNCIL OF
MILITARY JUSTICE UPHELD A SIX YEAR SENTENCE FOR
HURTADO, WHO WAS CONVICTED OF THE AUGUST 14,
1985, MASSACRE OF 69 NON-COMBATANT VILLAGERS IN
ACCOMARCA, AYACUCHO DEPARTMENT (REF A). IT WAS

Current Class: ▓▓▓   Page: 1

UNCLASSIFIED

Figure 1.5. Memo from the American Embassy in Lima, Peru to Secretary of State Warren Christopher.

UNCLASSIFIED

Current·Class: Page: 2
Current Handling: n/a
Document Number: 1993LIMA12846   Channel: n/a

ONE OF TWO HUMAN RIGHTS CASES DURING THE LAST 13
YEARS THAT HAD RESULTED IN THE CONVICTION OF AN
ARMY OFFICER (REF B). GOP POINTED TO BOTH CASES
AS PROOF OF ITS WILLINGNESS TO DISCIPLINE THOSE
RESPONSIBLE IN HUMAN RIGHTS CASES THAT INVOLVED
THE MILITARY.

3. [   ]STATED THAT THEN ARMY COMMANDER
GEN. PEDRO VILLANUEVA VALDIVIA (COMMANDER   B1
JANUARY-DECEMBER 1991) ORDERED HURTADO RELEASED
FROM CUSTODY OF THE MILITARY POLICE FOLLOWING
HIS INITIAL CONVICTION BY A LOWER MILITARY COURT.
DOCUMENTS [   ]ALSO SHOW THAT HURTADO
WAS AN ACTIVE DUTY CAPTAIN AS OF JULY 1992. [   ]   B1
INFORMATION SHOWS THAT HURTADO WAS AT THE ARMY   B1
TRAINING AND INSTRUCTION COMMAND (COINDE)
INFANTRY SCHOOL AS OF SEPTEMBER AND OCTOBER 1993
(SEP IIR).

PAGE 03   LIMA 12846 032114Z
4. COMMENT: WE CANNOT STATE CONCLUSIVELY THAT
HURTADO IS FREE. THESE TWO REPORTS, HOWEVER,
INDICATE THERE IS A HIGH POSSIBILITY HE IS FREE
AND ON ACTIVE DUTY. THE MILITARY IS FULLY AWARE
OF THE SIGNIFICANCE OF THE CASE TO THE USG AND
TO THE NATIONAL AND INTERNATIONAL HUMAN RIGHTS
COMMUNITY. THIS INFORMATION WOULD NEGATE THE
POSITIVE RESULTS GENERATED FROM HURTADO'S
CONVICTION AND RAISES SERIOUS QUESTIONS ABOUT
THE GOP'S WILL TO ADDRESS MILITARY IMPUNITY IN
HUMAN RIGHTS CASES IN THE FUTURE.
BRAYSHAW

NNNN

Current Class: ▮▮▮▮   Page: 2

UNCLASSIFIED

Figure 1.5. (*continued*)

generated from Hurtado's conviction and raises serious questions about the [government of Peru's] will to address military impunity in human rights cases in the future."[105]

Eduardo González, a senior official with Peru's Truth and Reconciliation Commission, saw the Accomarca Massacre as a military message to the civilian authorities. "There were a number of massacres, of which Accomarca was the most horrible." This was "a way of sending a very clear message from the military to the civilian government, that they were the ones taking the decisions and calling the shots, and that they would do as they considered fit, and that they would defend the impunity with which they operated."[106] González concluded that "Accomarca was the announcement that a horrible process of impunity was starting in Peru, and that, in fact, there wouldn't be … hope for justice for victims." Teófila and Cirila would have to search for the truth and for justice outside Peru.

[105] Ibid.
[106] Hurtado Transcript at 144.

2 RECONSTITUTING HUMAN DIGNITY AND THE PROCESS OF LEGAL JUSTICE

Maybe today love, I think she's coming home today ...

THE MÉNDEZ CASE AND ENTRENCHED GUATEMALAN IMPUNITY

On March 8, 1984, nine-year-old Wendy Méndez and her eleven-year-old brother, Igor, returned home to find ten members of Guatemala's military interrogating their mother, Luz Haydee Méndez. Wendy Méndez remembers that the soldiers quickly questioned the children as well. They then closed them in one of the bedrooms, where she and her brother could hear the soldiers questioning and beating their mother. Wendy remembers that after a while one of the soldiers came and took her into another room, where he locked the door, forced her onto her parents' bed, and raped her.[1] During her ordeal she "tried not to think of what was happening ... but concentrated on the coins resting on the bed ... it was as if I had gone to another world."[2]

Later, the soldiers brought the children out to the courtyard of the house, where Wendy saw her mother. At first she did not even recognize

---

[1] *José Miguel Gudiel Álvarez and others v. Guatemala* ("Diario Militar"), No. 116/10, Case No. 12.590, December 21, 2012, para. 113, translated by the author.

[2] Inter-American Commission on Human Rights, Ruling on Admissibility, Letter of Transmission to the Inter-American Court of Human Rights, *José Miguel Gudiel Álvarez and others v. Guatemala* ("Diario Militar"), Referral No. 116/10, Case No. 12.590, par. 216, p. 64.

her because of all the bruises on her face. The soldiers made the children watch as they pulled out their mother's fingernails with pliers and then they lined the children up against the wall with their mother. They pointed their machine guns at them, counted to three, and carried out a mock execution. The soldiers then took the family to the police station, where the abuse continued. Wendy remembers the soldiers hooked them up to a machine and shocked them. She remembers seeing her mother shocked over and over.[3] Days later soldiers returned the children to their home. They hid with their grandmother for two years and then escaped from Guatemala to Canada. Their mother was never seen again.

Guatemalan security forces killed an estimated two hundred thousand people during that country's thirty-year internal conflict.[4] Countless others, mostly members of Guatemala's indigenous community, were displaced.[5] One of the principal weapons used by Guatemalan security forces was forced disappearance. Security forces forcibly disappeared approximately forty thousand people during the conflict. The state targeted mostly leftist activists, labor leaders, students, academics, and human rights advocates. Though peace accords were signed in 1996, most of those responsible for these atrocities remain hidden behind a stubborn wall of impunity.

The United Nations Verification Mission in Guatemala (MINUGUA), charged with monitoring compliance with the peace accords, reported that "with regard to the allegations of threats, harassment and intimidation of judges ... these concerns are real [and] the Government ha[s] failed to provide the requisite protection or assistance to those who have complained."[6] MINUGUA cited "the large number of unsolved violent murders and the high incidence of impediments to investigations and prosecutions in these murders and

---

[3] Ibid., 64–65.
[4] U.S. Department of State, "Country Report on Human Rights Practices – Guatemala." http://www.state.gov/www/global/human_rights/. See also Recovery of Historical Memory Project, *Guatemala – Never Again! The Official Report of the Human Rights Office, Archdiocese of Guatemala* (Maryknoll, NY: Orbis Books).
[5] U.S. Department of State, "Country Report on Human Rights Practices – Guatemala."
[6] United Nations Verification Mission in Guatemala (MINUGUA), Report of the Special Rapporteur on the Independence of Judges and Lawyers: Report on the Mission to Guatemala. U.N. Commission on Human Rights, 56 Sess., Item 11(d), U.N. Doc. E/CN.4/2000/61/Add.1 (2000), at p. 30.

human rights-related crimes" as an "indication of the very high rate of impunity."[7] A later report stated that "harassment and threats to justice operators continue to be of serious concern [and that] rather than declining, these incidents have actually increased." This report found that "impunity is still widespread."[8] As Silvia Villacorta, the wife of an assassinated Guatemalan politician and activist, stated, "Guatemala is a country of deep wounds and shallow justice."[9]

Perhaps the case that is most emblematic of the systematic impunity present in Guatemala is that of Myrna Mack. On September 11, 1990, Guatemalan police assassinated Myrna Mack Chang, an anthropologist studying the displacement of thousands of indigenous Guatemalans. Though authorities told Myrna's sister, Helen, that Myrna had died in a car accident, Helen eventually discovered that her sister had been stabbed twenty-seven times. Helen Mack had never been extremely active in human rights issues, but after her sister was assassinated she devoted her life to human rights justice. She established the Myrna Mack Foundation, which has been a leading advocacy group for justice for Myrna Mack and the countless victims of the Guatemalan counterinsurgency.

From the beginning, the process of justice for Helen has been a difficult and life-threatening ordeal. State officials worked to block any efforts to discover who was responsible for the murder. Criminal investigators failed to take fingerprints, photographs, or blood samples from the crime scene. Although they did collect Myrna Mack's clothing and fingernail samples, officials threw them away before conducting any laboratory analysis. When one criminal investigator spoke openly about a report that linked Guatemalan security forces to the murder, he was assassinated.[10]

---

[7] Ibid., 31.

[8] MINUGUA, Report of the Special Rapporteur on the Independence of Judges and Lawyers: Report on the Mission to Guatemala. U.N. Commission on Human Rights, 58 Sess., Item 11(d), U.N. Doc. E/CN.4/2002/72/Add.2 (2001), at p. 24.

[9] Silvia Villacorta, Testimony before the Inter-American Court of Human Rights, San Jose, Costa Rica. Translated and transcribed by the author. See Jeffrey Davis and Edward H. Warner, "Reaching beyond the State: Judicial Independence, the Inter-American Court of Human Rights, and Accountability in Guatemala," *Journal of Human Rights* 6(2): 233–55.

[10] David Baluarte and Erin Chlopak, "The Case of Myrna Mack Chang: Overcoming Institutional Impunity in Guatemala," *Human Rights Brief* 10(3): 11–14.

Anyone associated with investigating the murder was at risk. In April 1994, when Guatemala's constitutional court was considering several human rights cases, including preliminary rulings in the Mack case, unknown attackers shot and killed the court's president, Epaminondas González Dubón.[11] Throughout the thirteen years of judicial proceedings, death threats have driven more than ten judges to drop the case, and several judges, prosecutors, and witnesses have fled the country. In July 1994, Helen Mack was forced to leave Guatemala for a time when activists discovered a plan to murder her. The next month, when attackers fired their weapons at Roberto Romero, a Myrna Mack Foundation lawyer, he fled the country as well.[12] One activist interviewed for this research who worked in Guatemala stated that judges and prosecutors associated with human rights cases suffered "harassment, threats [and] in a lot of cases their families have been threatened ... some of them have suffered attacks and some have suffered pressure from within the system."[13] Guatemalan officials used every weapon at their disposal to block the investigation and legal process in this case, as they did in virtually every attempt to pursue justice for human rights violations committed during and after the civil war.

This is an all too common strategy used by governments in the aftermath of widespread atrocities. In Chapter 1, I showed examples from El Salvador and Peru. In the following pages, I explore further examples from Latin America. However, because of the extent of the violations suffered and the depth of the impunity imposed, Guatemala is the ideal nation with which to study impunity and the efforts to overturn it.

TRANSITIONAL JUSTICE AS MORE THAN A LEGAL RESULT

When Wendy Méndez was twenty-five, she returned to Guatemala and cofounded HIJOS (Los Hijos por la Identidad y la Justicia contra el

---

[11] Human Rights First, "A Test of Justice," http://www.humanrightsfirst.org/wp-content/uploads/pdf/test_of_justice.pdf (Last accessed on December 19, 2012).

[12] Human Rights First, "A Test for Justice"; Human Rights Watch, "World Report – Guatemala," http://www.hrw.org/reports/world/reports/.

[13] Adriana Beltran, associate for Washington Office for Latin America, interview with the author, Washington, DC, June 4, 2004.

Olvido y el Silencio, or the Children for Identification, Justice, and against Forgetting and Silence), an nongovernmental organization (NGO) for children and family members of the disappeared who are dedicated to finding the truth and achieving justice. When asked to describe the justice she pursued, Ms. Méndez described it as a multifaceted process. "First of all our goal is to assure that the story of terror and repression never repeats again, this is a great task and it is understood as a medium and long term process where actors at HIJOS and other human rights organizations are not the only ones that must take action."[14] She understands justice on a societal level that prevents future violence. Moreover, she and her HIJOS colleagues see justice as a political movement. Ms. Méndez stated, "Youth and children as social, cultural and political actors must also take an important place in the struggle for justice in Guatemala, considering that impunity is a structural problem now that affects and will affect their lives in many ways for time to come if there are no clear changes today."[15] Of course, there is also an effort to achieve legal justice. "We understand justice in legal terms," Ms. Méndez continued, "that all those responsible for committing genocide, forced disappearances and other crimes must be brought to trial and sentenced accordingly, and fulfill their sentences in jail."[16]

In this book I endorse the conclusion that transitional justice is a complex system that includes political, social, economic, cultural, and legal factors, and I argue that the legal component of transitional justice is a similarly complex process consisting of varied elements. Scholars of transitional justice have found that it requires more than legal accountability. Legal justice is one part of transitional justice, but it is often thought of as a simple result – a guilty verdict, a prison sentence, or an exoneration. However, I expand on the idea of a multifaceted system of transitional justice, arguing that, like transitional justice, legal justice is more than a result; it is a multifaceted process (see Table 2.1).

Work for transitional justice has blossomed in the last decades. Indeed the field is "on an upward trajectory" and "has come to

---

[14] Wendy Méndez, interview with the author, May 26, 2010.
[15] Ibid.
[16] Ibid.

Table 2.1. *Definitions of Transitional Justice and Legal Justice*

Type of Justice	Definition
Transitional Justice	Transitional justice is a multifaceted system that includes social, political, economic, and legal elements to move a society from widespread human rights violations to a peaceful, democratic state in which the rule of law prevails, human dignity is recognized, and a system has been put in place to hold those responsible for violations accountable.
Legal Justice	Legal justice is one element of transitional justice. It is a process through which the truth of human rights violations is fully revealed, the victims and survivors are permitted to testify, a judicial or quasi-judicial institution issues public findings of fact, and those responsible for violations are subjected to legal accountability. The process should help reconstitute the human dignity of the victims while preserving the dignity of the accused.

dominate debates on the intersection between democratization, human rights protections and state reconstruction after conflict."[17] Examining the approaches to transitional justice reveals the clear "dominance of legalism."[18] Indeed even those who do the work of transitional justice in the field perceive it as "something which belongs to others – chiefly lawyers, policy makers and state officials."[19] However, Kieran McEvoy argued that excessive reliance on "legalism can cumulatively disconnect individuals and communities from any sense of sovereignty over transitional justice."[20] He pointed to the distinction identified by Paul Gready between "distant justice" and justice that is actually "embedded in the communities that have been directly effected [*sic*] by violence and conflict."[21]

---

[17] Kieran McEvoy, "Letting Go of Legalism: Developing a 'Thicker' Version of Transitional Justice," in *Transitional Justice from Below: Grassroots Activism and the Struggle for Change*, Kieran McEvoy and Lorna McGregor, eds. (Oxford: Hart Publishing, 2008), 15.

[18] Ibid., 16.

[19] Ibid. 17.

[20] Ibid., 29.

[21] Ibid.

McEvoy's work supports the conceptualization of transitional justice as a process of which legal justice is just a part. He argued that "an
international or local tribunal or a truth commission is self-evidently
but one element of a broader transitional process and should constantly
be articulated as such both in public utterances and in the working
practices of the legal professionals involved."[22] He cautioned against
giving too much credence to the retribution and deterrence justifications for legal justice stating that, "Individual responsibility fails to take
proper account of the complex collective factors which contribute to
violence." By finding a "small number of individuals officially guilty,"
McEvoy argued, we run the risk of "creating many more 'false inno-
cents.'"[23] I extend McEvoy's argument and contend that even legal
justice should not be understood narrowly as only the outcome of a
judicial proceeding.

Several other transitional justice scholars have demonstrated the
limitations of conceiving of justice simply in terms of legal judgments
and punishments.[24] Eric Stover concluded that transitional justice
must include "social justice, including finding the missing, providing
jobs and adequate housing, repairing factories and public buildings,
and reintegrating ethnically divided primary and secondary schools."[25]
Juan Méndez argued that, "It is a mistake for the human rights movement to allow itself to be painted into the corner of either a 'legalistic'
or a 'moralistic' position" on accountability for human rights violations.[26] Laurel Fletcher and Harvey Weinstein explained, "Although
billed by many advocates as critical to enable societies to recover from
mass violence, trials as justice are not the cure that all segments critical
to rebuilding seek."[27] Ruti Teitel acknowledged that, as "transitional
justice dilemmas" developed, they became "more comprehensive
than confronting or holding accountable the predecessor regime" and
asked "how to heal an entire society, and incorporate diverse rule of

[22] Ibid., 30.
[23] Ibid., 43.
[24] Laurel E. Fletcher and Harvey M. Weinstein, "Violence and Social Repair: Rethinking the
Contribution of Justice to Reconciliation," *Human Rights Quarterly* 24(3): 573–639.
[25] Eric Stover, *The Witnesses: War Crimes and the Promise of Justice in The Hague* (Philadelphia:
University of Pennsylvania Press, 2007), 145–46.
[26] Juan Méndez, "Accountability for Past Abuses," *Human Rights Quarterly* 19(2): 255–82.
[27] Fletcher and Weinstein, "Violence and Social Repair," 581.

law values, such as peace and reconciliation."[28] Brian Grodsky conceives of transitional justice not simply as criminal trials and punishment but as a continuum of transitional justice possibilities. The continuum begins with "cessation and codification of human rights violations" and "condemnation of the old system" and then "rehabilitation and compensation for victims." From these nonconfrontational mechanisms, Grodsky then places "creation of a truth commission" and "purging human rights abusers from public function" on the continuum. The pinnacle of Grodsky's continuum is "criminal prosecution of 'executors'" and "criminal prosecution of commanders." While this conceptualization recognizes different levels of transitional justice, it perceives the legal justice elements as results or outcomes instead of as a process.[29]

Understanding transitional justice as a process also better reflects the political reality of transitions. Political transitions are usually the product of compromise as they were in El Salvador, Chile, South Africa, and Guatemala. Many transitional justice scholars admit that state decisions on accountability mechanisms are based largely on political factors.[30] For example, a large number of scholars theorized that a regime's approach to transitional justice is determined by its power in relation to the deposed regime.[31] Luc Huyse, for example,

[28] Ruti Teitel, "Transitional Justice Genealogy," *Harvard Human Rights Journal* 16: 69, 70.

[29] Brian Grodsky, "Re-Ordering Justice: Towards A New Methodological Approach to Studying Transitional Justice," *Journal of Peace Research* 46(6) (November): 819–37, 824.

[30] Jamal Benomar, "Justice after Transitions," in *Transitional Justice*, vol. 1., Neil J. Kritz, ed. (Washington, DC: United States Institute of Peace Press, 1995), 32–41; Jack Donnelly, "International Human Rights: A Regime Analysis," *International Organization* 40(3): 599–642; Brian Grodsky, "Weighing the Costs of Accountability: The Role of Institutional Incentives in Pursuing Transitional Justice," *Journal of Human Rights* 7(4): 353–75; Brian Grodsky, *The Costs of Justice: Understanding How New Leaders Choose to Respond to Previous Rights Abuses* (South Bend, IN: Notre Dame Press, 2010); Naomi Roht-Arriaza, "Combatting Impunity: Some Thoughts on the Way Forward," *Law and Contemporary Problems* 59(4): 93–102; Daniel Sutter, "Settling Old Scores: Potholes along the Transition from Authoritarian Rule," *Journal of Conflict Resolution* 39(1): 110–28; Richard A. Wilson, *The Politics of Truth and Reconciliation in South Africa: Legitimizing the Post-Apartheid State* (New York: Cambridge University Press, 2001).

[31] Paloma Aguilar, "Justice, Politics and Memory in the Spanish Transition," in *The Politics of Memory: Transitional Justice in Democratizing Societies*, Alexandra Barahona De Brito, Carmen Gonzales-Enriquez, and Paloma Aguilar, eds. (Oxford: Oxford University Press, 2001); Luc Huyse, "Justice after Transition: On the Choices Successor Elites Make in

argued that "relative power tends to operate as a trump card where the greater the relative strength of the old elites compared to the new, the less likely we should see new elites pursue 'harsh' forms of justice."[32] Others emphasize the political nature of the courts trying human rights cases.[33] Justice is not the golden ring result of these political processes, and it is not won by overcoming the politics of these phenomena. It is achieved in increments as these political processes churn – the political processes themselves are the processes of justice. As McEvoy argued, "In the process, divorced from serious consideration of the wider political, social or cultural contexts which produced violence in the first place, the potential power of human rights institutions to prevent future violence is correspondingly reduced."[34] On the other hand, if we understand transitional justice as a system whose purpose must include the prevention of future violence, we can evaluate and calibrate it to require each element to take a logical step toward that end.

LEGAL JUSTICE AS A MULTIFACETED PROCESS

Using extensive interview data to study the effect of The Hague tribunal system on witnesses, victims, and survivors of the Yugoslav conflict, Eric Stover concluded that "for justice to play a meaningful role in post-war reconstruction it must be composed of several elements," and these elements go far beyond simple verdicts and sentences.[35] It must be a "consultive process" that considers the needs of those most

Dealing with the Past," *Law & Social Inquiry* 20(1): 51–78; Terence Roehrig, *The Prosecution of Former Military Leaders in Newly Democratic Nations* (Jefferson, NC: McFarland, 2002); Jose Zalaquett, "Balancing Ethical Imperatives and Political Constraints: The Dilemma of New Democracies Confronting Past Human Rights Violations," *Hastings Law Journal* 43: 1424–38.

[32] Huyse, "Justice after Transition," 78.

[33] Jeffrey Davis, *Justice across Borders: The Struggle for Human Rights in U.S. Courts* (New York: Cambridge University Press, 2008); Naomi Roht-Arriaza, *The Pinochet Effect: Transnational Justice in the Age of Human Rights* (Philadelphia: University of Pennsylvania Press, 2006); Michael J. Dodson and Donald W. Jackson, "Judicial Independence in Central America," in *Judicial Independence in the Age of Democracy*, Peter H. Russell and David M. O'Brien, eds. (Charlottesville: University of Virginia Press, 2001).

[34] McEvoy, "Letting Go of Legalism," 22–23.

[35] Stover, *The Witnesses*, 145.

affected by the violence.[36] Stover argued that justice must include judicial and nonjudicial elements such as truth commissions. Moreover, the judicial elements must be both international and domestic with clearly articulated goals and objectives. Similarly, McEvoy criticized the fact that in many legal justice efforts there "appears to be little cognizance here of the complex array of victims' needs beyond the punishment of perpetrators."[37] "Legal institutions associated with transitional justice can and should operate most effectively if they run in conjunction with properly managed, effective and accountable local or indigenous processes, which comply with basic international human rights standards."[38]

Defining legal justice solely as a result can foster the fundamental misapprehension that human rights come from the state or from state-created systems. Human rights are possessed by all people simply because they are human. Such rights do not rely on states, treaties, constitutions, or nongovernmental organizations (NGOs) for their existence. They are inherent. As Louis Henkin stated, "Human rights are universal: they belong to every human being in society."[39] Marko Milanović agreed that "rights are not gifts or privileges granted to individuals by generously disposed states, but rights which are inherent in the individuals' own dignity as human beings that cannot easily be sacrificed at the altar of security by overly eager states."[40] Systems of legal justice must therefore carefully articulate this truth and not imply that the court or tribunal will distribute human rights to the victims and litigants. Courts and tribunals can rule on violations of human rights law and can punish those who violate the law, but the rights in question exist regardless of the court.

According to philosophers like Locke, Rousseau, and Paine, people possess rights as a result of their creation rather than through any delegation by a government. As Thomas Paine concluded in the *Rights of Man*, "Society grants him nothing. Every man is a proprietor in society

---

[36] Ibid.
[37] McEvoy, "Letting Go of Legalism," 42.
[38] Ibid., 32.
[39] Louis Henkin, *The Age of Rights* (New York: Columbia University Press), 3.
[40] Marko Milanović, "Norm Conflict in International Law: Whither Human Rights?" *Duke Journal of Comparative & International Law* 20: 69, 99.

and draws on the capital as a matter of right." John Locke described humankind as born into a "state of perfect freedom," in which we possess all personal rights to the extent that no one tells us otherwise. Jean Jacques Rousseau emphasized that "what man loses by the social contract is his natural liberty and an unlimited right to everything he tries to get and succeeds in getting."[41] After World War II, nearly every nation adopted the Universal Declaration of Human Rights, which declared, "The inherent dignity and the equal and inalienable rights of all members of the human family is the foundation of freedom, justice and peace in the world."[42] In 1969, nations of the Americas signed the American Convention on Human Rights, which also endorsed the view that "the essential rights of man are not derived from one's being a national of a certain state, but are based upon attributes of the human personality."[43] Defining human rights justice exclusively as the result of a legal process can, often unintentionally, imply that the rights enforced arise from the state or from the court. This is especially perilous if the judicial system is extra-territorial or international.

As my overview of this scholarship demonstrates, defining transitional justice as a result – especially solely as the result of a legal process – misses essential elements of a multifaceted system. As all of these scholars acknowledge, legal justice is just one element of that system. In this book, I argue that this element is a process, rather than simply an outcome or result. Conceiving it as a dichotomous result misses the important contribution that each element of the legal process can make on legal justice for human rights violations. A limited, results-oriented view of legal justice also fosters a diminished view of the importance of legal justice in the transitional justice system. In other words, if we just focus on legal outcomes we miss the importance of the entire process on transitional justice. On the other hand, if we approach legal justice as a process we can fully appreciate how each step along that process contributes not only to legal justice, but also to

---

[41] Jean Jacques Rousseau, *The Social Contract, Or Principles of Political Right* (Whitefish, MT: Kessinger Publishing), Book 1, Section 8.
[42] Universal Declaration of Human Rights, G.A. Res. 217A (III), U.N. Doc. A/810 at 71 (1948), Preamble.
[43] American Convention on Human Rights, November 21, 1969, O.A.S. T.S. No. 36; 1144 U.N.T.S. 143; S. Treaty Doc. No. 95–21, 9 I.L.M. 99(1969), Preamble.

transitional justice and its ultimate goals of restoring human dignity and ending cycles of violence. The *process* of legal justice may indeed address the "complex collective factors that contribute to violence."[44] Moreover, while the result may be incapable of doing so, the legal process may actually contribute to justice that is "embedded in the communities that have been directly [affected] by violence and conflict."[45]

Kate Doyle, a senior analyst for the National Security Archive, has worked to obtain, analyze, and verify documentary evidence of human rights violations in Latin America. She is frequently called as an expert witness in human rights hearings and trials. She observed that legal justice is "not so much about the end result. The process of putting together a legal case, of having defendants, of having to bring evidence in, is such a radical step above what we were doing 15–20 years ago ... which was take testimony and mourn the dead." Ms. Doyle argued that the steps taken in a legal case are crucial in building justice for victims and survivors. "The experience of justice even when it doesn't result in someone going to jail is important." "The state has to come, they have to tell their side of the story, and the prosecution has to gather evidence." "In places like Guatemala where the judicial system is so dysfunctional this is an important part of learning to create justice."[46]

When we cling to the idea that transitional justice is a result – and a legal result at that – we reject any need to fully analyze the objective and subjective purpose of that result. The purposes of legal judgments are taken as given – retribution, deterrence, and enshrining the rule of law to name a few – but these are unsatisfactory when addressing widespread atrocities and transitions. For example, retribution is a gravely lacking basis for a system of legal justice after genocide. Punishment and deterrence are insufficient forms of justice for those whose family members have been disappeared and for the society born from a system of government that habitually disappeared its undesirables. As McEvoy argued, one pitfall of "the legalization of transitional justice is that in some transitional societies human rights concerns become a

---

[44] McEvoy, "Letting Go of Legalism," 43.
[45] Ibid., 29.
[46] Kate Doyle, senior analyst, National Security Archive, interview with the author, January 28, 2010.

byword for a retributive notion of justice."[47] When we grapple with the question of transitional justice for widespread egregious human rights violations, the purpose of our approach is far more complex, including societal, political, legal, and cultural elements. Similarly, when we examine the purpose of legal justice in postconflict societies, the purpose is more complex than retribution, deterrence, and the like. Tunnel vision focus on the narrow purposes of legal judgments can blind us to the multifaceted purposes of transitional justice and thus to how the legal process can achieve those purposes.

While retribution, deterrence, and elevating the rule of law are all necessary functions in legal justice, they are not the ultimate goal of legal justice for widespread human rights violations. Why is retribution needed? Why is respect for the rule of law desirable? Why is the truth required? Why do we need to express the wrongfulness of the rights violations? We certainly wish to deter future violations, but how does punishment do that, and is there a more comprehensive tool for deterrence? All of these purposes are worthwhile justifications for carrying out legal accountability and other justice mechanisms. However, they are not the overarching goal of legal justice, but partial and important elements of the ultimate goal. The overarching purpose of legal justice for human rights violations is to reconstitute the equilibrium of human dignity, or, in societies where it never existed, to build it. Through this, future violence can be deterred.

If Guatemala tried and punished every soldier, officer, and politician responsible for the massacres of Mayan Guatemalans, but left in place the presumption that the Maya were inferior – that they were the internal enemy and thus not worthy of life or physical integrity – the resulting justice would be vacuous. Instead, the process of justice must rebut the belief that certain people are not worthy of human dignity and elevate the victim or the victim's survivors to their rightful place as equal citizens of their society. By doing so, the process can prevent future violations. This can only be achieved by a multifaceted system of transitional justice that includes legal justice as one of its elements. A verdict or conviction alone cannot achieve this even if it meets its stated purposes. However, the *process* of legal justice, including the

[47] McEvoy, "Letting Go of Legalism," 24.

process that precedes, includes, and follows the verdict, can have a broad impact on reconstituting human dignity and contributing to the full transition from widespread human rights violations.

RESTORING HUMAN DIGNITY

Teófila Ochoa and Cirila Pulido described their suffering at the hands of the Peruvian military as a destruction of their human dignity (see Chapter 1). The conflict in Peru is an example of a tragically frequent phenomenon – a class of people is deemed less than human, or lacking human dignity and worth, to justify the extreme violence perpetrated against them. Eduardo González, an official for Peru's Truth and Reconciliation Commission (PTRC), concluded that the Accomarca massacre "was the result of disrespect for human life in general, but in particular is a mark of the great shame of Peru, which is racism against the indigenous population."[48] The officer commanding the attack on Accomarca, Lieutenant Telmo Hurtado, had asked his superiors "whether every civilian, any inhabitant, who was found in the area of the operation should be considered a terrorist criminal. And he was answered that, yes, every civilian in the area should be considered a terrorist criminal."[49]

Peruvian senator Javier Diez Canseco was among the senators who investigated the killings in the immediate aftermath of the massacre. He interviewed Hurtado, whose comments were recorded and transcribed. He asked him whether he just gave the order or participated. "I participated," Hurtado answered.[50] Then Senator Canseco asked whether Hurtado threw the grenades, and Hurtado answered, "To destroy, yes."[51] Senator Canseco concluded that "he was so clearly far away, distant from the people ... they were not human beings."[52] Regarding the people of the Ayacucho region, Hurtado asserted, "they cannot be changed and if I interrogate them, and I find that there's

---

[48] Hurtado Transcript at 127.
[49] González Testimony, Hurtado Transcript at 131.
[50] Testimony of Senator Javier Diez Canseco, Hurtado Transcript at 166.
[51] Ibid.
[52] Ibid.

nothing more useful in them, then I proceed.... I eliminate them."[53]
According to Peru's Truth and Reconciliation Commission, 75 percent of those who lost their lives in the conflict were native speak-
ers of indigenous languages and 40 percent of the crimes occurred in
the indigenous Ayacucho region, one of the poorest in Peru.[54] Clearly,
the security forces of the Peruvian state had accepted the notion that
indigenous Peruvians were not deserving of human dignity – that they
were not worthy of life or physical integrity.

The specific intent of brutal human rights violations, or at least
their known effect, is to strip human dignity from the victims. In a
public hearing, a victim of the political violence in Peru, Abraham
Fernández, stated that "Hopefully in ten or fifteen years' time we
too will be seen as Peruvians." As Magarrell Filippini pointed out,
this statement "sums up the feelings of the majority of the families
and victims" after the conflict in Peru.[55] Julissa Falcón's description
of the Truth and Reconciliation Commission in Peru demonstrated
how victims of atrocities, especially of sexual violence, were robbed
of their human dignity. He wrote, "The victims who did participate
in the PTRC's investigations would often talk about sexual violence
as if the victim were someone else. Others would use their own coded
language to tell their stories without mentioning explicit details [for
example] 'they affected my dignity as a woman' or 'my condition as
a woman.'"[56]

If, as I argue, the overarching purpose of the process of legal justice is to help restore an equilibrium of human dignity, this goal must
be kept in mind with each element of the process. For example, it is
true that the process of justice may fulfill the victim's desire for retribution, thus taking a step toward restoring the victim's dignity, but
that retribution must also preserve the dignity of the accused. Jaime
Malmud-Goti rejected retribution as a purpose of transitional justice
and argued that the dignity of a society and reforming the institutions

[53] Ibid.
[54] Lisa Magarrell and Leonardo Filippini, eds., "The Legacy of Truth Criminal Justice in the
Peruvian Transition," The Center for Transitional Justice, February 2006, p. 47.
[55] Ibid.
[56] Julissa Mantilla Falcón, "The Peruvian Truth and Reconciliation Commission's Treatment
of Sexual Violence Against Women," *Human Rights Brief* (12:2, Winter 2005).

responsible for the violations should be the primary goals.[57] Martha Minow held that retribution must include the guiding principle of the equal dignity of all persons. She acknowledged that by punishing those who commit atrocities, society corrects the defendant's view that the victim was less deserving of dignity. However, she argued that the dignity of the accused must be equally preserved in the punishment, because the "fantasy of revenge just reverses the roles of perpetrator and victim."[58] W. James Booth explained that "the absent victims of injustice are not 'dust and nothing' but retain a status and a presence as claimants on justice that gives rise to and shapes our efforts to address the wrongs done them. That presence calls on us to notice or recognize them as persons and not mere nullities owed no such acknowledgment."[59]

Placing the victim above the accused merely plants motivations for future violence. As Hannah Arendt observed, "The wrongdoer is brought to justice because his act has disturbed and gravely endangered the community as a whole, and because, as in civil suits, damage has been done to individuals who are entitled to reparation." She continued, "The reparation effected in criminal cases is of an altogether different nature; it is the body politic itself that stands in need of being repaired, and it is the general public order that has been thrown out of gear and must be restored, as it were. It is, in other words, the law, not the plaintiff, that must prevail."[60]

Deterrence is another oft-cited function of justice. Viewing victims as less than human or as beings without human dignity is a significant motivator for those who commit atrocities. Those in charge of operations that kill and disappear large numbers of people often claim it is justified because of their victims' lack of worth. For example, the governor of Buenos Aires province during Argentina's dirty war, General Ibérico Manuel Saint-Jean, boasted that "First, we are going to kill all

---

[57] Jaime Malmud-Goti, "Transitional Governments in the Breach: Why Punish State Criminals?" *Human Rights Quarterly* 12(1): 11–13.

[58] Martha Minow, *Between Vengeance and Forgiveness* (Boston, MA: Beacon Press, 1998), 13.

[59] James W. Booth, "'From This Far Place': On Justice and Absence," *American Political Science Review* 105(4): 750–64, 752.

[60] Hannah Arendt, *Eichmann in Jerusalem: A Report on the Banality of Evil* (New York: Penguin Classics), 9.

of the subversives, then their collaborators, then their sympathizers, then the indifferent; and finally the timid." He argued that subversives and collaborators were "useful idiots" whose ideology "converted [them] into automatons ... automatizing them like mechanical parts."[61] Of course, this is not strictly a Latin American phenomenon. At his genocide trial before the International Tribunal for the Former Yugoslavia, Bosnian Serb commander Ratko Mladic told the court, "I am General Mladic and the whole world knows who I am." One of his victims observed that she "saw him in court exactly as I saw him that day in Srebrenica 16 years ago ... he's still the big untouchable general, and we're so small."[62]

If this perceived lack of human dignity is one cause of atrocities, and one function of legal justice is deterrence, then how can justice confront this cause? How can justice convince society, not only that the act is deplored, not only that the act will be punished, but also that the foundation for it and all human rights atrocities is utterly false? It can do this only by convincing society of the victims' humanity. It must make humanization a central function of justice. Of course, in so doing justice must recognize the humanity – the human dignity – in those who carried out the atrocities as well. This is why, as I explain in Chapters 3 and 4, truth is a critical element in the process of legal justice. Stover recognized the need for the elements of justice to change the way members of society view each other. He argued that justice "requires a fundamental change to the social order which made possible the original crimes against humanity."[63] In his research on the former Yugoslavia, he found that "justice remains the event yet to come."[64] Minow pointed out that doctrines that often perpetuate impunity, like amnesties, privacy, and sovereign immunity are overcome by the demands of human dignity. She argued that, when "each individual is understood to be a rights

---

[61] Austin Sarat and Stuart Scheingold, *Cause Lawyering: Political Commitments and Professional Responsibilities* (Oxford: Oxford University Press, 1998), 503.
[62] Lauren Comiteau, "Defiance with a Smile: Mladic Faces Genocide Survivors in Court," *Time* (June 3, 2011). http://www.time.com/time/world/article/0,8599,2075747,00.html#ixzz1d8ypLpnX.
[63] Stover, *The Witnesses*, 15.
[64] Ibid.

bearer of equal dignity," governments will be less able to allow violations of human rights.[65]

Human dignity is the foundation of international human rights law. The three instruments making up the International Bill of Rights emphasize the importance of human dignity. The Universal Declaration of Human Rights, the International Covenant of Civil and Political Rights, and the International Covenant for Economic, Social and Cultural Rights place the dignity of humankind above all other values. The preamble of each instrument states that the "recognition of the inherent dignity and of the equal and inalienable rights of all members of the human family is the foundation of freedom, justice and peace in the world."[66] Louis Henkin, a renowned human rights scholar, defined human rights as "benefits deemed essential for the individual well-being, dignity, and fulfillment, and that reflect a common sense of justice, fairness and decency."[67] Similarly, Francis Fukuyama argued that rights allow citizens to require states to treat them with personal dignity.[68] Human dignity is also a foundation of humanitarian law. Article 3 of the Geneva Convention states that noncombatants "shall in all circumstances be treated humanely, without any adverse distinction founded on race, colour, religion or faith, sex, birth or wealth, or any other similar criteria." It prohibits "outrages upon personal dignity."[69] The Rome Statute of the International Criminal Court embraces the concept that the dignity of victims and witnesses is an essential function of the Court. Article 68 requires the Court to "take appropriate measures to protect the safety, physical and psychological well-being, dignity and privacy of victims and witnesses."[70]

---

[65] Minow, *Between Vengeance and Forgiveness*, 58.
[66] Universal Declaration of Human Rights, G.A. Res. 217A, at 71, U.N. GAOR, 3d Sess., 1st plen. mtg., U.N. Doc. A/180 (December 12, 1948) (emphasis added); International Covenant for Civil and Political Rights preamble, December 16, 1966, S. Ex. E, 95–2, 999 U.N.T.S. 171 (emphasis added); International Covenant for Economic, Social and Cultural Rights preamble, December 16, 1966, 993 U.N.T.S. 3 (emphasis added).
[67] Louis Henkin, *The Age of Rights* (New York: Columbia University Press), 2.
[68] Francis Fukuyama, *The End of History and the Last Man* (New York: Free Press, 1992).
[69] Geneva Convention, Article III (1949).
[70] Rome Statute of the International Criminal Court, Article 68 (July 17, 1998). http://www.unhcr.org/refworld/docid/3ae6b3a84.html.

The Appeals Chamber of the International Tribunal for the Former
Yugoslavia defined the international law violation of cruel treatment
as "an intentional act or omission … which causes serious mental or
physical suffering or injury or constitutes a serious attack on human
dignity."[71] The International Committee for the Red Cross (ICRC)
analyzed U.S. treatment of detainees in its wars in Afghanistan and Iraq
and found violations based on the treatment's impact on human dignity. The ICRC concluded that the U.S. "regime was clearly designed
to undermine human dignity and to create a sense of futility by induc-
ing, in many cases, severe physical and mental pain and suffering, with
the aim of obtaining compliance and extracting information, resulting
in exhaustion, depersonalisation and dehumanisation."[72] Courts have
repeatedly found violations of human rights law based on an action's
intrusion on human dignity. For example, the Federal District Court
in Massachusetts pointed out that "as with official torture, the practices of summary execution, 'disappearance,' and arbitrary detention
also have been met with universal condemnation and opprobrium."
The Court held that, "By international consensus, such practices have
been adjudged to be inconsistent with the 'inherent dignity and of the
equal and inalienable rights of all members of the human family.'"[73] In
another case, the Inter-American Court ruled that the state's denial of
Dominican nationality to the plaintiffs violated their human dignity.[74]

During Guatemala's thirty-year civil war, the "national security
doctrine" that dominated the state obliterated the human dignity of
anyone perceived as a threat. As the Inter-American Commission for
Human Rights has held, the national security doctrine was an "ideological manifestation of the struggle against the 'enemy within.'"[75] The

---

[71] *Prosecutor v. Tihomir Blaskic*, ICTY Appeals Chamber (July 29, 2004) at para. 595.
[72] International Committee for the Red Cross, "ICRC Report on the Treatment of Fourteen
'High Value Detainees' in CIA Custody," February 2007, p. 26.
[73] *Xuncax v. Gramajo*, 886 F. Supp. 162, 185 (D.MA 1995), quoting Universal Declaration
of Human Rights, Preamble & arts. 9–11, adopted December 10, 1948, G.A. Res. 217A,
U.N. Doc. A/811.
[74] *Yean and Bosico v. Dominican Republic*, Case 130, Inter-Am. C.H.R. (September 8, 2005),
available at http://www.cortei-dh.or.cr/serieic_ing/index.html (last accessed June 18,
2011).
[75] *Jose Gudiel v. Guatemala* ("Diario Militar"), Inter-Am. Comm. H.R. No. 12–590, Informe,
at par. 72 (February 2011).

concept of the "enemy within" or "internal enemy" rapidly expanded to include anyone perceived as dissenting, such as trade unionists, artists, educators, students, human rights activists, and the Mayan population.[76] At the start of the war, the humanity of the Mayan population was already threatened by historic racism, and this was exacerbated when Mayans were perceived as supporting the insurgency. State officials recently acknowledged that there was "irrefutable proof of the aberrant conduct and counterinsurgency logic applied by the state security forces against the so-called 'enemy within.'"[77]

One particularly vile tool security officials used to strike at the very dignity of the supposed "enemy within" was forced disappearance. In the Guatemalan trial of two officers who participated in the disappearance of Fernando García, Marina Villagrán testified about the psychological and social effects of disappearances. She referred to the "lingering anguish" of forced disappearance on the surviving families and argued that disappearance "creates an enormous fear and mistrust within society. One thinks, 'if this could happen to him, it could happen to me' and that produces in turn an absolute paralysis on political participation."[78] Disappearances cause people to feel that they are not safe – that their dignity as secure persons in a society is tenuous and that if they step out of bounds they could vanish. As Wendy Méndez recalled of her mother, "My last image of her remains her detention and this is so because there hasn't been any justice. Those responsible are still at large, free, enjoying their families, and grandchildren. That is something they took from me."[79]

The response must be the rebuilding of the truth that those deemed the "enemy within" have the same worth of those who

---

[76] Ibid. at pars. 74–76.

[77] Ibid. at par. 91, quoting report prepared by state officials.

[78] Kate Doyle, "'I wanted him back alive.' An Account of Edgar Fernando García's Case from Inside 'Tribunals Tower.'" Unredacted, October 26, 2010. http://nsarchive.wordpress.com/2010/10/26/i-wanted-him-back-alive-"-an-account-of-edgar-fernando-Garcías-case-from-inside-tribunals-tower/ (Last accessed February 15, 2013).

[79] HIJOS Guatemala, "Offensive for Remembrance: Where are the Disappeared?" http://www.mimundo-photoessays.org/2007/06/offensive-for-remembrance-where-are.html (Last accessed August 2, 2011).

carried out the campaign of oppression. Guatemalan rights advocate and Nobel Peace Prize recipient Rigoberta Menchu stated,
"The fundamental idea behind justice is to dignify the memory of
our deceased. It is to dignify the children, the women, the elders
who were annihilated through genocide, those who were kidnapped,
those who were disappeared, those who were tortured."[80] In a recent
bulletin, HIJOS argued: "According to our interpretation of the history and the memory of the resistance of the people, we understand justice to be a historical demand of the grassroots struggle for
dignity, sovereignty and self-determination."[81] Similarly, Almudena
Bernabeu, the Center for Justice and Accountability attorney representing the families in the Jesuits case in Spain, stated that one goal
of the prosecution in Spain was to win "respect for the dignity of all
the victims of the past."[82]

Victims and survivors express the need to restore dignity among
their objectives. In another case Ms. Bernabeu is litigating in Spain,
Feliciana M., a survivor of the genocide committed against Mayan
Guatemalans, testified, "We are trying to honor the memory of our
families, especially by exhuming their bodies so we can bury them with
dignity."[83] In a case in U.S. courts from El Salvador, Jose Calderon
testified at trial that his father's murder was part of an organized campaign against teachers. "On the part of the repressive core ... those who
never respected human dignity," he explained, "in the teacher, they
would see a potential enemy because a teacher can teach."[84] Verónica
Silva's husband, Winston Cabello, was disappeared by Chilean security officials. Upon winning a case in the United States against one
such official who was found liable for killing Mr. Cabello, Ms. Silva

---

[80] Rigoberta Menchu, in filmed interview, Amnesty International.
[81] HIJOS Guatemala, "Offensive for Remembrance."
[82] Center for Justice and Accountability, "Press Release: First International Witnesses to
Testify in Madrid in the El Salvador Jesuits Massacre Case," November 23, 2009.
[83] Kate Doyle, "Summary of Hearing Testimony of Feliciana M., Guatemala Genocide
Case," given to author June 30, 2008.
[84] *Chavez v. Carranza*, 2006 U.S. Dist. LEXIS 63257, 2 (W.D.Tenn. 2006) 15 Chavez,
Transcript of Trial, 696, lns 16–19. See *Chavez v. Carranza*, 413 F. Supp. 2d 891, 897
(W. D.Tenn. 2005).

stated, "This is but one step, but it's a step in the right direction to help us recover dignity in Chile."[85]

In 1982, Honduran security officials detained and tortured Óscar and Gloria Reyes for six months. In an interview, Mr. Reyes described justice in terms of equal dignity: "All people, regardless of their class, sex, race, political affiliation, religion, or any other special character-istic, receive the same treatment and respect that every human being deserves." He explained that justice also requires that an "individual who violates the above principle should be held responsible for his actions by the rule of law."[86] In 1980, Cecilia Moran Santos was a student at the National University and an employee of the Salvadoran Ministry of Education when Salvadoran security officials arrested her. They detained her at the National Police headquarters for eight days, tortured her repeatedly, and then kept her locked up for three years. To Ms. Moran, "justice is equivalent to equality … I have civil and human rights, and … I have the right to demand punishment for those who violate or break my rights, and I can bring them before a Court to judge their actions."[87]

Ms. Moran and Mr. Reyes also saw justice as a process to attain the goals they articulated. Ms. Moran explained, "individual cases are not sufficient for the pursuit of international justice, because they are part of the process." Mr. Reyes described the court ruling in his favor as only "one step towards our goal to get justice."

A Process to Restore Dignity

It is clear from the case studies I discuss in this chapter that the resto-ration of equal human dignity should be at least one of the chief pur-poses of any transitional justice mechanism – perhaps the overarching purpose. This finding necessitates the conceptualization of legal justice as a process. A guilty verdict alone cannot rehabilitate human dignity,

---

[85] Alfonso Chardy, "Crime against Humanity: Jury Finds Ex-Chilean Officer Liable in 1973 Slaying," *The Miami Herald*, October 16, 2003.
[86] Óscar Reyes, interview with the author, November 7, 2011. See *Reyes v. Grijalba*, Case No. 02–22046 (S.D.Fla. 2006).
[87] Cecilia Moran Santos, interview with the author, December 8, 2011. See *Chavez v. Carranza*, 413 F. Supp. 2d 891, 897 (W. D.Tenn. 2005).

but the revelation of the truth, the experience of testifying, seeing that the accused is subject to the law, and the countless other actions that allow victims and families to build their own process of justice can. By struggling to move the process along, advocates, victims, and families demonstrate convincingly that the victim and survivor is a person of equal worth, while preserving the dignity of the accused. The legal process overturns the contentions that the actions against the victim were justified and it rejects the argument that the victim or persons of the targeted group deserved their treatment.

The process of legal justice, like the system of transitional justice, is multifaceted and can be constructed based on objective and subjective demands. Several elements of this process can contribute significantly to rebuilding human dignity, and to transitional justice in general (see Table 2.2). Clearly, not every victim, survivor, or advocate will go through the same steps in the legal process, nor will they necessarily go through these elements in a particular order. Moreover, because my conceptualization embraces a subjective as well as objective definition of legal justice there may be elements that are not included in my analysis.

The first element in the process of legal justice is the forming of advocacy or victims groups (or joining one) to pursue the truth about the violations and to advocate for legal accountability. As I demonstrate in subsequent chapters, being part of such a group has been transformational for victims and survivors of human rights violations. It is an important element in the process of legal justice. After suffering the violation and hearing repeated state denials, joining with others who have suffered similar violations allows victims and survivors to find living proof that their experiences are true and that the denials are false. Through the group they can more effectively call for the release of information about the violations and litigate claims in domestic, foreign, regional, and international courts. I discuss the role of these groups further in Chapter 5. I demonstrate how they contribute to the multiple purposes of legal justice such as deterrence, reconciliation, and rebuilding human dignity.

In the next steps of the process, victims and advocates call on the state to investigate and reveal the truth about the violation and to prosecute those responsible. Asking the state to fulfill its obligations

Table 2.2. *Elements of Legal Justice*

Elements of the Process of Legal Justice
Forming advocacy groups to pursue the truth and legal accountability, or finding representation with an existing group.
Calling for the truth about the violations to be revealed and for prosecutions.
Calling on legal and judicial authorities to investigate violations and prosecute those suspected of criminal responsibility.
Uncovering the truth regarding the violations and finding hard evidence of that truth.
Participating in a truth commission investigation of the rights violations.
Pursuing criminal charges (in jurisdictions that allow private citizens to initiate criminal proceedings).
Proving the truth and legal accountability in a foreign, regional, or international court.
Having a foreign, regional, or international court issue findings of fact, conclusions of legal violations, and appropriate remedies.
Testifying before a foreign, regional, or international court.
Forcing government officials to respond to accusations before a foreign, regional, or international court.
Enforcing the foreign, regional, or international court ruling before domestic legal or political institutions.
Seeing those rulings obeyed.
Proving the truth and legal accountability in a domestic court.
Testifying before a domestic court.
Forcing government officials to respond to accusations before a domestic court.
Having a domestic court issue findings of fact, conclusions of legal violations, and appropriate remedies.
Seeing a domestic court issue convictions, sentences, and other remedies.
Participating in any appeals processes.
Working with community groups, local and international NGOs, and other venues to educate others on the violations, their causes, the legal process, and the current status of the legal process.
Taking foreign, regional, and international rulings and working to enshrine them in domestic law.
Taking judicial rulings and working to apply them to other violations either from the past or present, domestically or abroad.

to investigate and prosecute human rights violations is a crossroads in the process. When state officials are accused of human rights violations, most states choose the path of continued denials, obfuscation, and impunity instead of performing a full investigation and prosecution. This creates an additional rights violation by denying the rights to truth, information, investigation, and judicial protection. It exposes the extent to which the dignity of the victims and survivors is rejected by the state. The process of legal justice then becomes about overcoming state impunity in addition to seeking truth and accountability for the original violation. I explain this further in Chapters 3 and 4.

Victims and advocates can themselves uncover the truth about their violations and expose hard evidence of that truth despite resistance from the state. By interviewing witnesses, other victims, prisoners, and even soldiers and security officials, victims and advocates can find crucial evidence to advance the legal process. They often participate in truth commission investigations of rights violations. This step in the legal process can be instrumental in revealing the truth and enshrining it in an official report. Moreover, by combining the testimony of various victims, a truth commission can reach conclusions about the motives for the attacks and see patterns in the attacks. These conclusions can be persuasive and even controlling in subsequent judicial proceedings. The truth commission report can offer victims and advocates further evidence about the violations they have suffered. I explain the foundational importance of finding, exposing, and proving the truth in Chapters 3, 4, and 5.

In jurisdictions that allow private citizens to initiate criminal proceedings, victims and survivors can do so, thereby forcing police to investigate and judges to hear testimony. As a practical matter, however, courts in postconflict states are frequently instruments of impunity, and can shut down undesirable cases or bog them down with dilatory procedures. Moreover, as my brief discussion of the Myrna Mack case indicates, pursuing a human rights case in domestic courts can be exceptionally dangerous for the participants.

In such cases, advocates and surviving families can pursue truth and legal accountability in foreign, regional, or international courts. This can allow victims and survivors the opportunity to testify in court, to put forth and test evidence, and to prove their case, all crucial elements of the process of legal justice. Government officials must usually respond to the accusations in extra-territorial courts and officials often testify. This step in the process can result in a foreign, regional, or international court issuing findings of fact and conclusions of legal violations and even assessing appropriate remedies. Such a court ruling can then pressure government officials at home to allow the domestic legal process to go forward or to take positive steps in the investigation. Victims, advocates, and surviving families can work to enforce the foreign, regional, or international court rulings before domestic legal or political institutions. The extra-territorial ruling legitimizes the advocates' arguments and puts international pressure on states to comply. When states do so, by moving the domestic case or by awarding damages and other remedies, the victims' dignity and the truth of their arguments and accusations is further recognized. I discuss the impact of extra-territorial courts on the process of legal justice further in Chapters 6 and 7.

Proving the truth and winning legal accountability in a domestic court is an important aspect of the process of justice, perhaps the most important aspect. When victims and survivors testify before a domestic court, and have that court issue findings of fact, conclusions of legal violations, and appropriate remedies, the domestic legal system is at last overturning long-standing state denials and impunity. It is acknowledging the right of the victims and survivors to tell their story and accepting that the violations occurred and that those actions violated the law. Forcing officials to come before the court and answer accusations is in itself an important step. It demonstrates that those officials are subject to the law and subject to a legal proceeding initiated by the victims of violations. Of course, domestic trials can derail the process at any stage. Victims can be denied the right to testify, valuable evidence can be thrown out, the accused could claim immunity or amnesty, and the court could exonerate those who deserve conviction.

After a successful extra-territorial or domestic court case, participants can work with community groups, local and international NGOs, and in other venues to educate others on the human rights violations, their causes, and the results of the process. They can take foreign, regional, and international rulings and work to enshrine them in domestic law. Finally, participants can take judicial rulings and apply them to other violations from the past or present, in the country in question or in other states. In this way the process begins again and builds on itself. Each of these elements contributes to the purposes of legal justice. Each has an effect on retribution, reconciliation, deterrence, and each is a step toward reconstituting human dignity. Legal justice is this process, not simply the guilt or innocence stage of this process.

Wendy Méndez remembers her grandmother sitting on her front porch waiting for her daughter, Luz Méndez, to come home. "I remember her sitting outside her home, on a wooden chair, every day waiting, waiting for my mother to come home, 'maybe today love, I think she's coming home today, the peace treaties were signed and she's coming home, ask her to tell you the story of when she was little, my baby.' It broke my heart every time." The disappearance of Luz Méndez is an ongoing attack on her surviving family. The violation continues until the truth is revealed and acknowledged. Only through a process that recognizes the truth and that restores Luz Haydee's human dignity can Wendy Méndez and her brother begin to be restored. As I explain in the following chapter, finding and exposing the truth is the foundation of this process and the fuel that keeps it moving.

3 TRUTH AND THE PROCESS OF JUSTICE

THE GUDIEL CASES

The Guatemalan security forces came in four large jeeps. They burst into the small house José Miguel Gudiel was renting with his girlfriend and searched it. The agents beat Gudiel's girlfriend and landlord, but he escaped through a rooftop exit only to be chased down in a nearby park. It was September 22, 1983, and José Miguel Gudiel was never seen again.[1] For years his father, Florentín, and his sister Makrina demanded answers and campaigned for justice for his disappearance. In the nearly thirty years since, Guatemala has investigated neither Gudiel's whereabouts nor those responsible for ordering or carrying out his disappearance.[2]

Seven years earlier, when José lived with his family outside the capital, Florentín became a catechist and José went to work in the local mill to support his six brothers and sisters. Florentín taught his family the principles of liberation theology, which motivated José to join the union and work for social justice. Makrina recalled that "everyone who was organized in a union ... or who was a Christian who called for the dignity of life was identified as a communist, or as a guerrilla, or insurgent." "Our family did not escape that," she explained. "My dad and my brother were the first people in the community who were identified as being linked to a guerrilla movement."[3] One of the progovernment

---

[1] *José Miguel Gudiel Álvarez y otros v. Guatemala* ("Diario Militar Case"), Inter-Am. Comm. H.R., No. 12.590, Informe, para. 98 (February 2011).
[2] Ibid., Transmittal to the Court, pp. 3–4.
[3] Ibid., Informe, paras. 94–96.

paramilitaries distributed flyers accusing Florentín and José Gudiel of being communists and promising to kidnap them. In 1980, José moved to Guatemala City and joined the Organization of People in Arms. He disappeared three years later.[4]

The family was traumatized by José's disappearance. José's relatives fled to Mexico out of fear that others would be targeted. Makrina remembered the horror she felt thinking of the "torture that happened during his captivity." She felt "sure my brother cried, begged for mercy, for help, he thought of each of us, his family." José's sister Beatrice still feels that her greatest hope is to find her brother's remains. "It is sad not knowing where his remains are." She stated that she "just wants to know where the bones are, to give her brother the honor he deserves."[5] Truth is a large part of the process of justice demanded by the Gudiel family. The Gudiels brought Guatemala before the Inter-American Commission on Human Rights (the Commission), and it in turn has brought their case before the Inter-American Court of Human Rights (the case is discussed further in Chapter 6). Makrina described the justice she seeks this way: "Recounting the facts hurts, but at the same time is a healthy action." "For me, justice means that the state will accept that its policy resulted in the cruel and inhuman treatment of a person who was then disappeared." The remedies she envisions are linked with learning the truth. "We want information – what happened to my brother?"[6]

In this chapter, the work of Makrina Gudiel, Wendy Méndez, and other victims and advocates demonstrate that truth and information activates and sustains the process of justice. While the importance of truth for human rights justice is widely accepted, these case studies demonstrate the dynamic ways truth interacts with and fuels the justice process. Next, the case studies show how truth and information further the ultimate purpose of justice – the rebuilding of human dignity – and how the absence of truth perpetuates the fiction that the victims are not worthy of equal human dignity. In other words, denial of the truth allows the perpetrators to preserve their belief that the victims deserved their treatment. From here this chapter explains how

---

[4] Ibid., para. 96.
[5] Ibid., para. 100.
[6] Ibid., para. 104.

truth matters even without accountability. Truth alone can be the end of justice. Even if all the other reasons for justice have been vaporized by time and the mortality of man, the need for truth survives. Truth is immortal. In the following chapters, I demonstrate that victims and survivors have a right to truth protected by international human rights law and that this right includes the right to government documents and information. I then pick up with these case studies and tell the story of how advocates and victims uncover the truths their states work so hard to hide.

TRUTH AND THE PROCESS OF JUSTICE

Truth is the catalyst of justice. It starts when families of the disappeared demand answers about the fates of their loved ones, and when victims are driven to expose those responsible for ordering and carrying out crimes against them. Their first goal is the truth. A little truth does not quench this desire. It merely cracks the dam through which more facts must flow. Revealing and proving the truth sustains the process of justice and sometimes fulfills it.

State denial, obfuscation, and misinformation preserve entrenched impunity. Human rights crimes nearly always come with secrecy, denial, and forceful efforts to bury the truth, protect the guilty, and blame the victims. Argentine General Tomás Sánchez de Bustamenti argued during that country's Dirty War that, "In this type of struggle, the inherent secrecy with which our special operations must be conducted requires that we not divulge whom we have captured and whom we want to capture; everything has to be enveloped in a cloud of silence."[7] In another example, on April 9, 2012, Major Telmo Hurtado admitted to covering up the Accomarca Massacre when he testified in a criminal case in Peru. As I described in Chapter 1, Hurtado and members of Peru's military slaughtered sixty-nine villagers in Accomarca, Peru, including the families of Teófila Ochoa and Cirila Pulido. In the criminal case, Hurtado finally admitted that he was responsible for killing

---

[7] Austin Sarat and Stuart Scheingold, *Cause Lawyering: Political Commitments and Professional Responsibilities* (Oxford: Oxford University Press, 1998), 503.

thirty-one people during the attack and for covering up the massacre. He acknowledged that senior officials ordered him to hide their responsibility for the massacre so he "played the fool" when the Peruvian senate investigated the killings.[8] Often the goal of state oppression is to erase the victims from the history – the collective memory – of a society. Truth repairs this wrong. It fights back the years of repeated state denials and of blame for the victims.

While revealing the truth activates and nourishes the course of legal accountability, truth can also advance justice without or beyond legal accountability. To allege a crime, indict a suspect, prove a case, win a conviction, and justify a sentence, the truth of a human rights crime must be discovered, documented, and tested in a court of law. As the case studies outlined in this chapter show, some victims and families seek the truth at least in part to sustain criminal convictions against their attackers. Without truth there can be no legal accountability, but without legal accountability there can be truth. As Méndez argued, when we take a "sober and realistic view of political constraints in proposing accountability measures ... a program of truth and justice is not only the right thing to do, but also politically desirable because it goes a long way toward realizing our idea of democracy."[9] While the importance of truth for legal justice is axiomatic, its importance to justice goes beyond legal accountability. As Yasmin Naqvi found, truth "intersects with international criminal processes in various ways, at times strengthening the intended purpose to prosecute persons accused of international crimes and at times overriding the focus on the individual defendant and instead turning the attention of a case to the broader implications of international criminal trials."[10] Human rights justice often sets its sights on bigger goals than simply convicting the guilty, such as the facilitation of peace, reconciliation, the rule of law, retribution, deterrence, and the eradication of impunity. Again, Naqvi pointed

---

[8] The Center for Justice and Accountability, "Telmo Hurtado Testifies to Cover-Up of Accomarca Massacre in Peruvian Court" (April 9, 2012). http://cja.org/article. php?id=1080 (Last accessed August 20, 2012).

[9] Juan Méndez, "Accountability for Past Abuses," *Human Rights Quarterly* 19(2): 255–82, 255.

[10] Yasmin Naqvi, "The Right to the Truth in International Law: Fact or Fiction?" *The International Review of the Red Cross* 88(862) (2006): 245–73, 246.

out that "the significance of this by-product of legal truth has taken on a new dimension, owing no doubt to the unique objectives that international criminal law is supposed to fulfill and that go way above and beyond merely finding guilt or innocence of particular individuals."[11] Truth is the electricity that drives the machine, and sometimes it is enough just to turn the light on, and sometimes that is all the machine can do. Extra-territorial legal cases are exceptional vehicles for revealing and testing the truth because they allow advocates to evade the mechanisms of state impunity while using judicial fora to extract the truth and test its reliability under legal scrutiny. For these reasons, I examine the work of extra-territorial legal actions in Chapter 6.

Scholars embrace the importance of revealing the truth for both the narrow and broad purposes of human rights justice. Fuyuki Kurasawa pointed out that "bearing witness to past, present and future structural injustices and atrocities is necessary for forgiveness to be envisaged, for farsighted warnings about potential catastrophes to be heeded, for aid to those in need to be forthcoming and for solidarity with distant others to be built."[12] Ruti Teitel found that "establishing knowledge of past actions committed under color of law and its public construction as wrongdoing is the necessary threshold to prospective normative uses of the criminal law."[13] Diane Orentlicher argued that by exposing the truth about violations of the past and condemning them, prosecutions could deter potential lawbreakers and inoculate the public against future abuses.[14] W. James Booth agreed, arguing that when survivors uncover the truth, "their stories would be part of a repository of lessons for the future, or among 'the political-cultural resources' needed for resistance to injustice in the here and now."[15] Brian Grodsky contended that an essential element of transitional justice is to reach "consensus on the historical wrongs" and help

---

[11] Ibid., 246.

[12] Fuyuki Kurasawa, *The Work of Global Justice: Human Rights as Practices* (Cambridge: Cambridge University Press, 2007), 23.

[13] Ruti Teitel, "Transitional Jurisprudence: The Role of Law in Political Transformation," *Yale L.J.* 106 (2009): 2050–51.

[14] Diane F. Orentlicher, *Settling Accounts: The Duty to Prosecute Human Rights Violations of a Prior Regime*, *Yale L.J.* 100: 2537, at 2540.; Diane F. Orentlicher, *Genocide, in Crimes of War: What the Public Should Know 2d. ed.* (New York: W. W. Norton Press, 2007).

[15] James W. Booth, "'From this Far Place': On Justice and Absence," *American Political Science Review* 105(4): 750–64, 754.

form a "new societal bond."[16] Hearing the victims' stories and enshrining them in the judicial or historical record are essential parts of achieving justice for human rights violations.[17] From his interviews with victims and survivors of the Yugoslav conflicts, Eric Stover found that they believed justice "meant piercing the veil of denial about past war crimes that had shrouded divided communities since the war."[18]

Vaclav Havel told the story of a greengrocer in communist Czechoslovakia who hung "in his window, among the onions and carrots, the slogan: 'Workers of the world, unite!'"[19] He does this, Havel recounted, because "if he were to refuse, there could be trouble." Survivors and citizens in states torn apart by widespread human rights violations are asked to mount similar slogans – the slogans of amnesty, of moving on, of reconciliation, of national unity, and of democracy. Like the greengrocer, they are asked to ignore the truth – they are asked to forget the atrocities they have suffered. Havel went on:

> Let us now imagine that one day something in our greengrocer snaps and he stops putting up the slogans merely to ingratiate himself. He stops voting in elections he knows are a farce. He begins to say what he really thinks at political meetings. And he even finds the strength in himself to express solidarity with those whom his conscience commands him to support. In this revolt the greengrocer steps out of living within the lie. He rejects the ritual and breaks the rules of the game. He discovers once more his suppressed identity and dignity. He gives his freedom a concrete significance. *His revolt is an attempt to live within the truth.*

By rejecting the lie, the greengrocer has:

> shattered the world of appearances, the fundamental pillar of the system. He has upset the power structure by tearing apart what holds it together. He has demonstrated that living a lie is living a

---

[16] Brian Grodsky, "Re-Ordering Justice: Towards a New Methodological Approach to Studying Transitional Justice," *Journal of Peace Research* (46)6: 820.

[17] Jeffrey Davis and Edward H. Warner, "Reaching beyond the State: Judicial Independence, the Inter-American Court of Human Rights and Accountability in Guatemala," *Journal of Human Rights* 6(2): 250.

[18] Eric Stover, *The Witnesses: War Crimes and the Promise of Justice in The Hague* (College Station: University of Pennsylvania Press, 2007), 143.

[19] Vaclav Havel, "The Greengrocer." http://www.ppu.org.uk/learn/infodocs/people/pp-havel.html.

lie. He has broken through the exalted facade of the system ... he has said that the emperor is naked. And because the emperor is in fact naked, something extremely dangerous has happened: by his action, the greengrocer has addressed the world. He has enabled everyone to peer behind the curtain. He has shown everyone that it is possible to live within the truth.

It is similar with the victims of human rights violations. They are asked to forget their own pain or the son, daughter, brother, sister, husband, or wife who disappeared to let the new regime govern. They are expected to pretend the state is clothed in the innocence of past atrocities, in the endorsement of their necessity, or at least in the forgiveness of the victims. But the state is naked, and when a survivor exposes the truth the world can "peer behind the curtain" and see the lie upon which the system of impunity is based.

Cecilia Moran Santos, who was tortured for days in El Salvador in 1980, emphasized the importance of exposing the truth in her search for justice. "We are taking on an educational task," she explained, "so the history of violations and injustices does not continue repeating."[20] Juan Romagoza Arce sued the Salvadoran generals who ordered his torture during El Salvador's civil war in U.S. federal court. The generals had retired in Florida, and Romagoza and two other victims sued them for human rights violations under the Alien Tort Statute. In testifying, Romagoza reflected, "I am lucky to be alive, not like many friends and fellow doctors who died at that time through the death squads, through the guards, through the Army, [in] many ways." He felt it was his duty to expose the truth. "I am one of the few who can tell this story, and it is not fair for me to remain silent. It hurts to be here telling my story and reopening my wounds, but the truth can't be hidden, and it can't be buried."[21]

Without Truth, Impunity

José Gudiel's father, Florentín, a former revolutionary like his son, worked in community education after the Guatemalan Civil War

---

[20] Cecilia Moran Santos, interview with the author, December 8, 2011. See *Chavez v. Carranza*, 413 F. Supp. 2d 891, 897 (W.D.Tenn. 2005).
[21] *Romagoza v. Garcia*, 99–8364-CIV-HURLEY (SDFL 2002), Trial Transcript, pp. 154–55.

ended in 1996 and the family returned from self-imposed exile in Mexico. He organized housing projects for combatants who had been demobilized. For this work, the United Nations Development Program named him an "Anonymous Hero" in 2002. He was elected mayor of his city, Cruce de la Esperanza, about forty miles from Guatemala City.[22] On December 20, 2004, he was cycling home from work when two other cyclists approached, followed by a grey pickup truck with tinted windows. Armed men in the truck shot Mr. Gudiel in the back and knocked him off his bicycle. They got out of the truck and then "shot him in the forehead, and then shot him once more for good measure in the left temple." The killers took nothing and used hollow point bullets. Florentín Gudiel had been assassinated.[23]

This is the effect of state denial and impunity. Guatemala preserved its denial of any state responsibility for the disappearance of Florentín Gudiel's son, José. By failing to legally condemn it, the state maintained its justification for the atrocities committed against perceived enemies during the civil war. Florentín Gudiel, as a former revolutionary and as someone seeking to overturn those state denials, was seen as the enemy within and as a legitimate target. The Inter-American Commission for Human Rights concluded that Guatemala's withholding of the truth in José's case was in itself an attack – a violation of the survivors' human rights. It held that the "sum of years" that the information was concealed was a continuous part of the counterinsurgency.[24] The absence of truth and the persistence of impunity set the stage for the assassination of Florentín Gudiel.

Guatemalan law enforcement officials have neither arrested nor questioned any suspects. According to José's sister and Florentín's daughter, Makrina, the investigation has gone nowhere.[25] From the moment of Florentín's murder, there have been death threats and attacks against the family. Armed men in an unmarked car parked outside the family home during the wake.[26] Unidentified men threatened

---

[22] *Florentín Gudiel v. Guatemala*, Inter-Am. Comm. H.R. Report No. 109/10, Petition 1420–05, Ruling on Admissibility, para. 9 (September 8, 2010).
[23] Ibid., para. 10.
[24] Diario Militar Case, Transmittal Letter at p. 5.
[25] Gudiel, Admissibility, paras. 12–16.
[26] Ibid., para. 11.

anyone visiting the family during the traditional nine days of mourning, saying that they would "sufriran la misma suerte" (suffer the same fate).[27] Armed men wearing shirts with the insignia of the former right-wing ruling party, El Frente Republicano Guatemalteco (Guatemalan Republican Front), parked by the family home in the weeks following the murder.[28] Later several men attacked Makrina and tried to set fire to her car as she drove home.[29] Amnesty International released an alert warning that the family members, especially Makrina, were in "grave danger."[30] Amnesty International has concluded that these attacks against "human rights defenders and others involved in human rights cases may be part of a systematic campaign to silence those who have spoken out against impunity for human rights abuses."[31] Amnesty International recognized that, as a result of entrenched impunity, "Serving and ex-military personnel, some of whom have been implicated in these human rights abuses, are widely suspected of belonging to criminal networks that have enormous influence in both the government and the army."[32]

The Gudiel case demonstrates two fundamental points. When the state buries the truth in denials, impunity persists and new violations will occur. As the UN special rapporteur on the right to freedom of opinion and expression, Frank LaRue, observed, "The key issue in Guatemala even today ten years after signing the peace is impunity – the lack of justice."[33] The Guatemalan Historical Clarification Commission found that the state "allowed impunity to become one of the most important mechanisms for generating and maintaining a climate of terror."[34] The Inter-American Court of Human Rights has pointed out that many victims of forced disappearance "were captured in the plain light of day, in

[27] Ibid.
[28] Ibid.
[29] Ibid., para. 17.
[30] Amnesty International, "Fear for safety," AI Index: AMR 34/004/2005, p. 1 (January 10, 2005).
[31] Ibid., 2.
[32] Ibid.
[33] Frank LaRue in Rigoberta Menchu, *Granito: How to Nail a Dictator*, Skylight Pictures, 2011.
[34] Guatemalan Historical Clarification Commission Report, Conclusions I, para. 56. (1998). http://shr.aaas.org/guatemala/ceh/report/english/toc.html.

public streets, and this is evidence of the impunity with which the captors acted."[35]

J. Patrice McSherry and Raul Mejia stated that "Impunity allows the continuation of a state policy of terror as a political weapon; it serves to protect individual torturers and murderers in the military, who often continue to occupy high-ranking posts in civilian government."[36] Truth is the first step – the opening – that begins a process of dismantling impunity. Human rights scholars have embraced the idea that truth is essential to overturn impunity. Naomi Roht-Arriaza made this argument and quoted the presidential decree establishing the Chilean Truth Commission: "Only upon a foundation of truth will it be possible to meet the basic demands of justice and create the necessary conditions for achieving true national reconciliation."[37] Mark Amstutz similarly contended, "for without truth-telling there can be no accountability, and without accountability there can be no forgiveness."[38] Inga Genefke made similar arguments, stating that denial is "a tangible continuing injury" and moreover "an impediment in the individual's and society's healing process."[39] After months of fieldwork exhuming victims of mass killings in Guatemala, Victoria Sanford stated that denial and "amnesty creates an 'official story' that denies individual victims of violence, as well as their families and society in general, a forum for truth. Without truth, there is no chance of justice and accountability."[40]

In 2012, Dr. Efraim Zuroff helped track down ninety-seven-year-old alleged Nazi war criminal László Csizsik-Csatáry for the Simon Wiesenthal Center. Dr. Zuroff explained why it remains necessary to

[35] *José Miguel Gudiel Álvarez and others v. Guatemala* ("Diario Militar"), Referral No. 116/10, Case No. 12.590, IntAmCtHR, Sentencia, November 20, 2012, para. 214.

[36] J. Patrice McSherry and Raul Molina Mejia, "Confronting the Question of Justice in Guatemala," *Social Justice* (September 22).

[37] Naomi Roht-Arriaza, *Impunity and Human Rights in International Law and Practice* (Oxford: Oxford University Press), 179.

[38] Mark R. Amstutz, *The Healing of Nations, The Promise and Limits of Political Forgiveness* (Rowman & Littlefield Publishers, 2005), 25.

[39] Inga Genefke, "Statement on the United Nations International Day in Support of Victims of Torture," Secretary-General, International Rehabilitation Council for Torture Victims, Copenhagen, Denmark, June 26, 1999; quoted in Stover, *The Witnesses*, 12.

[40] Victoria Sanford, *Buried Secrets: Truth and Human Rights in Guatemala* (New York: Palgrave Macmillan Press, 2003), 396.

prosecute Nazi war criminals even though they are very old and even though the war ended more than sixty-five years ago. Among other reasons, Dr. Zuroff explained that "the trials of Nazi war criminals and collaborators are a very powerful tool in the ongoing fight against Holocaust denial and distortion." "They are an important addition to the existing documentation of the mass murders and emphasize the necessity of identifying those responsible."[41] The effort is necessary, in other words, to establish and preserve the truth regarding the genocidal crimes of the Holocaust, especially against those who would deny or distort that truth.

When the UN Commission on Human Rights appointed Louis Joinet to investigate the problem of impunity after widespread violations, he concluded that truth was necessary to prevent impunity. He argued that states have a "duty to remember" and "to be forearmed against the perversions of history that go under the name of revisionism or negationism." Joinet concluded that "full and effective exercise of the right to the truth is essential to avoid any recurrence of such acts in the future."[42] Antonio García, a Spanish lawyer working to bring high-level Guatemalan officials to justice for genocide, commented on the prominence of violence committed by clandestine groups in today's Guatemala. "Guaranteeing the impunity of the past, does not help the impunity of today," he observed.[43] Helen Mack, whose sister Myrna was assassinated by a Guatemalan death squad in 1990, observed that "Twenty years later we continue the fight against impunity ... because the impunity of the past is what has generated the impunity of the present."[44] In an interview, Ms. Mack explained

[41] Efraim Zuroff, "Why Nazi Hunting is Still a Worthy Pursuit," CNN (September 24, 2012), http://edition.cnn.com/2012/09/24/opinion/zuroff-nazi-hunting/ (last accessed September 24, 2012).

[42] Louis Joinet, "Question of the impunity of perpetrators of human rights violations (civil and political)," 1996/119, UN Doc. E/CN.4/Sub.2/1997/ 20/Rev.1., Annex I, Principle 1.

[43] Ivan Briscoe, "Guatemala's Court Wars and the Silenced Genocide," North American Congress on Latin America (February 4, 2008), http://www.nacla.org/news/guatemala's-court-wars-and-silenced-genocide (Last accessed December 12, 2012).

[44] Gerson Ortiz, "Recuerdan a Myrna Mack, a Veinte Años de su Muerte," La Hora, September 11, 2010, https://lahora.com.gt/index.php/nacional/guatemala/actualidad/134746-recuerdan-a-myrna-mack-a-veinte-anos-de-su-muerte (Last accessed May 30, 2012).

that this impunity has resulted in an overall "incapacity of the state to protect the most fundamental of human rights like the right to live."[45] Almudena Bernabeu, a lawyer for the Center for Justice and Accountability, stated that "if there is no justice, history repeats and repeats and repeats."[46] Cecilia Moran Santos, a Salvadoran torture victim, described the situation this way: "We have been forced to forget, to forgive and to reconcile with the idea that there are no rights, that we have to assimilate and recognize that nothing will happen to the perpetrators, that there is no need to impart justice."[47]

Truth and Dignity

As I argued in Chapter 2, the purpose of the process of human rights justice is to establish an equilibrium of human dignity destroyed by widespread atrocities and violations. When the truth is revealed and proved, the dignity of the victims and survivors is healed at least a little. Truth serves "to aid the healing process," according to Naqvi, and "among other things, it would offer a sense of closure, enable their dignity to be restored."[48] In Chapter 2 I told the story of Wendy Méndez and her siblings. Since that night when she was just nine years old, when Guatemalan forces captured her mother, she has been searching for the truth. She explained:

> One of the things that affect me the most is not having a place to take her flowers. I don't know what her final destination has been. It's a story without an end – like a badly made film without an end. It's not that we did not like the ending. It did not end! Until we find the disappeared, they will remain in their hands. The crime continues. She is still being forcibly disappeared today.[49]

Ms. Méndez frequently emphasizes the lack of truth more than the disappearance itself when discussing the effects of her loss through

---

[45] Helen Mack, Interview at the Washington Office for Latin America, May 15, 2008.
[46] Menchu, *Granito.*
[47] Cecilia Moran Santos, interview with the author, December 8, 2011.
[48] Naqvi, "The Right to the Truth in International Law," 249.
[49] HIJOS Guatemala, "Offensive for Remembrance: Where are the Disappeared?" http://www.mimundo-photoessays.org/2007/06/offensive-for-remembrance-where-are.html (Last accessed August 2, 2011).

the years. The dominant element of the holistic view of justice she described was truth – to learn the truth about what happened to her mother. She has argued that justice must "rescue and recover historical memory" and demands "historical memory and truth." "For us it is important to rescue our history not only as victims and survivors of genocide but also our history of resistance, struggle, life and joy that were lived and practiced during the war," she explained. Ms. Méndez recognized that "the clarification of truth is done through understanding the diverse experiences and points of view."[50] Marcia Méndez, Wendy's aunt and Luz Haydee Méndez's sister, publicly demanded the truth in a national newspaper article, "The army, the high command, the police, they know where the remains are."[51] The demand for truth is a universal one for human rights victims, especially for those whose loved ones have disappeared. Soberanis Natalia Galvez's son Carlos Guillermo Ramirez disappeared in Guatemala on February 15, 1984. "This is a problem that we carry within our soul," she observed. "Since he disappeared my life has been cut short. What I most want is to embrace even his bones. This is the only thing that keeps me alive."[52]

Psychologists and psychiatrists have demonstrated that victims and survivors heal somewhat when they testify about the truth of the violations they and their loved ones have suffered.[53] Dumisa Ntsebeza argued that by testifying and enshrining their experiences in the official record, victims gained a sense of "civil dignity as an equal citizen

---

[50] Wendy Méndez Interview.

[51] Daniela Castillo, "Lo que más deseo en esta vida es volver a abrazarlo aunque sea su osamenta," El Periódico (Guatemala), April 27, 2012, http://www.elperiodico.com.gt/es/20120427/pais/211390/ (Last accessed May 1, 2012).

[52] Castillo, "Lo que más deseo en esta vida es volver a abrazarlo aunque sea su osamenta."

[53] Inger Agger, The Blue Room: Trauma and Testimony among Refugee Women: A Psychosocial Exploration (London: Zed Books, 1992); Stevan M. Weine, Alma D. Kulenovic, Ivan Pavkovic, and Robin Geldons, "Testimony Psychotherapy in Bosnian Refugees: A Pilot Study," American Journal of Psychiatry 151: 1720–25; Patricia K. Robin Herbst, "From Helpless Victim to Empowered Survivor: Oral History as a Treatment of Survivors of Torture." Refugee Women and Their Mental Health 13: 141–54; Adrianne Aron, "Testimonio: A Bridge between Psychotherapy and Socio-Therapy," Refugee Women and Their Mental Health 13: 173–89; Ana Julia Cienfuegos and Cristina Monelli, "The Testimony of Political Repression as a Therapeutic Instrument," American Journal of Orthopsychiatry 53: 43–51.

before the law."[54] In her book about transitions in Eastern Europe, Tina Rosenberg wrote:

> Nations, like individuals, need to face up to and understand traumatic past events before they can put them aside and move on to normal life. This is important for the victims, who can truly heal and resume their contributions to society only when their dignity and suffering have been officially acknowledged.[55]

As it emerged from the violent oppression of apartheid, South Africa adopted a constitution expressly to build "a historic bridge between the past of a deeply divided society characterized by strife, conflict, untold suffering and injustice, and a future founded on the recognition of human rights, democracy and peaceful co-existence."[56] In their founding document, South Africans held that "to transcend the divisions and strife of the past, which generated gross violations of human rights, the transgression of humanitarian principles in violent conflicts and a legacy of hatred, fear, guilt and revenge ... there is a need for understanding but not for vengeance, a need for reparation but not for retaliation."[57] The constitution embraces a justice based largely on truth that sought to reestablish the human dignity of an entire population of victims.

After her sister Myrna was killed by a Guatemalan death squad, Helen Mack spent her life campaigning for truth and justice for her sister and countless other victims. She argued that "truth is powerful and that is why what really happened is coming to light."[58] "Myrna gave her life for the masses and that is why I continued with the case ... we must think about the dignity of all Guatemalans – those who have

---

[54] Dumisa B. Ntsebeza, "The Use of Truth Commissions: Lessons for the World," in *Truth v. Justice*, Robert I. Rotberg and Dennis Thompson, eds. (Princeton, NJ: Princeton University Press, 2000).

[55] Tina Rosenberg, *The Haunted Land: Facing Europe's Ghosts after Communism* (New York: Vintage Press, 1996), xviii.

[56] *Azanian Peoples Org.* (AZAPO) *v. The President of South Africa*, 1996 (4) SALR 637 (CC) para. 3.

[57] Ibid.

[58] Helen Mack, Interview with Beatriz Manz, "The Myrna Mack Case: Challenge to Military Impunity in Guatemala," Center for Latin American Studies, University of California, Berkeley, November 12, 2002.

never been recognized or taken into account."With regard to her efforts for legal justice, she stated: "What the case does precisely is to rescue the human side of Guatemala's history; the story of the masses. It has to be rescued, because of the many who refuse to recognize or admit that hundreds of thousands of innocent civilians died."[59] I discuss the Myrna Mack case in more detail in Chapter 5, but Helen Mack's comments here clearly indicate how truth nourishes the rebuilding of human dignity.

Alejandra García, the daughter of disappeared labor activist Fernando García (discussed further in Chapter 5), also stressed the fundamental importance of truth in recognizing not only her father's dignity but her own and her mother's. "For us moral reparation will be when the government recognizes that yes, something did happen and that the disappearance of Fernando was forced, and that our fight and our protests were valid; not like they called my mom back then that she was a revolutionary and crazy."[60] When the Guatemalan "government acknowledges what happened, that will dignify my mother's fight, my father's name, and even my own name," Alejandra stated.[61] She explained, "I have no words to describe how difficult it was for my mom to explain to a little girl that her father had disappeared, without knowing if he is dead or alive, if he will return home or not." "These things are not easy to explain," she reflected, "much less to a little girl that lost her father when she was a year and nine months old, and kept asking for him every moment."[62] Her mother, Nineth Montenegro, reiterated the link between truth, justice, and dignity. "I want to emphasize that life doesn't have ideologies; it's not about being left or right – it's about the right to live in dignity as human beings."[63]

---

[59] Ibid.

[60] Alejandra García, Radio Interview, "Corte IDH podría dictar sentencia en Caso de Desaparición de Fernando García en Ocho Meses," Emisoras Unidas 89.7, Guatemala City, May 2, 2012, http://noticias.emisorasunidas.com/noticias/primera-hora/corte-idh-podria-dictar-sentencia-caso-desaparicion-fernando-García-ocho-meses (Last accessed May 27, 2012).

[61] Ibid.

[62] Alejandra García, Statement.

[63] Nineth Montenegro, Radio Interview, "Corte IDH podría dictar sentencia en Caso de Desaparición de Fernando García en Ocho Meses," Emisoras Unidas 89.7, Guatemala

Truth is an essential part of the process of justice. Alejandra García tells us why. "My heart cannot rest and be at peace without the truth, as harsh as it may be, the truth always heals the soul."[64]

After being with the victims as they testified in the Guatemalan genocide case in Spain, Kate Doyle commented on the desire of the victims and survivors to pursue the truth. "A lot of these people have never been on a plane, never left Guatemala – it is an amazing act of will and bravery and endurance to be here [in Madrid] 27 years later to once again talk about seeing your brother's head smashed against a rock, to once again talk about seeing your baby killed."[65] The victims' lawyer, Almudena Bernabeu, commented about another case in the Spanish courts seeking justice for the assassination of the six Jesuit priests in El Salvador. Ms. Bernabeu stated, "This first round of testimony in Spain seeks justice on behalf of the victims' relatives and for the people of El Salvador. Guaranteeing justice and respect for the dignity of all the victims of the past is the only way that El Salvador can make the transition towards reconciliation and a stronger society."[66] The link between truth, justice, and human dignity is clearly established in the experiences of these advocates, survivors, and victims who have made its pursuit their life's work.

Truth as Justice

The pursuit of truth within the process of justice is not just a Latin American phenomenon. Victims and survivors the world over seek to uncover the truth about violations they have suffered even when time has erased all possibility of legal accountability. In 2010, thirteen Polish citizens and the Polish government sued Russia for the 1940 Katyn massacre. After the Soviet Union invaded Poland in 1939, agents of the Soviet secret police, the People's Commissariat for Internal Affairs

City, May 2, 2012, http://noticias.emisorasunidas.com/noticias/primera-hora/corte-idh-podria-dictar-sentencia-caso-desaparicion-fernando-García-ocho-meses (Last accessed May 27, 2012).

[64] Alejandra García, Statement.

[65] Kate Doyle, senior analyst, National Security Archive, Interview with the author, May 30, 2008.

[66] Center for Justice and Accountability, "Press Release: First International Witnesses to Testify in Madrid in the El Salvador Jesuits Massacre Case," November 23, 2009.

(NKVD), executed more than twenty-one thousand Polish officers, police, prisoners of war, and others. At the time, the Soviets blamed the massacre on Nazi forces, and for years the Soviet Union worked to hide the truth about the killings. In 1989, Soviet scholars revealed that Stalin ordered the NKVD to massacre the Poles. Advocates then uncovered a memorandum, signed by Stalin, ordering the execution of Polish officers and police (see Figure 3.1). In response Soviet General Secretary Mikhail Gorbachev invited a delegation of Polish survivors to the Katyn memorial, but he still refused to release all the records or formally accept responsibility. Among those invited was former U.S. National Security Advisor Zbigniew Brzezinski. Brzezinski gave a speech in which he emphasized the importance of revealing the truth surrounding the massacre. "It seems very important to me that the truth should be spoken about what took place, for only with the truth can the new Soviet leadership distance itself from the crimes of Stalin and the NKVD. Only the truth can serve as the basis of true friendship between the Soviet and the Polish peoples. The truth will make a path for itself."[67]

Since the fall of the Soviet Union, the Russian government has released additional information about the massacre, but it has kept most of the records classified. Polish survivors and the Polish government are demanding these records to identify the victims and to determine whether the massacre amounted to genocide. Thirteen family members and the Polish government have sued in the European Court of Human Rights alleging that the Russian government failed to provide an adequate investigation into the killings. The language of the complaint demonstrates the importance of the truth and how its absence facilitated impunity. It states that the families were "denied an effective remedy which would have been able to reveal the true circumstances in which their relatives had been killed," and the "above-mentioned deficiencies of the criminal investigation undermined the efficiency of other remedies, as the success of civil-law measures was made dependent on the result of criminal investigation."[68] This case

---

[67] "Commemoration of Victims of Katyn Massacre," BBC News, November 1, 1989.

[68] Ewa Losińska, "The Polish Government will Support the Relatives of the Victims of the NKVD in Strasbourg," *Rzeczpospolita* (February 18, 2010), Zack Zagger, "Poland government joins suit against Russia for 1940 Katyn massacre," *Jurist Legal News and Research, Paper Chase* (February 18, 2010).

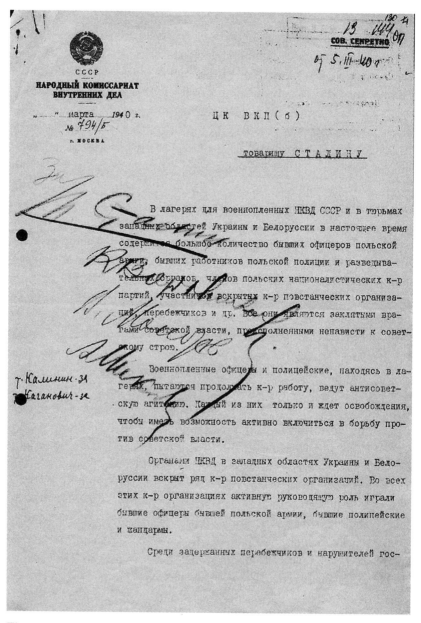

Figure 3.1. Memo planning the execution of Polish officers with Stalin's signature.

demonstrates the preeminence of the truth in the process of justice because the other oft-cited aspects of justice are necessarily absent. There can be no punishment, no retribution, and no deterrence when all those responsible have died in the intervening seventy years. Truth is the justice the victims seek – they are one and the same.

MISSING CHILDREN CASES – SERRANO CRUZ SISTERS

The search for the truth is particularly desperate in cases involving young children. On June 2, 1982, Salvadoran soldiers captured Ernestina and Erlinda Serrano and they were never seen again.[69] They were only seven and three years old.[70] Their parents, Dionisio Serrano and Maria Victoria Cruz Franco, are now dead. Their older sister, Suyapa Serrano Cruz, was with the girls the day that they were taken. Her family members had fled from their home that day because they heard gunshots and soldiers coming, but were separated when only her mother and two siblings, Fernando and Rosa, were able to cross the river to reach the town of Chichilco. Suyapa, with her own baby, father, brother, and Ernestina and Erlinda, took refuge in a wooded area known as "Los Alvarenga." Her father and brother went to find water while she, her baby, and the girls waited. When Suyapa heard the sounds of more soldiers approaching, she left the girls in fear that her crying baby would give them away. Unfortunately, the soldiers found Ernestina and Erlinda, and after much discussion, they took the girls. Suyapa heard the soldiers as they talked about what to do with her sisters, and after they left, she came out of hiding to look for them. When her father and brother returned, they continued looking for the girls to no avail.[71] A month later, once the family had reunited, Ms. Cruz finally learned about the disappearance of her two daughters. She would never see them again.

---

[69] Research on this and the Gelman case was conducted in part by my excellent research assistant, Micaela Perez Ferrero.

[70] *Serrano-Cruz Sisters v. El Salvador.* Preliminary Objections and Judgment of November 23, 2004, Inter-Am. Ct. H. R. (Ser. C) No. 118 (2004).

[71] Ibid.

The Salvadoran military captured dozens of children during this operation, and more than 800 disappeared during the war.[72] In these situations, the military refused to make any effort to reunite these children with their families. Instead soldiers took the children to army barracks far from their homes and occasionally turned them over to the Salvadoran Red Cross. The Red Cross in turn gave the children to orphanages or group homes that took care of these children, but did not try to find their families. Many children were assigned new identities, given fake birth certificates, and offered for adoption or given to military officers. Adoptions frequently involved the exchange of large sums of money.[73] According to El Salvador expert Margaret Popkin, after the war ended in 1992, families whose children were taken first turned to the Salvadoran Truth Commission. However, because the Commission was only empowered for a short time, it concentrated on egregious cases and "was unable to carry out the necessary research or reach conclusions about the fate of the children who disappeared in the context of military operations."[74]

On April 30, 1993, the girls' mother, Maria Victoria Cruz, filed a complaint before the Chalatenango Trial Court demanding justice for her missing daughters. The case went nowhere, however, as state officials refused to offer any information on the disappearance. Like many families whose children were taken, Ms. Cruz turned to the Asociación Pro Búsqueda, a human rights organization dedicated to finding the missing children of El Salvador.[75] The organization was founded in part by Father Jon Cortina, a Jesuit priest who, but for a visit to a rural parish on November 16, 1989, would have been among the victims of the Jesuits massacre discussed in Chapter 1. Despite the complete lack of state cooperation, Pro Búsqueda has found more than 245 missing children. Some were found in group homes or orphanages in El

---

[72] Ken Ellingwood, "Salvadoran Group Dogged in Search for Children Missing Years Ago in Civil War," *Los Angeles Times* (July 13, 2011).

[73] See Margaret Popkin, "The Serrano Sisters: El Salvador in the Inter-American Court of Human Rights," Equipo Nizkor (September 30, 2004), at: http://www.derechos.org/nizkor/salvador/doc/serrano.html (Last accessed February 9, 2012).

[74] Popkin, "The Serrano Sisters."

[75] Asociacion Pro-Búsqueda de Ninas y Ninos Desaparecidos. "Mision y Vision," at: http://www.facebook.com/PROBUSQUEDA (Last accessed February 9, 2012).

Salvador; others had been adopted in Europe, Latin America, or the United States. According to Popkin, "Almost without exception, they have wanted to learn about their families of origin and most have chosen to meet their relatives, even if they have grown up without speaking Spanish in a completely alien middle class world."[76] Moreover, the "others, who have grown up in Salvadoran institutions, discover they do, in fact, have a family."[77]

In the case of the Serrano Cruz sisters, like in numerous other cases, the Salvadoran state has aggressively blocked any attempt to learn the truth. It has denied the existence of any military operations in the area where the girls disappeared.[78] It has tried to discredit Ms. Cruz by claiming that she was merely seeking financial gain, and the state has even claimed that the sisters never existed.[79] Ms. Cruz carried on, however, and with the help of Pro Búsqueda she took the case of her missing daughters to the Inter-American Commission for Human Rights and then to the Inter-American Court of Human Rights. In 2005, the court ordered El Salvador to fully investigate what happened to Ernestina and Erlinda and to punish those found responsible.

Ms. Cruz's struggle continued, however, as the state was extremely slow in responding to the judgment.[80] Even President Mauricio Funes admitted that the state's institutions have not investigated the cases properly. He acknowledged that the victims and the society have the right to know what truly happened and the failure to make progress has been a failure to provide justice.[81] However, not until January 18, 2010 did President Funes apologize and ask for forgiveness from the

---

[76] Popkin, "The Serrano Sisters."

[77] Ibid.

[78] "Pro-Búsqueda Press Release on Serrano Cruz Case," (January 7, 2005) at: http://www.ediec.org/news/newsitem/article/pro-busqueda-press-release-on-serrano-cruz-case/ (Last accessed February 9, 2012).

[79] Popkin, "The Serrano Sisters."

[80] "United Nations Recommends El Salvador to Investigate the Whereabouts of the Serrano Cruz Sisters." *CEJIL*. Center for Justice and International Law, April 7, 2011. http://cejil.org/en/comunicados/united-nations-recommends-el-salvador-investigate-whereabouts-serrano-cruz-sisters.

[81] EFE. "Funes Reclama Falta de Investigación en los Casos de los Infantes Desaparecidos." *Que.es*. Factoría de Información, April 7, 2011. http://www.que.es/ultimas-noticias/sucesos/201103300154-funes-reclama-falta-investigacion-casos-efe.html.

victims of the human rights violations.[82] Estar Alvarenga, coordinator of Asociacion Pro-Búsqueda, claims that to date the government has still failed to diligently investigate the fates of the missing children.[83] Ernestina and Erlinda are still missing and Ms. Cruz, who fought for two decades to find her children, passed away on March 30, 2004.[84] Another mother seeking a lost child with the help of Pro Búsqueda, Enma Orellana, expressed her need to know the truth this way: "One suffers so by not knowing.... I dream that one day before I die, I might see that she has been found."[85]

MISSING CHILDREN CASES – THE GELMAN CASE

On August 24, 1976, security forces of the Argentine dictatorship broke into the home of the Gelman family.[86] They were seeking Juan Gelman, an ardent political activist and poet, but were unaware that he had already fled Argentina. In his place the security forces took Gelman's daughter, Nora Eva Gelman Schubaroff, his son, Marcelo Ariel Gelman, and his daughter-in-law, Maria Claudia García Iruretagoyena de Gelman, who was seven months pregnant at the time. Only his daughter would return.

Officials took the three victims to "Automotores Orletti," a car repair shop that had been turned into a secret detention and torture center in Buenos Aires. A week later, they freed Nora Gelman but continued to hold and torture Marcelo and Maria Claudia in separate cells. Neither one ever knew the fate of the other. At the end of September 1976, officials transferred Marcelo to an unknown destination and

---

[82] Castro, Eugenio, and Zoraya Urbina. "Gobierno Conmemora Día de la Niñez Desaparecida Durante el Conflicto Armado." *DiarioCoLatino.com*. Diario Co Latino, April 7, 2011. http://www.diariocolatino.com/es/20110329/nacionales/90949/Gobierno-conmemora-D%C3%ADa-de-la-Niñez-Desaparecida-durante-el-conflicto-armado.htm.

[83] EFE, "Funes Reclama Falta de Investigación en los Casos de los Infantes Desaparecidos."

[84] *Serrano-Cruz Sisters v. El Salvador*, Preliminary Objections and Judgment of November 23, 2004, Inter-Am. Ct. H. R. (Ser. C) No. 118 (2004).

[85] Ellingwood, "Salvadoran Group Dogged in Search for Children Missing Years Ago in Civil War."

[86] *Gelman vs. Uruguay*, Judgment of February 24, 2011, Inter-Am. Ct. H.R. (Ser. C) No. 221 (2011), paras. 79–90; Inter-American Commission on Human Rights. *Petition 438–06 Admissibility: Juan Gelman, Maria Claudia Garcia De Gelman, and Maria Macarena Gelman Garcia Iruretagoyena v. Uruguay*. Issue brief no. 30/07. 2007.

eventually killed him with a shot to the neck. They hid his body in a 200-liter drum filled with cement and sand. Years later, in 1989, the Argentine Forensic Anthropology Team found his remains in a suburban cemetery in the province of Buenos Aires.[87]

Officers of the Uruguayan Air Force transferred Maria Claudia to Montevideo, Uruguay. There, the Information Service of the Uruguayan Department of Defense (SID) held her despite the fact that she had no connection with Uruguay and had never been active in a militant organization that had anything to do with Uruguay. Near the beginning of November, they took her to a military hospital, where she gave birth to a baby girl. Both she and the baby returned to the detention center and stayed there until December 1976, when Uruguayan forces took the child and transferred Maria Claudia once again.[88] Maria Claudia's family has no concrete information about what happened to her after she was transferred, but they believe she is dead. They have worked tirelessly to discover what happened to Maria Claudia's little girl.

From 1976 to 1983, Argentina was in the midst of its "Dirty War." During this time, it is estimated that about thirteen thousand people were disappeared, but other estimations have been as high as thirty thousand.[89] The majority of the victims were never seen again. In 1986, the Argentine government enacted the Ley de Punto Final, an amnesty law that protected those who had committed atrocities during the Dirty War. In 1987, the government passed another amnesty law, the Ley de Obedience Debida, further protecting those who were subordinates from accusation for violations committed under orders. In 2003, the Argentine congress revoked both laws, and in 2005, the Supreme Court declared both unconstitutional.[90] As this case demonstrates, Uruguay worked with Argentina in carrying out its political repression. And like Argentina, Uruguay enacted the Ley de Caducidad (Amnesty Law) in 1986, which provided amnesty for those involved in human rights violations during the 1970s to the

---

[87] *Gelman*, para. 83.
[88] Ibid., para. 89.
[89] Sam Ferguson, "Argentina's 'Disappeared:' Justice at Last or Reneging on Amnesty?" *The Christian Science Monitor*, April 6, 2011. http://www.csmonitor.com/World/2009/1224/Argentina-s-disappeared-Justice-at-last-or-reneging-on-amnesty.
[90] Ibid.

1980s.[91] This law has been an insurmountable obstacle for victims attempting to obtain justice for the wrongs done to them and their families by the Uruguayan government.

On January 14, 1977, Angel Taurino, a policeman, and his wife found a baby in a basket on their front doorstep. All that was left with the baby was a note saying that she was born November 1, 1976 and that the mother could not take care of her. The couple took her in and baptized her as Maria Macarena Taurino.[92] While Maria Macarena grew and lived her life, never knowing the identity of her biological parents, Marcelo Ariel Gelman and Maria Claudia García, their father, Juan Gelman, aggressively searched for his lost granddaughter. After twenty-three years of searching, Juan Gelman came into contact with Maria Macarena's adoptive mother. Four months after the death of her adoptive father, Maria Macarena's adoptive mother finally told her how they found her.[93] After learning of her past identity and the forcible disappearance of her biological parents, Maria Macarena sought judicial nullification of her birth certificate and its re-issuance confirming her true identity as the biological child of Marcelo and Maria Claudia Gelman. This is not to say that she has rejected her adoptive family. On the contrary, Maria Macarena continues to live with her adoptive mother, who has been extremely supportive throughout this entire process.[94] Like the Katyn massacre case, these cases demonstrate the prominence of truth in the process of justice. It is the truth that the families seek above all – what happened to their children? Where are they now? Punishment, retribution, vengeance, and deterrence were all of lesser value to these families.

The experiences of the Serrano Cruz family, the Gelman family, and the Gudiel family show how exposing the truth is an essential function of the process of justice. To some survivors truth is justice, and to all it is a catalyst to the process. State denial keeps the wounds

[91] Ekaterina Sivolobova, "URUGUAY: Approaches to the Expiry Law." *Jurist: Legal News & Research*. U of Pittsburgh: School of Law, April 13, 2011. Web. April 6, 2011. http://jurist. org/dateline/2010/06/uruguay-approaches-to-the-expiry-law.php.

[92] *Gelman*, para. 107.

[93] Gabriela Canas, "Macarena Gelman: 'Fui un regalo robado.'" *Lanacion.com*. SA LA Nacion, 2011. Web. April 6, 2011. http://www.lanacion.com.ar/nota.asp?nota_id=1038048.

[94] Ibid.

open and keeps the violation going. Makrina Gudiel Álvarez testified before the Inter-American Court on the meaning of justice. For her, justice "is for the nation to know, to be able, through the testimony of what they did to my brother, [to know] that they did it to thousands who don't have the same opportunity as those of us who are in [this case who] have a connection through which we can seek justice."[95]

As these case studies suggest, exposing the truth is the essential ingredient of justice – it is the most important step in achieving the purpose of any justice process. States, courts, and international organizations have recognized this and accepted the right of victims and survivors to know the facts about their violations. As I demonstrate in the next chapter, victims and survivors have the right to truth recognized in international law, and this can be exercised through the right to government information.

---

[95] "Diario Militar Case," para. 104.

4 THE FOUNDATION OF JUSTICE: THE RIGHTS TO TRUTH AND INFORMATION

THE RIGHT TO TRUTH

In this chapter, I show that truth is a human right, and that it includes the right to government information. Exploring the legal foundations of the right to truth in the context of my case studies makes it clear that without information from the state, truth is illusive. I show that international human rights law requires states to unlock their archives and open their files to provide victims with the information required for them to know the full truth.

Truth is fundamental to the inherent dignity of the human person, and has developed into a human right of its own. As the United Nations Office of the High Commissioner on Human Rights (OHCHR) has held, victims of gross human rights violations, families of victims, and society have the fundamental human right to know "the full and complete truth as to the events that transpired, their specific circumstances, and who participated in them, including knowing the circumstances in which the violations took place, as well as the reasons for them."[1] In addition, "In cases of enforced disappearance, missing persons, children abducted during the captivity of a mother subjected to enforced disappearance, secret executions and secret burial place, the right to the truth also has a special dimension: to know the fate and whereabouts of the victim."[2] The OHCHR report concluded, "The right to

---

[1] United Nations Office of the High Commissioner on Human Rights (OHCHR), "Study on the Right to the Truth: Report of the Office of the United Nations High Commissioner for Human Rights" (UN/ Doc. E/CN.4/2006/91 2006), para. 59.
[2] Ibid.

the truth about gross human rights violations and serious violations of humanitarian law is an inalienable and autonomous right."[3] Despite this straightforward conclusion, however, the OHCHR report is not an enforceable source of international law – it merely recognizes that these enforceable sources exist. The legally enforceable right to truth comes from a multifaceted set of fundamental standards of international law.

The Foundations of the Right to Truth

The seeds of the right to truth come from humanitarian law. Article 33 of the 1977 Additional Protocol 1 of the Geneva Convention of 1949 requires parties to armed conflict to search for missing persons and communicate information about those persons. The United Nations General Assembly spurred the addition of this article by passing resolutions calling on states to acknowledge that families need to know the fate of those missing in armed conflict.[4] The right to the truth is closely linked with other rights, such as the right to an effective remedy, the right to legal and judicial protection, the right to family life, the right to an effective investigation, the right to a hearing by a competent, independent, and impartial tribunal, the right to obtain reparation, and the right to seek and impart information. Most important among these is the right to an investigation – as it obligates states to search for the disappeared, to uncover evidence of torture and killings, and to do so in a systematic way.[5] For example, in 1982 the Human Rights Committee interpreted the obligation to provide a remedy listed in the International Covenant on Civil and Political Rights as including the duty to investigate allegations of violations.[6] The European Court of Human Rights also found the "right to a remedy" provision in the European Convention to include the obligation to investigate.[7]

---

[3] Ibid., para. 55.
[4] General Assembly resolutions 3220 (XXIX), 33/173, 45/165, and 47/132; 20 ICRC commentary on article 32 of Protocol I of the Geneva Conventions, of August 12, 1949, para. 1211; UNHCHR Report at 6.
[5] Promotion and Protection of Human Rights, Study on the Right to the Truth, Report of the Office of the United Nations High Commissioner for Human Rights, Distr. GENERAL, E/CN.4/2006/91, February 8, 2006.
[6] 37 UN GAOR Supp. No. 40, UN Doc No. A/37/40 (1982) at 94.
[7] *Case of Klass and Others* (F.R.G.), 28 Eur. Ct. H.R. (ser. A) (1978).

The Inter-American System

The right to truth was born from the struggle to overcome denial and impunity. After her brother Manfredo Velásquez was disappeared by Honduran forces, Zenaida Velásquez tirelessly searched for information on her brother's whereabouts.[8] Manfredo Velásquez had been an elementary schoolteacher and university student when Honduran security officials captured him.[9] In all likelihood they targeted him because he was a leader in the Student Union and a political activist.[10] Velásquez left his home and wife and four children on September 12, 1981, and was never seen again.[11]

In the days, weeks, and months immediately after her brother's disappearance, Zenaida Velásquez pursued every avenue to get him back, including filing a petition for habeas corpus and seeking help from the U.S. Embassy. She even met with the head of the Honduran intelligence unit (DNI), Colonel Lopez Grijalba, but he denied any knowledge of Manfredo Velásquez. She and the family knew that if they did not find Manfredo soon he would be lost forever, but officials blocked her efforts at every turn. With no options in Honduras, Zenaida and other family members filed a complaint with the Inter-American Commission on Human Rights (Commission) on October 7, 1981.[12] Seven days later, the Commission asked the Honduran government to respond to the complaint with information on the disappearance, but the state did not reply. In the meantime, at tremendous risk, Zenaida managed to find out what happened to Manfredo in the hours and days after his abduction by conducting her own investigation. He was captured by the DNI in broad daylight, in the parking lot of a movie theater, and then held, interrogated, and tortured in Station II of the State Security Force. On September 17, officials moved him to the Infantry First Battalion headquarters. With this information in

---

[8] For a detailed account of this case, see Jeffrey Davis, *Justice across Borders: The Struggle for Human Rights in U.S. Courts* (New York: Cambridge University Press, 2008), 71–74.

[9] *Reyes v. Grijalba*, Case No. 02–22046 (S.D.Fla. 2006) (Statement of Facts and Conclusions of Law), 4.

[10] *Reyes v. Grijalba*, CJA Case Summary, http://www.cja.org/cases/grijalba.shtml.

[11] *Reyes v. Grijalba*, Statement of Facts and Conclusions of Law, 4.

[12] CJA, *Reyes v. Grijalba*, Plaintiff Profile, http://cja.org/article.php?id=469 (Last accessed September 5, 2012).

hand, the family petitioned the Commission to "intercede with the pertinent authorities so that justice may prevail and guarantee the life and safety of Angel Manfredo Velásquez Rodríguez."[13] To some extent the demand for information, the demand for truth, was a demand for Manfredo's life.

Despite repeated entreaties from the Commission, Honduran officials continued to delay and deny, and they did so for five years. In 1983, the Commission laid the foundation for the legal establishment of the right to truth and demanded that Honduras "undertake a complete and impartial investigation to determine the persons responsible for the acts denounced."[14] Finally, in 1986, the Commission referred the case to the Inter-American Court of Human Rights (IACtHR). (I describe the procedures of the Inter-American system further in Chapter 6).

Shortly before the IACtHR hearing, Honduran intelligence officials assassinated two important witnesses. The Court heard the case anyway and ruled in favor of the Velásquez family in 1988. In so doing, it recognized the human right to truth as emanating from several other rights protected by the American Convention. The IACtHR held that states have the duty of "juridically ensuring the free and full enjoyment of human rights."[15] "As a consequence," the IACtHR pointed out, "the states must prevent, *investigate* and punish any violation of the rights recognized by the Convention." The Court ruled that "even in the hypothetical case that those individually responsible for crimes of this type cannot be legally punished under certain circumstances, the State is obligated to use the means at its disposal to inform the relatives of the fate of the victims and, if they have been killed, the location of their remains."[16] The IACtHR explained that the right to an investigation and truth emanates from a state's obligation to protect its people from rights violations and to protect the right to judicial process. "The State is obligated to investigate every situation involving a violation of the rights protected by the Convention."[17] It outlined the meaning of this

---

[13] *Velásquez Rodriguez v. Honduras*, Inter-Am. Comm. H.R., para. 3.
[14] Ibid. (N 30/83 OEA/Ser.L/V/II.61, doc.44).
[15] Ibid. (ser. C) No. 4 (July 29, 1988) at para. 166.
[16] Ibid., para. 181.
[17] Ibid., para. 176.

right, explaining that it is "not breached merely because the investigation does not produce a satisfactory result." However, the investigation "must be undertaken in a serious manner and not as a mere formality preordained to be ineffective."[18]

Typically, the prosecutor, plaintiff, or complainant has the burden of proving culpability when litigating a case before a court of law. However, in the Velásquez case, the IACtHR ruled that the burden should be reduced because the state had exclusive access to the truth about what happened to the victims. The Court reasoned that "the policy of disappearances, supported or tolerated by the Government, is designed to conceal and destroy evidence of disappearances."[19] Therefore, if the complainants can demonstrate a policy and pattern of disappearances, "the disappearance of a particular individual may be proved through circumstantial or indirect evidence or by logical inference."[20] The IACtHR pointed out, "Otherwise, it would be impossible to prove that an individual has been disappeared."[21] Unlike in domestic criminal proceedings, the Court held that "in proceedings to determine human rights violations the State cannot rely on the defense that the complainant has failed to present evidence when it cannot be obtained without the State's cooperation."[22] Therefore, not only did the IACtHR establish the right to truth in this case, it recognized the control the state has over evidence of that truth, and it allowed complainants to establish culpability based on the evidence available to them. The effect of this ruling is to place the burden on state officials to reveal the evidence in their control or face international culpability based on circumstantial evidence.

The case is exemplary of the importance of truth in the process of justice as well. Zenaida continued to search for answers about her brother's disappearance and she risked her life to do so. In 1987, she was kidnapped by Honduran police forces. As they drove her away she saw a friend on the side of the street. Zenaida lifted her arms and showed her friend the shackles that bound her. Her friend notified

[18] Ibid., para. 177.
[19] Ibid., para. 124.
[20] Ibid.
[21] Ibid.
[22] Ibid., para. 138.

several human rights organizations, and groups all over the world protested Zenaida's capture and demanded her release. As a result, she was released unharmed. Her efforts to uncover the truth paid off. Ms. Velásquez helped her lawyers track down an eyewitness who had met Manfredo in a Honduran prison. The eyewitness eventually testified in a U.S. court in a civil human rights case that he had been in a prison cell near Velásquez, and heard him say, in a painful voice, "Help me, fellow. My name is Manfredo Velásquez."[23] The U.S. Court found Colonel Juan López Grijalba liable for the detention, torture, and death of Manfredo Velásquez.

"We did not want money," Zenaida Velásquez explained. "We wanted to find Manfredo's remains so that we could give him a proper burial." She explained how without the truth, the violation continued: "Our wounds will continue to bleed until we can bury our loved ones." The eyewitness testimony – that truth – was the link between Manfredo's disappearance, the Honduran security forces, and the colonel in charge, Juan López Grijalba. The truth Zenaida discovered led to legal accountability in the United States – crucial elements in the justice process.

Development and Expansion of the Right

The Inter-American Court further established the right to truth in a case from Peru that echoed the Accomarca Massacre case. Peru's government had passed an amnesty law that blocked all attempts to prove who was responsible for massacres committed against indigenous Peruvians. In the *Barrios Altos* case, the IACtHR ruled that "all amnesty provisions ... designed to eliminate responsibility are inadmissible, because they are intended to prevent the investigation and punishment of those responsible for serious human rights violations such as torture, ... forced disappearance, all of them prohibited because they violate non-derogable rights recognized by international human rights law."[24] The court went further and held that "owing to the manifest incompatibility of self-amnesty laws and the American

[23] *Reyes v. Grijalba*, Statement of Facts and Conclusions of Law, 4.
[24] *Barrios Altos* Case (*Chumbipuma Aguirre v. Peru*), Inter-Am.Ct. H.R. (ser. C) No. 87. (2001), para. 41.

Convention on Human Rights, the said laws lack legal effect."[25] In so ruling, the Court enforced the right to truth. It held that the amnesty law was void because through it "the surviving victims, their next of kin and the next of kin of the victims who died were prevented from knowing the truth about the events that occurred in Barrios Altos."[26] Once again, the IACtHR explained that the right to truth arises from the rights to "investigation and prosecution that are established in Articles 8 and 25 of the Convention."[27] In his concurring opinion, Judge Trindade expressed the Court's holding clearly: "Self-amnesties are, in sum, an inadmissible offence against the right to truth and the right to justice."[28]

In the *Serrano Cruz* case, the Inter-American Court ruled "that the State must ensure that the domestic proceedings to investigate what happened to Ernestina and Erlinda and, if appropriate, punish those responsible, has the desired effect."[29] The Court ruled that the family had the right to know the truth about what happened to the girls. It also held that those who preserve the wall of impunity and denial violate the Convention. "The Court has also established," the judges wrote, "that public officials or individuals who hinder, deviate, or unduly delay the investigations to clarify the truth about the facts must be punished."[30] The Court explained El Salvador's duties under the Convention. The state "must investigate the facts reported in this case effectively, in order to trace Ernestina and Erlinda, find out what happened to them and, if appropriate, identify, prosecute, and punish all the masterminds and perpetrators of the violations committed against them."[31] Also, El Salvador must conduct a "genuine search for the victims, and eliminate all the obstacles and mechanisms *de facto* and *de jure*, which prevent compliance with these obligations in the instant case."[32] The right to the truth is not owed simply to the family,

---

[25] Ibid., para. 44.
[26] Ibid., para. 47.
[27] Ibid., para. 46.
[28] Ibid., Judge Trindade concurrence, para. 5.
[29] Case of the *Serrano-Cruz Sisters v. El Salvador*, Inter-American Court of Human Rights, March 1, 2005.
[30] Ibid.
[31] Ibid.
[32] Ibid.

but to the entire nation. "The Court decides that the result of the criminal proceedings must be publicized, so that Salvadoran society may know the truth of what happened."[33]

In the case of *Heliodoro Portugal v. Panama*, the IACtHR reiterated its ruling that the denial of truth and information to the family of a disappeared man constituted a human rights violation. On May 14, 1970, Heliodoro Portugal was in the Coca-Cola café in Panama City when men in civilian clothes forced him into an unmarked vehicle and took him away. Twenty years later, when Panama restored its democratic government, Portugal's daughter began legal proceedings arising from the disappearance of her father. In 1999, officials from the attorney general's office found Portugal's remains outside a military barracks, and reported this finding to his family in 2000. Nobody has been prosecuted or convicted for kidnapping and killing Mr. Portugal, however. His family filed a complaint in the Inter-American system, but when the case reached the Inter-American Court, Panama argued the Court did not have jurisdiction because the alleged violation took place in 1970, twenty years before Panama accepted the jurisdiction of the Court. The IACtHR agreed that it only had the authority to rule on violations that occurred after 1990, and that because Mr. Portugal was killed before that date it could not consider the alleged extrajudicial killing claim. However, the IACtHR held that it could rule on the forced disappearance complaint because "forced disappearance of persons is characterized by being a violation of a continuing or permanent nature."[34] The forced disappearance of Mr. Portugal continued from the moment of his abduction in 1970 until officials told his family that they found his remains in 2000. In other words, the violation continued until the truth was discovered and communicated to Mr. Portugal's family. The violation of Article 7, the right to liberty, did not simply occur in 1970, and it did not simply have one victim. The violation goes on from the moment of capture until the truth is revealed.

The Court also ruled that Panama violated the family's right to humane treatment by refusing to reveal the truth. Mr. Portugal's daughter, Patria, testified that she has "suffered so much from the loss of my

---

[33] Ibid.
[34] *Portugal v. Panama*, Inter-Am.Ct. H.R. (ser. C) No. 87. (2008), para. 34.

father, not from his death itself ... more than from his death, from
his disappearance, the fact that he was beaten, tortured, disappeared,
leaving his family unprotected and not knowing where he was. This
is the greatest crime of all because we did not know where he was."[35]
The IACtHR held that the "uncertainty and absence of information
from the State regarding what happened to Mr. Portugal, which to a
great extent continue to this day, have been a source of frustration and
anguish for his next of kin, in addition to causing feelings of insecurity,
frustration and powerlessness in the face of the failure of the authorities to investigate the facts."[36] Denying the truth and hiding the facts
was in itself a human rights violation.

The European Court of Human Rights

In 1996, the European Court of Human Rights (ECHR) ruled that victims and family members had the right to an effective investigation in a
case called *Aksoy v. Turkey*. Mr. Aksoy was arrested during an uprising
of the Kurdistan Workers' Party in southern Turkey. Turkish officials
crammed him in a five-foot by three-foot cell with two other inmates,
and then tortured him by hanging him from his wrists with his arms
behind his back. After his release, he reported his torture to the public
prosecutor, but that office did nothing. Two years later, Mr. Aksoy was
murdered. The European Court ruled that Article 13 of the European
Convention on Human Rights "imposes ... an obligation on States
to carry out a thorough and effective investigation of incidents of
torture."[37] The Court explained that victims and their families have
a right to "a thorough and effective investigation capable of leading to
the identification and punishment of those responsible."[38] This holding
established a right to truth under the European Convention on Human
Rights by requiring States not only to investigate but also to share the
results of that investigation with the victims and families. As the Court
held, states must conduct an effective investigation "including effective
access for the complainant to the investigatory procedure."[39] The Court

[35] Ibid., para. 168.
[36] Ibid., para. 174.
[37] *Aksoy v. Turkey*, 21987/93 (Eur. Ct. H.R. November 26, 1996), para. 98.
[38] Ibid.
[39] Ibid., para. 98.

also placed the burden of revealing the truth about what happened to Aksoy in custody on the state, and not on Aksoy as the complainant. It held that "where an individual is taken into police custody in good health but is found to be injured at the time of release, it is incumbent on the State to provide a plausible explanation as to the causing of the injury."[40]

During the Chechnya conflict in 2000, Russian forces captured and disappeared hundreds of civilians they claimed were connected with Chechnyan terrorists. Russian soldiers stopped Said-Khuseyn Imakayev, a dentist, at a road block in Chechnya on December 17, 2000. Imakayev was last seen as troops forced him into a military all-terrain vehicle, while other soldiers drove his car. Imakayev's parents tried to get prosecutors to investigate the disappearance, and the prosecutors started and adjourned a kidnapping case several times. Seeing no hope of progress with the domestic investigation, they filed a claim in the European Court of Human Rights in February 2002. Four months later, troops barged in to the family home, confiscated documents and disks, and arrested Said-Magomed Imakayev, Said-Khuseyn's father. Mrs. Marzet Imakayeva went directly to the military officials in the area and in Grozny demanding information about her husband's whereabouts. At first military officials assured Mrs. Imakayeva that her husband would be released shortly. She notified the human rights groups helping her with her son's case and the ECHR. The ECHR contacted Russian officials and demanded information on Mr. Imakayeva. The Russian government responded by claiming that no government or military units were responsible for Mr. Imakayev's arrest. They claimed he was abducted by unidentified armed men.

A few weeks later, Mrs. Imakayeva and family members of other men who were disappeared with Mr. Imakayeva met with the area military commander. While on the base, they spotted one of the military vehicles that had been at the Imakayeva home. The commander questioned a crew member from that vehicle and, while Mrs. Imakayeva and the others watched, he confirmed his unit conducted operations in their town on the June night in question. He also confirmed his unit transported two prisoners in his vehicle, but claimed they were removed at a military

---

[40] Ibid., para. 61, citing *Tomasi v. France* (Eur. Ct. H.R. August 27, 1992, Series A no. 241–A), paras. 108–11; and *Ribitsch v. Austria* (Eur. Ct. H.R. December 4, 1995, Series A no. 336), para. 34.

checkpoint. With this information the Russian authorities transferred the case to the military prosecutor, who stalled the case yet again. Said-Magomed and Said-Khuseyn Imakayev were never seen again.

Russia refused the ECHR's repeated demands for information, arguing that responding would interfere with the domestic investigation or that it would violate Russia's Suppression of Terrorism Act. The ECHR acknowledged in a case where there has been no factual hearing in domestic court, "The Court is inevitably confronted [with] establishing the facts of the case."[41] In previous cases where disappearances and extrajudicial killings were alleged, officials connected to the Court "regularly undertook fact-finding missions for the purpose of taking depositions from witnesses, in addition to assessing the parties' observations and the documentary evidence submitted by them."[42] Citing earlier cases, the Court held that, because the facts of Imakayev's disappearance were exclusively in the control of the state, the state had the burden of proving what happened to him.[43] If a missing person was last seen in the custody of state officials, or "he or she entered a place under their control ... the onus is on the Government to provide a plausible explanation as to what happened on the premises and to show that the person concerned was not detained by the authorities, but left the premises without subsequently being deprived of his or her liberty."[44]

The Court confronted the challenge of exposing the facts of the disappearance in light of the Russian government's refusal to release any information. As the Court pointed out, "The Government refused to disclose any documents which could shed light on the fate of the applicant's son and husband and did not present any plausible explanation concerning their alleged detention or subsequent fate." The Court refused to allow Russia's stonewalling to stand in the way of issuing a ruling with findings of fact. "In view of this patent denial of cooperation, the Court is obliged to take a decision on the facts of the case with the materials available."[45] The ECHR held Russia's refusal

---

[41] *Imakayeva v. Russia*, App. no. 7615/02 (Eur. Ct. H.R. November 9, 2006), para. 113.
[42] Ibid., para. 117.
[43] Ibid., para. 114, citing *Tomasi v. France* (Eur. Ct. H.R. August 27, 1992), Series A no. 241–A, para. 108–111, and *Selmouni v. France*, no. 25803/94 (Eur. Ct. H.R. 1999), para. 87.
[44] Ibid., para. 115.
[45] Ibid., para. 119.

to cooperate was in itself evidence of its government's culpability, stating that, "it can draw inferences from the Government's conduct."[46] Therefore, the Court found that the applicant, Imakayev's mother, had proved beyond a reasonable doubt that Russian security forces captured her son. Imakayev's mother also convinced the Court that Russia deprived her son of his right to life. It held that because he disappeared in a war zone more than five years before the Court's decision, and because there had been no information on his whereabouts since that time, he could be presumed dead. The applicant convinced the Court that "in the context of the conflict in Chechnya, when a person is detained by unidentified servicemen without any subsequent acknowledgement of detention, this can be regarded as life-threatening."[47] Therefore, the Court ruled that Russia was responsible for Imakayev's death and that it violated the right to life articulated in Article 2 of the Convention.

As in the Inter-American system, the right to truth in the European system is expressed as arising from the right to an investigation and is derived from other rights expressed in the Convention. In the *Imakayeva* case, the ECHR held that the right to life "in conjunction with the State's general duty under Article 1 ... to 'secure to everyone within [its] jurisdiction the rights and freedoms defined in [the] Convention,' also requires by implication that there should be some form of effective official investigation."[48] For the investigation to be sufficient, "the persons responsible for and carrying out the investigation [must] be independent from those implicated in the events [and] must also be effective in the sense that it is capable of leading to a determination of whether the force used in such cases was or was not justified."[49] The Court ruled that the state must also take all the steps to secure the essential evidence and must complete the investigation promptly.[50]

Article 13 of the European Convention guarantees to those whose rights have been violated "an effective remedy before a national

---

46 Ibid., para. 133.
47 Ibid., para. 141.
48 Ibid., para. 146.
49 Ibid., para. 147.
50 Ibid., para. 148.

authority." The Court ruled that this includes the right to "a thorough and effective investigation capable of leading to the identification and punishment of those responsible ... including effective access for the complainant to the investigation procedure."[51] This right, according to the Court, is "broader" than the right to an investigation that arises from the violation of a substantive right and the duty to protect that right – the right to life in the *Imakayeva* case.

The *Imakayeva* ruling advanced the right to truth in five ways. First, it placed the burden on the government to prove what happened to people under its control, recognizing that the state often has exclusive control over the evidence in these situations. Second, it ruled that if the state refuses to release information about an incident, the Court can rely on other evidence – even circumstantial evidence – to make factual findings. Third, the ECHR held that the state's refusal to cooperate allows the Court to "draw inferences" about the government's actions in the case. These two developments not only allow the Court to issue findings of fact, they also prevent states from sabotaging legal proceedings by refusing to release evidence. They put pressure on states to release evidence to prevent the Court from drawing inferences from its failure to do so. Fourth, the Court ruled that when a victim disappeared from a conflict area like Chechnya, and when there has been no information from the government on the victim's status, it can presume the victim is dead and that the state is responsible for that death. Finally, the ECHR ruled that victims and survivors have a right to an effective investigation, they have a right to access that investigation, and they have a right to an effective remedy.

Treaties and International Agreements

On December 23, 2010, the International Convention for the Protection of All Persons from Enforced Disappearance came into force. At this writing, ninety-two nations have signed the Convention and forty have ratified it. The Preamble affirms "the right of any victim to know the truth about the circumstances of an enforced disappearance and the fate of the disappeared person, and the right to ... receive and

---

[51] Ibid., para. 193.

impart information to this end."[52] Article 24(2) states "Each victim has the right to know the truth regarding the circumstances of the enforced disappearance, the progress and results of the investigation and the fate of the disappeared person." It goes on to place the duty to reveal the truth on the state by requiring that "each State Party shall take appropriate measures in this regard."[53]

The legal right to truth is grounded in the right to information expressed in the International Convention on Civil and Political Rights (ICCPR). One hundred sixty-seven nations have ratified the ICCPR, and Article 19 of that treaty states, "Everyone shall have the right to freedom of expression; *this right shall include freedom to seek, receive and impart information* and ideas of all kinds."[54] The institution charged with interpreting and applying the ICCPR, the Human Rights Committee (HRC), held that denying families of those forcibly disappeared or secretly executed access to the facts regarding the fate of their loved ones constituted psychological torture in violation of Article 7.[55] Mariya Staselovich claimed that Belarus violated the ICCPR by failing to tell her anything about the fate of her son, who had been sentenced to death. In response the HRC wrote that it "understands the continued anguish and mental stress caused to the author, as the mother of the condemned prisoner, by the persisting uncertainty of the circumstances that led to his execution, as well as the location of his gravesite."[56] The "failure to notify the author of the scheduled date for the execution of her son, and their subsequent persistent failure to notify her of the location of her son's grave amounts to inhuman treatment."[57] In two cases from Tajikistan, the HRC emphasized that the ICCPR obligates states to provide information to families, including the location of victims' gravesites.[58]

---

[52] International Convention for the Protection of All Persons from Enforced Disappearance, Preamble, December 23, 2010. http://www.unhcr.org/refworld/docid/47fdfaeb0.html.
[53] Ibid. at Article 24(2).
[54] International Covenant on Civil and Political Rights, Article 19(2).
[55] *Lyashkevich v. Belarus*, Human Rights Committee, No 887/1999, UN Doc. CCPR/C/77/D/950/2000, para. 9.2.
[56] Ibid.
[57] Ibid.
[58] *Khalilova v. Tajikistan*, Communication No. 973/ 2001, UN Doc. CCPR/C/83/D/973/2001; *Valichon Aliboev v. Tajikistan*, Communication No. 985/2001, UN Doc. CCPR/C/85/D/985/2001 (2005).

The United Nations

The Inter-American and European courts have firmly established the right to truth. In both, the right arises from the right to an effective investigation and remedy. The United Nations and its instrumentalities have also articulated the right. The Office of the High Commissioner for Human Rights (OHCHR) concluded that, "The right to the truth about gross human rights violations and serious violations of humanitarian law is an inalienable and autonomous right, recognized in several international treaties and instruments as well as by national, regional and international jurisprudence and numerous resolutions of intergovernmental bodies at the universal and regional levels."[59] The OHCHR pointed out that while the right has developed in disappearance cases, "international law on the right to the truth has evolved to apply in all situations of serious violations of human rights."[60]

Clearly the right belongs to victims and their immediate families, but as the OHCHR pointed out, "the notion of 'victim' may have a collective dimension ... the right to the truth may be understood as both an individual and a collective right."[61] The society that has suffered widespread human rights violations has the right to know the full facts about who orchestrated and carried out the violations and the circumstances surrounding the violations. The right to truth means the right to know the causes of and circumstances surrounding the rights violations, as well as the results of any subsequent investigation. As we have seen from the cases discussed in this chapter, there is a right to know the fate of those who have disappeared and the whereabouts of their remains.[62] The OHCHR concluded that the right requires "knowing the full and complete truth as to the events that transpired, their specific circumstances, and who participated in them, including knowing the circumstances in which the violations took place, as well as the reasons for them," and where applicable, the right "to know the fate and whereabouts of the victim."[63]

---

[59] OHCHR, "Study on the Right to the Truth: Report of the Office of the United Nations High Commissioner for Human Rights," para. 55.
[60] Ibid., para. 38.
[61] Ibid., para. 36.
[62] Ibid., para. 38.
[63] Ibid., para. 59.

As Yasmin Naqvi pointed out in her study, in 1996, the UN Human Rights Commission ordered a study of impunity and concluded that "every people has the inalienable right to know the truth about past events and about the circumstances and reasons which led, through the consistent pattern of gross violations of human rights, to the perpetration of aberrant crimes."[64] In 2005, the UN Human Rights Commission adopted an updated Set of Principles for the Protection and Promotion of Human Rights through Action to Combat Impunity.[65] Principle 1 declares that states are required "to ensure the inalienable right to know the truth about violations." Principle 2 states that "every people has the inalienable right to know the truth about past events concerning the perpetration of heinous crimes and about the circumstances and reasons that led, through massive or systematic violations, to the perpetration of those crimes." Finally, Principle 4 holds that "irrespective of any legal proceedings, victims and their families have the imprescriptible right to know the truth about the circumstances in which violations took place and, in the event of death or disappearance, the victims' fate."[66]

Secretary General of the United Nations Ban Ki-moon endorsed the right to truth for victims of gross human rights violations. "Knowing the truth offers individual victims and their relatives a way to gain closure, restore their dignity and experience at least some remedy for their losses," Mr. Ban stated. "Exposing the truth also helps entire societies to foster accountability for violations ... and since the process of determining the truth often involves fact-finding inquiries and public testimony by victims and perpetrators, it can provide catharsis and help produce a shared history of events that facilitates healing and reconciliation." UN High Commissioner for Human Rights Navi Pillay declared: "The right to the truth implies knowing the full and complete

---

[64] Louis Joinet, "Revised final Report, Prepared Pursuant to Sub-Commission decision 1996/119, Question of the impunity of perpetrators of human rights violations (civil and political)," UN Doc. E/CN.4/Sub.2/1997/20/Rev.1, Annex II (October 2, 1997).

[65] Updated Set of Principles for the Protection and Promotion of Human Rights through Action to Combat Impunity, UN Doc. E/CN.4/2005/102/Add.1 (February 8, 2005). See Yasmin Naqvi, "The Right to the Truth in International Law: Fact or Fiction?" *The International Review of the Red Cross* 88(862) (2006): 245–73, 247, footnote 8, and 260.

[66] "Updated Set of Principles."

truth about events that transpired, their specific circumstances, and who participated in them, including knowing the circumstances in which the violations took place as well as the reasons for them."[67]

Customary International Law

From its foundations in humanitarian law to its enforcement in regional courts, such a wide variety of legal institutions have established the human right to truth that the right has reached the status of a customary rule of international law. Customary international law can be defined as a "customary practice of states followed from a sense of legal obligation."[68] Nations must obey a rule out of a sense of legal obligation, and this compliance must be widespread for that rule to be considered customary international law. Evidence of customary international law can be found in "the works of jurists, writing professedly on public law; or by the general usage and practice of nations; or by judicial decisions recognizing and enforcing that law."[69]

Juan Méndez was one of the first scholars to chart the emergence of the customary human right to truth. In 1997, he argued there was an emerging right in which states had an "obligation to disclose to the victims and to society all that can reliably be known about the circumstances of the crime, including the identity of the perpetrators and instigators."[70] Méndez also pointed out that "experts convened by the United Nations have argued that the right to know the truth has achieved the status of a customary international law norm."[71] Even in 2006, Naqvi acknowledged that "there have been repeated inferences of this right in relation to other fundamental human rights by human rights bodies and courts." Furthermore:

> Cumulatively, the effect of these decisions, taken together with the widespread practice of instituting mechanisms to discover the

---

[67] "UN Officials Underline the Right to Truth for Victims of Gross Human Rights Abuses," March 24, 2011, http://www.un.org/apps/news/story.asp?newsID=37878&Cr=human+r ights&Cr1 (Last accessed November 7, 2012).

[68] Restatement (Third) of the Foreign Relations Law of the United States § 102(2) (1986).

[69] *United States v. Smith*, 18 U.S. (5 Wheat.) 153, 160–61, 5 L. Ed. 57 (1820).

[70] Juan E. Méndez, "Accountability for Past Abuses," *Human Rights Quarterly* 19(2): 255–82, 261.

[71] Ibid., 262.

truth in countries where serious crimes have been committed, as well as some national legislation and the constant reiteration of the importance of knowing the truth by international and national organs, suggests the emergence of something approaching a customary right.[72]

Since that time ninety-two nations have signed and forty have ratified the International Convention for the Protection of All Persons from Enforced Disappearance. The Inter-American and European human rights courts have continued to issue rulings citing the rights to truth and investigations. Several national courts have also recognized the right in disappearance cases, such as the constitutional courts of Colombia and Peru, and the high criminal court in Argentina.[73] Moreover, the Constitutional Court of South Africa endorsed the right in the landmark case, *Azanian Peoples Organization v. The President of South Africa* (discussed later in this chapter).

OBSTACLES TO THE RIGHT TO TRUTH

National security secrecy doctrines like the State Secrets Privilege and Public Interest Immunity can obstruct the right to truth. In 2002, Binyam Ahmed Mohamed was arrested in Pakistan and swept up in the United States' extraordinary rendition program. He was transferred first to Morocco and then to Guantanamo Bay, where he was interrogated and tortured. When the United States charged Mohamed with aiding terrorism, British officials refused Mohamed's request that they turn over exculpatory evidence and evidence of his torture, claiming the evidence was protected by Public Interest Immunity. When Mohamed was released, he filed a civil case in the United States against the aviation company involved in his extraordinary rendition and torture. U.S. courts dismissed Mohamed's case under the States Secrets Privilege. While these doctrines allow states to conceal evidence and even terminate legal proceedings to protect national security, there is considerable risk that they will be used to avoid embarrassment or

---

[72] Naqvi, "The Right to the Truth in International Law," 267.
[73] OHCHR, "Study on the Right to the Truth: Report of the Office of the United Nations High Commissioner for Human Rights," para. 23.

even to protect those guilty of human rights crimes. States all over the world use these doctrines with different legal rules and institutional arrangements governing their use and applicability.[74]

As I explained previously, in the *Barrios Altos* case, the Inter-American Court of Human Rights held that amnesty laws are unlawful because they violate the right to truth and the right to a judicial remedy. Like national security doctrines, amnesties continue to be formidable barriers to learning the truth about human rights violations. In the Jesuits' case discussed in Chapter 1, El Salvador's amnesty law continues to hide the full truth about who planned, ordered, and carried out the assassinations. This same law of course blocks progress in thousands of human rights cases, including the investigation into the assassination of Archbishop Óscar Romero and the *Serrano Cruz* case. However, as Naqvi pointed out, the "general de-legitimization of any amnesties for international crimes in the international community is slowly closing the window on this limitation to truth-seeking."[75]

Not all amnesties are alike, and some types may not interfere with the right of victims and survivors to learn the truth. The clearest example of an amnesty that encouraged truth telling is the South African truth and reconciliation system. After decades of oppressive apartheid rule, and brutal suppression of any dissent, the South African government negotiated a peaceful transition to democratic governance. Its constitution states that it:

> Provides a historic bridge between the past of a deeply divided society characterised by strife, conflict, untold suffering and injustice, and a future founded on the recognition of human rights, democracy and peaceful co-existence.... The pursuit of national unity, the well-being of all South African citizens and peace require reconciliation between the people of South Africa and the reconstruction of society.... In order to advance such reconciliation and reconstruction, amnesty shall be granted in respect of acts, omissions and offences associated with political objectives and committed in the course of the conflicts of the past. To this end, Parliament under this Constitution shall adopt a law ... providing for the mechanisms, criteria and procedures, including tribunals,

---

[74] See also *Arar v. Ashcroft and others*, 414 F. Supp. 2d 250 (E.D.N.Y. 2006).
[75] Naqvi, "The Right to the Truth in International Law," 267.

if any, through which such amnesty shall be dealt with at any time after the law has been passed.

In 1995, the South African parliament passed the Promotion of National Unity and Reconciliation Act (the Act) establishing the Truth and Reconciliation Commission (TRC). The TRC's purpose was to promote unity and reconciliation by "establishing as complete a picture as possible of the causes, nature and extent of the gross violations of human rights."[76] This system embraced the idea that truth, and truth alone, could build unity and reconciliation from the rubble of decades of human rights violations. To establish this truth, South Africa granted "amnesty to persons who make full disclosure of all the relevant facts relating to acts associated with a political objective."[77]

Immediately after the parliament passed the Reconciliation Act, several victims of apartheid violations sued the government. They argued the Act violated the constitutional provision guaranteeing that "every person shall have the right to have justiciable disputes settled by a court of law or, where appropriate, another independent or impartial forum."[78] The South African Constitutional Court acknowledged that "every decent human being must feel grave discomfort in living with a consequence which might allow the perpetrators of evil acts to walk the streets of this land with impunity, protected in their freedom by an amnesty."[79] However, it upheld the Reconciliation Act, including the amnesty provision. In doing so, the justices recognized that the regime that perpetrates atrocities must also work to conceal them. "Much of what transpired in this shameful period is shrouded in secrecy and not easily capable of objective demonstration and proof." Like all societies in the aftermath of widespread atrocities, "secrecy and authoritarianism have concealed the truth in little crevices of obscurity in our history."[80] The South African Parliament and the Constitutional Court were willing to sacrifice traditional elements of legal justice like retribution and punishment to reveal the truth.

---

[76] *Azanian Peoples Org.* (AZAPO) *v. The President of South Africa*, 1996 (4) SALR 637 (CC), para. 4.
[77] Ibid.
[78] Ibid., para. 8.
[79] Ibid., para. 17.
[80] Ibid.

By granting amnesty, the Act eliminated the possibility of criminal or civil legal action against those accused of planning and carrying out human rights violations. However, it did so in exchange for
an enforcement of the right to truth because the TRC "may grant
amnesty in respect of the relevant offence only if the perpetrator of
the misdeed makes a full disclosure of all relevant facts."[81] The South
African Constitutional Court explained, "If the offender does not,
and in consequence thereof the victim or his or her family is not able
to discover the truth, the application for amnesty will fail."[82] In the
Barrios-Altos case, the IACtHR ruled that self-amnesties violate the
American Convention's rights to justice and truth. The South African
amnesty provision is not a self-amnesty enacted solely by the government accused of violations. On the other hand, it was proposed in
transitional negotiations and passed, upheld, and carried out by the
new democratic administration.

Whether the TRC achieved the ideal balance between accountability and reconciliation, and whether the system violated victims' rights
to legal justice are the subjects of numerous writings. It is important to
note that there are powerful criticisms of the TRC and of how it carried
out its mandate.[83] For example, it has been accused of failing to use its
subpoena power in important cases for fear of upsetting important parties. Also, the TRC only received 7116 applications for amnesty, a small
number given the length, pervasiveness and intensity of the oppressive
regime.[84] Dullah Omar, South Africa's Minister of Justice, observed
that "the perpetrators of apartheid crimes have not been as forthcoming as they should have been."[85] Most of the applications came from
people already in prison, which suggests the TRC system did not have
the effect of encouraging disclosure from those who were outside the
justice system. Most importantly perhaps is the TRC system's failure

---

[81] Ibid., para. 20.
[82] Ibid.
[83] See Richard Wilson, *The Politics of Truth and Reconciliation in South Africa: Legitimizing
the Post-Apartheid State* (Cambridge: Cambridge University Press, 2001); Audrey R.
Chapman, "Truth Recovery Through the TRC's Institutional Hearing Process," in *Truth
and Reconciliation: Did the TRC Deliver*, Audrey Chapman and Hugo van der Merwe (eds)
(Philadelphia: University of Pennsylvania Press, 2008).
[84] Jeremy Sarkin, "An Evaluation of the South African Amnesty Process," in *Truth and
Reconciliation: Did the TRC Deliver*, Audrey Chapman and Hugo van der Merwe (eds)
(Philadelphia: University of Pennsylvania Press, 2008).
[85] Quoted in Sarkin, "An Evaluation…" at 94.

to encourage top political and military officials to come forward and exchange truth for amnesty. As Priscilla Hayner observed, "many former perpetrators took the risk not to apply, particularly political leaders of the apartheid government and senior officers in the army."[86]

For our purposes here, however, it is sufficient to demonstrate that, unlike Peru's self-amnesty, the TRC enabled victims to discover truths that may have remained forever hidden. And as we have seen, the Constitutional Court's holding is further evidence of the importance of truth in the process of justice even in the absence of any hope for legal accountability. Naqvi emphasized this point, writing that "these types of 'accountable amnesties' may be considered valid and can be recognized under international law, which adds leverage to the notion that a right to the truth has a legal value, not merely a moral or narrative one."[87]

The most destructive obstacles to the truth are, of course, state denial, obfuscation, misinformation, and intimidation. With the exception of South Africa, all of the aforementioned cases include the same tragic story of state officials denying any knowledge of what happened to the disappeared, to the killed, or to the tortured. That denial frequently harnesses the many mechanisms of the state, including the investigators, the police, the judiciary, and the media. In Chapter 1, I described the investigation of the Jesuits' massacre in El Salvador in which the chief investigator actively worked to cover up the military's responsibility for the crimes. I also described the Accomarca Massacre in Peru in which the commander who led the attack concealed the involvement of senior officials who ordered the operation. Each case study I have cited, and each I will discuss later, includes efforts by states and state actors to conceal the truth.

DEFINING THE RIGHT – THE RIGHT TO INFORMATION

My analysis has established that victims of serious human rights violations and their families have the right to the truth about what happened to them or their loved ones. *Truth*, however, can be an imprecise term. The perpetrator's truth may be quite different from the victim's

---

[86] Priscilla B. Hayner, *Unspeakable Truths: Facing the Challenge of Truth Commissions* (New York: Routledge, 2002), at 43.
[87] Naqvi, "The Right to the Truth in International Law," 267.

truth. The right, therefore, must be to objective truth, or at least to a truth that is as objective as possible. That is, victims and their families have the right to know who was responsible for planning and carrying out the violation, and to know why they or their loved one was targeted. Families have the right to know where the remains of the deceased have been buried. In short, victims and families have the right to know the entire story of the violation committed against them. It follows from this definition of truth that the right must entitle victims and families to information, documents, testimony, images, and other forms of recorded evidence with which an empirical analysis can be conducted. Only through this information can the full truth be constructed. Caroline Elkins pointed out that "The process of redemptive justice, and with it the documentation and arbitration of historical trauma, has developed a momentum of its own over the last several decades."[88] Of the right to truth, Naqvi argued that "Like procedural rights, it arises after the violation of another human right has taken place, and would appear to be violated when particular information relating to the initial violation is not provided by the authorities, be it by the official disclosure of information, the emergence of such information from a trial or by other truth-seeking mechanisms."[89]

Wendy Méndez stressed the importance of getting records and documents from Guatemala regarding the disappearance of her mother and others disappeared by the state. She argued that gaining "access to this information for our own analysis and interpretation" was crucial in her search for justice. She did not seek information simply to form the basis for legal justice, but to derive the full truth for herself. "This is important especially for younger and future generations," she explained, "giving them the tools to analyze that truth and have them come to their own conclusions and political positions."[90]

On November 18, 2011, Brazil enacted a law guaranteeing the right to public information (Lei da Acesso a Informação) and a law creating a truth commission (Lei da Comissão da Verdade). The fact

---

[88] Caroline Elkins, "Alchemy of Evidence: Mau Mau, the British Empire, and the High Court of Justice," *The Journal of Imperial and Commonwealth History* 39(5) (December): 731–48, 732.
[89] Naqvi, "The Right to the Truth in International Law," 249.
[90] Méndez, Interview with the author.

that President Dilma Rousseff signed the two landmark laws on the same day demonstrates the connection between the right to truth and the right to government information. The laws also demonstrate the increasing prominence of the rights to truth and information as well as the continued strength of those who continue to preserve denials and impunity. While the truth commission was empowered to investigate human rights crimes committed by the government and by Brazil's insurgency between 1946 and 1988, by calling witnesses to testify under oath and by having unlimited access to government documents, its findings cannot be used in future prosecutions. The amnesty law was left in place. Granting this concession was the only way to over-come staunch military opposition to the creation of the commission. As a result, advocates have criticized the commission as merely a way of covering up the military's abuses. Torture Never Again leader Victoris Gabois complained that "Brazil's former companions in the armed resistance are making deals with the military and the oligarchs of Brazil."[91] For her part, President Rousseff emphasized the positive. "For generations of Brazilians who died, we honour them today not through a process of revenge, but through a process of rebuilding truth and memory," she stated. "The truth about our past is fundamental, so those facts that stain our history will never happen again."[92]

The IACtHR played a vital role in the passage of these laws. Brazil passed them one year after the IACtHR ruled Brazil had violated the American Convention on Human Rights during its Dirty War. Surviving family members won their case against Brazil, in which they claimed numerous rights violations stemming from the disappearance and execution of their family members. In that case, as in the other cases discussed previously, the Court upheld the survivors' right to truth, ruling that "the absence, lack of justice and information after the passage of thirty years and the omission of the authorities to act have

[91] Traci Tong, "Brazil's Truth Commission Under Fire from Military and Torture Victims," Public Radio *International, The World*, October 30, 2012. http://www.theworld.org/2012/10/brazils-truth-commission-under-fire-from-military-and-torture-victims/

[92] Erin Maskell, "Brazil Takes Steps on Truth, Human Rights, and the Right to Know," National Security Archive, November 22, 2011, http://nsarchive.wordpress.com/2011/11/22/brazil-takes-steps-on-truth-human-rights-and-the-right-to-know/ (Last accessed November 12, 2012).

created a state of anxiety, restlessness, lack of trust, despair, impotence, and anguish for the family members, seriously harming their emotional stability and right to personal integrity."[93] The Court not only held that the survivors had the right to truth, but it went further and tied it to the right to government information. For example, it stressed that "the harm they have lived has increased given the State's omission regarding the lack of information and investigation and the *denial of access to State archives*."[94] The Court pointed out that Brazil's refusal to reveal information on the disappeared "kept alive the hope of finding them" and has "prevented … their family members from providing a proper burial, disturbing their healing process and perpetrating suffering and uncertainty."[95]

During the hearing, psychologist Paulo Cesar Endo testified that "one of the situations that makes up a large part of the suffering for decades is the absence of a proper burial, the disappearance of the bodies and the unwillingness of the … governments to search for the bodily remains of their next of kin."[96] According to Dr. Endo, this "hampers the psychological detachment from said person and the next of kin that remain alive," and prevents closure.[97] The Court agreed and held that "the deprivation of access to the truth of the facts of the location of a disappeared person constitutes a form of cruel and inhumane treatment."[98] Moreover, "ascertaining the final whereabouts of the disappeared victim will permit the next of kin to heal from the anguish and suffering caused by uncertainty of the location of their disappeared family member."[99] This anguish and suffering has increased, "given the constant failure of the State authorities to offer information regarding the whereabouts of the victims or to initiate an effective investigation in order to ascertain information on what occurred."[100]

As a result of these findings, the Court ordered Brazil to conduct investigations into the whereabouts of the disappeared and into who was

---

[93] *Gomes Lund v. Brazil*, IntAmCtHR, Serie C No. 219, at para. 232 (November 24, 2010).
[94] Ibid., para. 238 (emphasis added).
[95] Ibid.
[96] Ibid., para. 239.
[97] Ibid.
[98] Ibid., para. 240.
[99] Ibid.
[100] Ibid., para. 241.

responsible for planning and carrying out these crimes. It ruled that Brazil should create a truth commission and that amnesty laws and statutes of limitations cannot preclude the investigations. It went further, however, and required "the State to adopt the legislative and administrative measures, and any other measures, that are necessary to strengthen the normative framework of *access to information*, pursuant to the Inter-American standards of protection on human rights, such as those indicated in the present Judgment."[101] The Court thus forged the connection between the rights to personal integrity, to truth, and to government information. One year later, Brazil passed its freedom of information law.

Four years earlier, in 2006, the Inter-American Court handed down its landmark ruling on the right to information in *Claude-Reyes v. Chile*. In this case, the Court held that "by expressly stipulating the right to 'seek' and 'receive' 'information,' Article 13 of the Convention protects the right of all individuals to request access to State-held information, with the exceptions permitted by the restrictions established in the Convention." Moreover, because Article 2 of the Convention requires states to protect the rights expressed in the other articles, government officials have an obligation to eliminate obstacles to the right to obtain information. As the Court explained, the two Articles taken together results in "the right of the individual to receive such information and the positive obligation of the State to provide it." The Court went on to explain the full meaning of the right. It pointed out that "information should be provided without the need to prove direct interest or personal involvement in order to obtain it." This has clear implications in human rights cases – all citizens, not only victims and their families, have the right to seek and receive information about rights violations. The Court explained that "the right to freedom of thought and expression includes the protection of the right of access to State-held information, which also clearly includes the two dimensions, individual and social, of the right to freedom of thought and expression that must be guaranteed simultaneously by the State."[102]

Numerous regional and international organizations and treaties have embraced the right to government information. Like the

---

[101] Ibid., para. 293.
[102] *Claude-Reyes et al. v. Chile*, Judgment of September 19, 2006. Series C No. 151, para. 77.

American Convention, Article 19 of the International Covenant on Civil and Political Rights recognizes the "right to freedom of expression; [and] this right shall include freedom to seek, receive and impart information and ideas of all kinds." The European Convention on Human Rights (Article 10) and the European Charter of Fundamental Freedoms (Article 42) each express the right to receive public information. The Inter-American Democratic Charter expresses the need for citizens to be fully informed to ensure a transparent and accountable democratic government. The UN Convention against Corruption and the Rio Declaration on Environment and Development make similar statements.[103] Moreover, according to the Open Society Justice Initiative, at least ninety-three countries had laws protecting the right to request and receive government information as of September 2012.[104]

The right to government information – freedom of information – is a potent tool for discovering, exposing, and proving the truth, and for activating the process of justice. Because government information can directly impeach years of state denials, it has a potent effect on reestablishing human dignity. The actions and motives of those responsible can be exposed in black and white for all to see. Of course, the challenge of enforcing this right, especially in human rights cases, is extremely difficult to overcome. However, Kate Doyle, her colleagues at the National Security Archive, and other advocates have confronted and overturned decades of state denial and obfuscation with documents and evidence. Ms. Doyle argued that they are "constructing a new story about what happened – an historical truth based on facts and documents and evidence."[105]

In the following chapter, I study the struggle of victims and advocates to extract records and documents from regimes that have dug in deep trenches of denial and impunity, and I examine their work in constructing the truth using those sources. Through this work, advocates and victims have sparked a small revolution in the process of human rights justice.

---

[103] United Nations Convention against Corruption, Articles 10 and 13, Resolution 58/4 of the General Assembly, October 31, 2003; Rio Declaration on Environment and Development, Principle 10, United Nations Conference on Environment and Development, June 3–14, 1992.

[104] Open Society Justice Initiative, "Access to Information Laws: Overview and Statutory Goals," http://www.right2info.org/access-to-information-laws (Last accessed December 17, 2012).

[105] Kate Doyle, interview with the author.

5   MOVING THE PROCESS AND PROVING THE TRUTH

UNCOVERING AND PROVING THE TRUTH

For victims, survivors, and their advocates, proving the factual truth is a crucial element of legal justice and can be a monumentally difficult task because of repeated state denials, cover-ups, and obfuscation. Advocates are revolutionizing the concept of justice by convincing jurists that truth is an essential component of human rights, and they are reforming the pursuit of justice by uncovering and analyzing documentary evidence that often contradicts decades of state denial. Moldy police files, clandestine communiqués, and lost bureaucratic records are being pieced together to elevate truth over the din of impunity. Human rights nongovernmental organizations (NGOs) are the moving force behind this process.

THE ENGINE OF THE PROCESS – NONGOVERNMENTAL ORGANIZATIONS

Human rights NGOs push the process of justice forward by revealing truth, demanding legal justice at home, pursuing their cases abroad, and using those cases to force the domestic process along. On April 26, 2012, Nineth Montenegro testified before the Inter-American Court of Human Rights that her husband, Edgar Fernando García, was "a man who always resisted the idea of living in a country where we were completely silenced by the military dictators."[1] He was a twenty-six-year-old engineering student outraged by the poor pay and working conditions for factory workers in Guatemala. He became a union leader and a member of the Guatemalan Workers' Party (PGT). In an interview before she testified, his wife recalled that he opposed the Guatemalan government "as a political activist not as a guerrilla."[2] Nevertheless any opposition, in fact any association with a labor union, was enough to make Fernando García an "internal enemy." On February 18, 1984, he left for work and never returned.

"When he didn't return for lunch – in this atmosphere when the military dictatorship takes, assassinates and massacres Guatemalans for their opposition daily – we began to feel afraid." All that day Ms. Montenegro looked and waited, and then at 3 A.M. the next day there was a sound outside her door. Thinking her husband had returned, she opened the door to find armed men outside. They pointed their weapons at her and demanded to be let inside. The armed men searched everywhere, pointed their guns at her, at her mother-in-law, and even at her eighteen-month-old daughter. They told Ms. Montenegro that they needed to take all the documents Fernando had in his possession and that her life and Fernando's life depended on those documents. "I wanted to believe that they were there to help, I don't know why," Ms. Montenegro recalled at the Court. "But when they were leaving I saw heavily armed men on the rooftops climbing down, and they got into cars without license plates," she testified. "At that moment I understood that something grave had happened."[3]

She knew then that the men were after any documents related to the labor union and that they would use them to compromise her husband. In the days following her husband's disappearance, Ms. Montenegro tracked down her husband's friends and they told her what had

[1] Testimony of Nineth Montenegro, *Edgar Fernando Garcia and Others v. Guatemala,* Hearing, April 25, 2012, Inter-Am. Ct. H.R. No. 12.343, 117/10, transcribed and translated by the author.

[2] Nineth Montenegro, Radio Interview, "Corte IDH podría dictar sentencia en Caso de Desaparición de Fernando García en Ocho Meses," Emisoras Unidas 89.7, Guatemala City, May 2, 2012, http://noticias.emisorasunidas.com/noticias/primera-hora/corte-idh-podria-dictar-sentencia-caso-desaparicion-fernando-García-ocho-meses (Last accessed May 27, 2012).

[3] Montenegro Testimony, Inter-Am. Ct.

happened; twenty-eight years later she told the Inter-American Court. Fernando and his friend, Danilo Chinchillo, were walking down 3rd Avenue in Guatemala City at 10 o'clock on a Saturday morning when Danilo spotted armed men in civilian clothing and ran. The streets were full of people, but Danilo and Fernando knew that would not stop Guatemalan security forces from attacking if they had come for them. Fernando also started to run, and the police opened fire. Danilo was hit and Fernando probably was too, but while Danilo was taken to a hospital in an ambulance, Fernando was thrown in an unmarked car and never seen again. They had been on their way to meet a fellow PGT member, Ana Lucrecia Molina Theissen.[4] From his hospital bed Danilo gave a taped interview in which he described his escape and Fernando being taken away in a car belonging to the Fourth Corps (Cuatro Cuerpo) of the national police – a unit known for forced disappearances.

As Ms. Montenegro told the Inter-American Court, her husband's case became emblematic in Guatemala because "not one single day did we rest in our struggle for my husband, not one single day." In the first week, Ms. Montenegro went to Fernando's factory and to the union and demanded that those in charge intercede on his behalf. When, by the end of the week, she had not heard a single answer, she gave a press conference with her baby daughter in which she told the story of Fernando's capture. To publicly accuse the government like this during a time when the slightest opposition justified the harshest government reprisals was an act of extreme courage. Ms. Montenegro went to the government officials themselves, including the head of the Fourth Corps of the national police, Jorge Alberto Gomez, the head of the national police, Hector de la Cruz, and even the head of state, General Óscar Humberto Mejía Victores. She brought her daughter so she could talk to the head of state. "I wanted to appeal to his heart because the only thing I wanted was for Fernando to return home

---

[4] Ana Lucrecia Molina Theissen, Testimony before the Guatemalan Criminal Court, Guatemala City, reported by Kate Doyle, "'I wanted him back alive.' An Account of Edgar Fernando García's Case from Inside 'Tribunals Tower,'" National Security Archive, October 26, 2010, http://nsarchive.wordpress.com/2010/10/26/i-wanted-him-back-alive-"-an-account-of-edgar-fernando-Garcías-case-from-inside-tribunals-tower/ (Last accessed May 22, 2012). When Ms. Theissen showed up late, the men were nowhere to be found. Later she discovered what happened and was devastated.

alive – nothing else." Instead he told her, "Lady, get used to this, we're in a dirty war."[5] When Ms. Montenegro went to the Fourth Corps of the national police, she received an answer that tragically exemplified the mindset of the Guatemalan security forces and the impunity with which they operated. An armed and masked man told her: "Look Señora, I'm going to tell you one thing, here we do detain people, but only the guerillas, the communists, the perverts of this country. You say your husband is a good father, that he was a good worker, that he was honest. Do you really believe we could have your husband?"[6]

The García Case and the Founding of the Grupo de Apoyo Mutuo

In June 1984, after running into continuous rebukes and denials from the Guatemalan state, Ms. Montenegro decided that to find her husband she needed to organize. Along with several other families of the disappeared she cofounded the Mutual Support Group (Grupo de Apoyo Mutuo or GAM), possibly the first human rights organization in Guatemala. When she testified before the Inter-American Court, Ms. Montenegro recalled that in the months after Fernando disappeared many people supported her in her search, and many people drew closer "because we were all living in the same situation" with loved ones disappeared. "So we decided to organize for support, for solidarity, and we were the voice of those who had been silenced."[7] GAM pushed the Guatemalan government to turn over information about Fernando García and other disappeared victims by organizing demonstrations, meeting with government officials, and coordinating with international human rights groups. However, the state never replied to repeated requests for information, telling Ms. Montenegro at various times that her husband did not exist or that he had moved to Canada.[8]

---

[5] *Edgar Fernando García and Others v. Guatemala*, Report, October 22, 2010, Inter-Am. Comm. H.R. No. 12.343, 117/10 at 20, http://www.cidh.oas.org/demandas/12.343esp.pdf (Last accessed June 1, 2012).
[6] *Guatemala: Memoria y Silencio*, Caso Ilustrativo No. 48, Part III.
[7] Montenegro Testimony, Inter-Am. Ct.
[8] Montenegro, Radio Interview.

GAM grew quickly as the families of victims of state violence in the cities and Mayan victims of the army counterinsurgency in rural regions joined the group. "I don't have words to explain – how we were treated was devastating, ferocious and demonic." "When we organized," Ms. Montenegro explained, "we were seen as an objective to destroy." "I was at the point of losing my life many times," she recalled. To stay alive she hid in the house of an international human rights organization, "and for nine years I could not be alone, not in my house nor at work." All along the state conducted a "campaign to discredit us, to marginalize us … to portray us as crazy seditious liars," she testified.[9] Óscar Mejía Víctores publicly condemned GAM as a tool of the guerillas, and his government set out to destroy the organization. A GAM witness told the Guatemalan truth commission that "To discredit us they called us communists, subversives, enemies of the state. Us, women who before were workers, housewives, who are suffering, who are victims of this violence."[10]

During Easter week of 1985, the government launched a bloody offensive against the leadership of GAM. Security forces kidnapped, tortured, and murdered one of the senior GAM members, Héctor Gómez Calito. Then, after GAM cofounder Rosario Godoy de Cuevas gave the eulogy at Gómez's funeral, security forces captured her. Her body and those of her two-year-old baby and her brother were found in a ditch outside Guatemala City. It was clear they had been tortured. Despite these attacks and countless others, GAM members continued their struggle, eventually bringing cases in the Inter-American system and before Guatemalan courts.

Their story is not unique. Wendy Méndez, whose mother was disappeared, cofounded HIJOS, an organization supporting children and other family members whose loved ones had disappeared. In her testimony before the Inter-American Court, Ms. Méndez recalled that "she knew other children of the disappeared and we shared the dream and objective of organizing ourselves."[11] She went on, "So we founded HIJOS and for thirteen years we have been working for historical

[9] Montenegro Testimony, Inter-Am. Ct.
[10] *Guatemala: Memoria y Silencio*, Caso Ilustrativo No. 48, Part III.
[11] Wendy Méndez, Testimony before the Inter-American Court, *José Miguel Gudiel Álvarez and others v. Guatemala* ("Diario Militar"), Referral No. 116/10, Case No. 12.590.

memory, truth and justice." Ms. Méndez testified: "This was really important for me and for all of us to be organized and to express to society the need to find the remains of our loved ones, and have justice so that never again will any family have to go through this." Like members of GAM they suffered threats and attacks from the government, but persevered. NGOs like the Myrna Mack Foundation and the University of California, Berkeley Human Rights Clinic represented Ms. Méndez and the other families in her case before the Inter-American Commission and Court.

Feliciana M., a survivor of the genocide committed against Mayans in Guatemala, testified in the case litigated in Spain. She told the court of her involvement in the National Organization of Widows of Guatemala (CONAVIGUA), an organization made up of widows and young people who suffered in the armed conflict. The organization has about fifteen thousand members, most of whom lost relatives during the conflict. As Feliciana testified, "The work is in defense of the right to life, the rights of children and human rights."[12]

Pro-Búsqueda works with families whose children disappeared during El Salvador's civil war. The organization has found more than 300 children in its eighteen years. It uses standard detective work and receives DNA testing help from universities in the United States. Teófila Ochoa Lizarbe and Cirila Pulido, childhood survivors of the Accomarca Massacre in Peru, started the Victims of Political Violence in Accomarca (Asociación de Familiares Afectados por la Violencia Política del Distrito de Accomarca). Their organization worked with Peru's truth commission and eventually with the criminal trials of those responsible for planning and carrying out the massacre. Every case study in this book tells the story of victims and survivors who have organized or been part of similar organizations. Their work with NGOs has enabled them to chip away at the many pillars of impunity and to take the incredible steps they have taken.

Human rights groups have actively promoted rights issues in various political arenas worldwide. Charles Epp illustrated that an active rights-oriented legal sector is crucial if a nation is to undergo an individual

---

[12] Alfonso Chardy, "Crime against Humanity: Jury Finds Ex-Chilean Officer Liable in 1973 Slaying," *The Miami Herald*, October 16, 2003.

rights revolution.[13] He found that the "growth of a support structure for legal mobilization," including "rights-advocacy organizations," has been the primary driving force when nations embrace human rights.[14] Kathryn Sikkink argued that human rights groups are effective in their work because they construct highly connected networks and coordinate their efforts. She pointed out how the "human rights issue network" is "bound by shared values and by dense exchanges of information and services."[15] These shared values, she stated, "are embodied in international human rights law."[16] Scholars have also found that victims and survivors represented by human rights groups are far more successful when they bring their cases to court.[17] Again, this success is due in large part to the relationships forged between the organization and its clients and to the networks constructed by these organizations across borders.[18] Fuyuki Kurusawa concluded, "Indeed, without the labour of groups and persons struggling to give voice and respond to mass abuses of both civil-political and socio-economic rights, the pursuit of global justice would rapidly grind to a halt."[19]

    In Chapter 2, I told the story of the Guatemalan police assassination of Myrna Mack Chang on September 11, 1990. Guatemalan officials made every effort to stop the investigation into this murder – including killing lawyers and judges. The case is an excellent example of the effectiveness of human rights groups in this area. After her sister was assassinated, Helen Mack founded the Myrna Mack Foundation, which evolved into an advocacy group campaigning for justice and rights and against clandestine powers in Guatemala. Guatemalan officials tried to obstruct Helen Mack and the foundation through attacks, threats, and dilatory pleadings. While the foundation pressed the case in Guatemala, Human Rights First (HRF) and the Center for Justice and International Law (CEJIL) pursued justice internationally. CEJIL

---

[13] Charles R. Epp, *The Rights Revolution* (Chicago, IL: University of Chicago Press, 1998).
[14] Ibid., 69.
[15] Kathryn Sikkink, "Human Rights, Principled Issue Networks and Sovereignty in Latin America," *International Organization* 47, no. 3 (1993): 411–441.
[16] Ibid., 416.
[17] See Jeffrey Davis, *Justice across Borders: The Struggle for Human Rights in U.S. Courts* (New York: Cambridge University Press, 2008);, chapter 3.
[18] Ibid.
[19] Fuyuki Kurasawa, *The Work of Global Justice: Human Rights as Practices* (Cambridge: Cambridge University Press, 2007), 23.

and HRF lawyers filed claims with the Inter-American human rights system alleging violations of rights embodied in the Inter-American Convention on Human Rights. The expertise, resources, and commitment of these groups sustained the case – and its principles – throughout the more than thirteen years of litigation.

In an interview with Roxanna Altholz, a former lawyer for CEJIL who was the lead counsel in the Mack case before the Inter-American Court, she expressed the importance of group involvement. "We're the blood of the system, we keep it alive, we make it work," she stated.[20] She argued that the limited light of justice that filters through obscuring impunity does so because of the "blood and sweat" of human rights activists and the victims they represent. Ms. Altholz pointed out that the Myrna Mack Foundation "raised funds to bring 13 witnesses to the Inter-American Court" in San Jose, Costa Rica, which was a "huge expense." Moreover, she described how HRF recruited pro bono private counsel to donate their time and the considerable resources of their private law firm to assist in litigation. CEJIL's expertise was crucial to the case because it is the "only NGO dedicated exclusively to the Inter-American system." It has high levels of "credibility and expertise" as well as a strong "regional operation."[21]

Human rights groups also coordinate lobbying and public relations campaigns with litigation efforts. These groups broadcast the voices of human rights victims internationally. The Myrna Mack Foundation, HRF, and the Washington Office for Latin America (WOLA) worked closely with CEJIL lawyers litigating the Mack case in the Inter-American system to conduct a public relations campaign to ensure that the case moved Guatemala toward domestic justice and increased global awareness of the human rights situation there. As Adriana Beltran, the head of this campaign, stated in an interview, "We used the Mack case as a way of highlighting the inefficiencies of the judicial system."[22] The purpose of the media campaign was to "illustrat[e] the

---

[20] Roxanna Altholz, attorney, Center for Justice and Accountability, Interview with the author, Washington, DC, May 11, 2004. Ms. Altholz is now the associate director of the International Human Rights Law Clinic at the University of California, Berkeley Law School.

[21] Ibid.

[22] Beltran interview.

impunity that the military enjoyed, the weaknesses and the failures of the judicial system, the human rights situation and the fact that so many witnesses, lawyers, judges were being threatened, harassed, murdered." This group orchestrated a well-organized campaign to use the case to bring pressure to bear on Guatemala from members of the U.S. government. Ms. Beltran recalled, "if the case was stalling – or if security was necessary – we would organize a campaign involving 'dear colleague' letters or remarks on the floor, [we] would then circulate it to U.S. and international media."[23]

In addition to coordinating litigation with lobbying and public relations, groups are most effective when international activists coordinate their efforts with those on the ground in the country of origin. In the *Mack* case, for example, CEJIL, HRF, and the Myrna Mack Foundation worked together in planning their domestic and Inter-American litigation strategies. As Ms. Altholz of CEJIL stated, "we looked at what they did domestically when we were preparing for trial." In fact, domestic and international attorneys "used some of the same witnesses, some of the same evidence, some of the same strategy, some of the same techniques."[24] Lawyers litigating in Guatemala would use orders of the Inter-American Court in their arguments domestically. In addition to issuing press releases and lobbying internationally, WOLA was active in training Guatemalan human rights NGOs to effectively advocate domestically.

Another vital way group activity operates to improve the chances of accountability is by protecting human rights defenders and those seeking justice. As Ms. Beltran pointed out, her group would mobilize a media campaign or alert members of congress "if security was necessary." She explained that "when [Helen Mack's] lawyer was receiving a number of threats – right before the case actually went to trial – [Helen] called me and said we're receiving threats and everybody was on the phone with the State Department, with the embassy, with members of congress or their staff, saying please call and tell them that you're really concerned." In this effort "we were sending the message that she's not alone."[25] Human rights organizations have also been instrumental in

[23] Ibid.
[24] Altholz, interview with the author.
[25] Beltran interview.

discovering evidence of what happened to victims of human rights violations and of government responsibility.

TRUTH COMMISSIONS

As we have already seen with the Accomarca case, truth commissions play an important role in exposing the truth about human rights viola- tions. Truth commissions take many forms. Some are merely mecha- nisms to cover up a regime's culpability for human rights – to show the rest of the world that it is doing something about its shameful past. Some are the product of brittle compromises and exist as the only mechanism a new and fragile peace can sustain. Scholars have thoroughly analyzed the many variations and functions of truth commissions around the globe.[26] This book is not among those studies, but instead examines truth commissions through the lens of its research questions. What has been the role of truth commissions in the process of legal justice in the case studies I analyze? I address this question throughout the book.

While the South African Truth and Reconciliation Commission (TRC) is the subject of significant criticisms (see Chapter 4), its man- date is perhaps a model for using truth commissions to extract infor- mation from the perpetrators of violations. Unlike most subsequent commissions, the South African Commission relied on and spot- lighted individual victims and perpetrators. When the South African Constitutional Court considered the system's legality, it recognized that "all that often effectively remains is the truth of wounded memo- ries of loved ones sharing instinctive suspicions, deep and traumatising to the survivors but otherwise incapable of translating themselves into objective and corroborative evidence which could survive the rigours of the law."[27] The South African TRC:

> Seeks to address this massive problem by encouraging these sur- vivors and the dependants of the tortured and the wounded, the

---

[26] See Priscilla B. Hayner, *Unspeakable Truths: Facing the Challenge of Truth Commissions* (New York: Routledge, 2002); Robert I. Rotberg and Dennis Thompson, eds., *Truth v. Justice: The Morality of Truth Commissions* (Princeton, NJ: Princeton University Press, 2000).

[27] *Azanian Peoples Org.* (AZAPO) v. The President of South Africa, 1996 (4) SALR 637 (CC), para. 17.

maimed and the dead to unburden their grief publicly, to receive the collective recognition of a new nation that they were wronged, and crucially, to help them to discover what did in truth happen to their loved ones, where and under what circumstances it did happen, and who was responsible.[28]

The TRC system promised complete amnesty for all perpetrators who came forward and testified in full about their role in the violations. Some characterize this as a choice between truth and justice, but in actuality it is a choice between different elements in the process of justice. The TRC process valued truth over punishment. As the Constitutional Court observed, "truth, which the victims of repression seek so desperately to know is, in the circumstances, much more likely to be forthcoming if those responsible for such monstrous misdeeds are encouraged to disclose the whole truth with the incentive that they will not receive the punishment which they undoubtedly deserve if they do."[29]

Truth commissions in Latin America have been instrumental in revealing the truth about human rights violations in the region, but they are fundamentally different institutions from the South African TRC. They base their findings almost exclusively on witness and victim testimony, and rarely enjoy the full cooperation of their governments. Furthermore, they are rarely empowered to name those responsible for committing the violations but instead are limited to merely finding that the violations occurred.

The 1996 Guatemalan Peace Accords and subsequent law of national reconciliation established the Historical Clarification Commission (CEH), but the Guatemalan government and military often refused to cooperate with the CEH's investigation. In a case stemming from forced disappearances during the war, the Inter-American Court of Human Rights found that the government repeatedly refused to provide requested documents and evidence to the CEH. It pointed out that "the Ministry of Defense denied the existence of documents such as [the] Diario Militar, which appeared through unofficial channels three months after the Commission issued its final report."[30] The CEH

[28] Ibid.
[29] Ibid.
[30] *José Miguel Gudiel Álvarez and others v. Guatemala* ("Diario Militar"), No. 116/10, Case No. 12.590, December 21, 2012, para. 113, translated by the author. at para. 296.

informed the Court that "this lack of information adversely impacted the performance of its mandate." For example, it "could not determine the chain of command regarding enforced disappearances committed during the conflict."[31] Valencia Villa, a former CEH official, testified that if the CEH "had had access to all the documents it requested ... many borderline cases would have been clarified."[32] The Court reiterated previous rulings that while "states may establish truth commissions to contribute to the construction and preservation of historical memory, the clarification of facts and determination of institutional, social and policies in certain historical periods of a society ... these committees do not replace the State's obligation to establish the truth through judicial proceedings."[33] The CEH did determine that the state was responsible for acts of genocide against the Mayan people, and this has had an impact on building the case against former officials in Spain and Guatemala. Almudena Bernabeu, the lawyer working on the genocide case in Spain, stated, "After the truth commission, people said it was not enough, this is a compromise, justice is being crippled."[34]

Peru's Truth Commission tried to lay the foundation for future prosecutions. As former commission member Eduardo González stated, its mission was to "establish the truth about crimes that occurred in a violent or dictatorial past ... that are supposed to help further judicial [action]."[35] He pointed out, however, that a "truth commission is a nonjudicial body ... a panel of experts or persons of investigations, to help victims channel their voices in the public sphere [who] are supposed to also help explain the facts and try to find some kind of recommendation, so that there is a measure of deterrence in the future."[36] The commission worked for almost two years and it heard testimony from approximately seventeen thousand witnesses. Mr. González recalled that "there were a number of cases that had created a very deep impact

---

[31] Ibid.
[32] Ibid., para. 297.
[33] Ibid., para. 298.
[34] Elisabeth Malkin, "Ex-Dictator Is Ordered to Trial in Guatemalan War Crimes Case," *New York Times*, January 28, 2013.
[35] Transcript of Trial at 44, *Ochoa Lizarbe v. Hurtado*, No. 07–21783-CIV-JORDAN, 2008 U.S. Dist. LEXIS 109517 (S.D. Fla. March 4, 2008), 106.
[36] Ibid.

in the national psyche, in the national consciousness, events that had been extremely traumatizing for our society."[37] He explained that, because these cases were so important, the commission "decided that it was fair to ensure that a number of very exemplary cases of brutality would be deeply studied, reconstructed, and that the results of our investigation should be put in the hands of the prosecutorial services of Peru so that justice will have a chance to be served."[38] One of these cases was the Accomarca Massacre.

SECRET DOCUMENTS

Kate Doyle is a senior analyst for the National Security Archive (the Archive), a U.S. nongovernmental organization that secures and publicizes government information and documents. She has been instrumental in discovering, analyzing, and validating documentary evidence in numerous Latin American human rights cases. She was deeply involved in the Myrna Mack case, one of the foundational human rights cases in Guatemala. Advocates in that case discovered a major problem in trying to prove their allegations. "How do you talk to the judge about the military, and military intelligence, and military intelligence operations and death squad operations – all that stuff, when there is nothing on paper about that, nothing official," Ms. Doyle observed.[39] "What is incredible is that you go into a case like that and you can't even say in an official way 'judge, here are the structures of the Estado Mayor Presidencial' [the Guatemalan secret police].You can't do that because there is no such thing as an official document proving that." "Human rights investigators traditionally have had to rely almost exclusively on testimony – witnesses, survivors," she explained. "The fact is when you want to make a case, when you want to indict a dictator, you need evidence and you can't build an entire case … on testimony."[40] Ms. Doyle had an idea. "So I said let's see if we can get documents through the U.S., through FOIA [the Freedom of Information Act], something

---

[37] Ibid., 109.
[38] Ibid.
[39] Kate Doyle, interview with the author, January 28, 2010.
[40] Kate Doyle, *Granito: How to Nail a Dictator* (film), Skylight Pictures, 2011.

to get us started ... let's gather these documents and do this for the [Guatemalan] genocide case and then broaden it."[41]

Similarly, when the United Nations truth commission for El Salvador began its work after the 1992 peace accords, the Archive tried to help its work by forcing the declassification and release of U.S. intelligence and diplomatic documents. The State Department, Central Intelligence Agency, and military intelligence agencies eventually released numerous documents that occasionally served as the only government documentary evidence to support claims of human rights violations. As I demonstrated in Chapter 1, these documents tell the story of the massacre of the Jesuits and of the subsequent cover-up.

The Archive also released documents that refuted the Guatemalan government's denial of culpability for the murder of GAM leaders in 1985 by reporting the Guatemalan government's surveillance of and attacks on GAM members (see Figure 5.1). In the document, the U.S. Embassy stated that its source has "no doubt that the GOG [Government of Guatemala] was directly responsible for Gomez's murder" referring to Héctor Gómez Calito, the GAM member discussed earlier. This source "had seen Gomez's body" and "it had been subjected to more abuse to make a point to GAM."[42]

The Archive has also received, analyzed, and released documents used to build cases against Salvadoran officials in several cases in the United States and Spain. In one such case, mentioned previously, Juan Romagoza sued Salvadoran generals who had presided over his capture and torture. Dr. Romagoza explained the importance of the State Department documents at trial. "One [U.S.] ambassador did testify, wanting to defend them [the generals]. But when he was asked about the very cables he had written to the State Department, he sounded like one of the witnesses against them. The ambassador couldn't defend the generals because he himself had documented their crimes."[43]

---

[41] Doyle, interview with author.

[42] Kate Doyle and Jesse Franzblau, "Historical Archives Lead to Arrest of Police Officers in Guatemalan Disappearance," National Security Archive Electronic Briefing Book No. 273 (March 17, 2009), http://www.gwu.edu/~nsarchiv/NSAEBB/NSAEBB273/index.htm (Last accessed December 20, 2012).

[43] Juan Romagoza Arce, "Reflections on the Verdict," http://www.cja.org/forSurvivors/reflect.doc (Last accessed September 12, 2007).

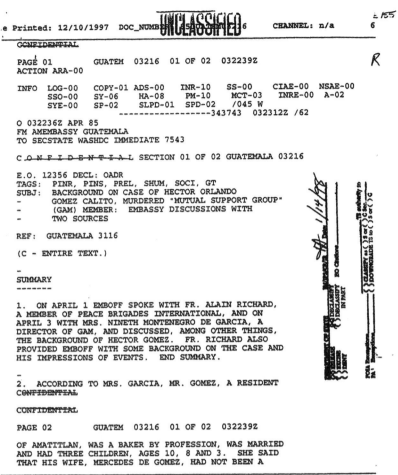

Figure 5.1. Cable from U.S. Embassy in Guatemala to U.S. Secretary of State Regarding the Attacks on GAM.

The Archive began its Guatemala Documentation Project in 1994 to support the Guatemalan Historical Clarification Commission. The peace accords signed in July of that year established the commission to investigate the human rights violations committed during the war.

e Printed: 12/10/1997   DOC_NUMB~~ER 00~~6   CHANNEL: n/a   6

MEMBER OF GAM, BUT THAT SHE INTENDED TO JOIN FOLLOWING .
HER ,HUSBAND'S DEATH. MRS. GARCIA SAID GOMEZ WAS NOT
THE SPOKESMAN FOR THE GROUP, NOR A MEMBER OF THE BOARD
OF DIRECTORS, BUT HAD ACTED AS A PUBLICIST AND INFOR-
MATION OFFICER FOR THE GROUP. SHE SAID HE HAD BEEN
AFFILIATED WITH THE GROUP FOR SOME TIME, AND HAD
JOINED BECAUSE HIS BROTHER, RENE ARNOLDO GOMEZ HAD
DISAPPEARED ON JULY 16, 1983.

NOTE: LIST OF DISAPPEARED PREVIOUSLY PROVIDED BY GAM
DID NOT LIST GOMEZ, ALTHOUGH A SECOND LIST SUPPLIED
BY FR. RICHARD DOES INCLUDE HIS NAME. IT SAYS HE
DISAPPEARED JULY 26, 1982, NOT 1983, AS MRS GARCIA SAYS.

3. FR. RICHARD SPOKE OF GOMEZ' ROLE ALSO. HE SAID
THAT GOMEZ, WHOM HE DESCRIBED AS AN EXTREMELY
NON-VIOLENT PERSON, HAD APPARENTLY ONLY RECENTLY
BECOME ACTIVE IN THE GAM. HE CONFIRMED THAT GOMEZ
WAS NEITHER A MEMBER OF THE BOARD OF DIRECTORS NOR THE
GROUP'S SPOKESMAN. HE SAID THAT GOMEZ HAD SOME VISI-
BILITY AT SOME GROUP EVENTS, AND THAT HE AND FOUR OTHER
GAM MEMBERS HAD ATTENDED A MEETING WITH THE PRESIDENT
OF THE GUATEMALAN CONSTITUENT ASSEMBLY. RICHARD
ADDED THAT NEWSPAPER CHARACTERIZATIONS OF GOMEZ AS
"THE GAM LEADER" WERE INACCURATE REPORTING. GOMEZ
WAS DESCRIBED IN ACCOUNTS OF THE DEATH CARRIED IN THE
GUATEMALA CITY NEWSPAPERS AS THE "CHIEF LEADER" AND
AS A "MANAGER" OF GAM. A NEWSPAPER ANNOUNCEMENT OF
APRIL 2, SPONSORED BY GAM, HOWEVER, CALLED GOMEZ
~~CONFIDENTIAL~~

~~CONFIDENTIAL~~

PAGE 03   GUATEM 03216   01 OF 02   032239Z

"OUR COMPANERO (ASSOCIATE)".

4. FR. ALAIN RICHARD TOLD EMBOFF THAT HE IS A
FRANCISCAN PRIEST AND FRENCH CITIZEN. HE SAID HE
HAD SERVED IN GUATEMALA IN THE PAST AS A PBI ADVISOR,
BUT HAD JUST RECENTLY RETURNED TO THE COUNTRY.
RICHARD TOLD EMBOFF THAT HE UNDERSTOOD THAT ABOUT
MARCH 25, MEMBERS OF THE GOG'S DEPARTMENT OF TECHNICAL
INVESTIGATIONS (DIT) HAD ASKED THE MAYOR OF THE TOWN
OF AMATITLAN, WHERE GOMEZ LIVED, FOR INFORMATION
ABOUT THE VICTIM. THE MAYOR WAS SAID TO HAVE PROVIDED
NO INFORMATION. AT ABOUT THE SAME DATE, GOMEZ'S

Page - 2

Figure 5.1. (*continued*)

e Printed: 12/10/1997 DOC_NUM... UNCLASSIFIED 216   CHANNEL: n/a   6

HOUSE WAS REPORTED TO HAVE BEEN UNDER SURVEILLANCE BY
MEN .IN AUTOMOBILES. RICHARD SAID THAT ON MARCH 30
GOMEZ HAD ATTENDED A WEEKLY GAM MEETING HELD AT PBI
HEADQUARTERS IN ZONE 11 OF GUATEMALA CITY. HE SAID
APPARENTLY GOMEZ HAD BEEN ABDUCTED AFTER THE MEETING,
BUT IT WAS NOT CLEAR IF THIS HAD OCCURRED IN GUATEMALA
CITY OR IN AMATITLAN.

5. RICHARD HAD NO DOUBTS THAT THE GOG WAS DIRECTLY
RESPONSIBLE FOR GOMEZ'S MURDER. HE TOLD EMBOFF THAT HE
HAD SEEN GOMEZ'S BODY AND THAT IT HAD BEEN BADLY
BEATEN. HE BELIEVED THAT WHILE IN THE PAST PEOPLE
ABDUCTED BY THE GOG HAD BEEN KILLED QUICKLY, GOMEZ HAD
BEEN SUBJECTED TO MORE ABUSE, TO MAKE A POINT TO THE
GAM GROUP.

WHEN ASKED IF ONLY CERTAIN MEMBERS OF GAM HAVE BEEN
SINGLED OUT TO RECEIVE THREATS OR SURVEILLANCE, HE

CONFIDENTIAL

NNN

CONFIDENTIAL

PAGE 01   GUATEM 03216   02 OF 02   032239Z
ACTION ARA-00

INFO LOG-00   COPY-01 ADS-00   INR-10   SS-00   CIAE-00 NSAE-00
      SSO-00   SY-06   HA-08   PM-10   MCT-03   INRE-00 A-02
      SYE-00   SP-02   SLPD-01   SPD-02   /045 W
                       ------------------343744 032325Z /62
O 032236Z APR 85
FM AMEMBASSY GUATEMALA
TO SECSTATE WASHDC IMMEDIATE 7544

Page - 3

UNCLASSIFIED

Figure 5.1. (*continued*)

Kate Doyle and her colleagues at the Archive knew from their experience in El Salvador that "there was one issue about which the truth commission would have virtually no primary information but which is well documented by U.S. agencies: the Guatemalan intelligence and security apparatus."[44] While they were immersed in the FOIA back and forth with the U.S. government, the "Clinton administration helped significantly when it released in June 1996 its Intelligence Oversight Board (IOB) Report on U.S. intelligence operations in Guatemala, accompanied by approximately 6,000 State Department, CIA and Defense Department documents."[45]

For years, Guatemala denied any knowledge of or responsibility for the thousands of people disappeared during its thirty-year civil war. While the Guatemalan truth commission provided detailed accounts of how many of the victims were disappeared, its report was based largely on the testimony of family members and other witnesses and thus more was needed to mount a legal case. Then, in 1999, Kate Doyle was working in Washington, DC when a contact from Guatemala brought her a package. Inside was what is now called the "Diario Militar" or death squad dossier. It is a document containing photographs and data on 183 disappeared victims. As Ms. Doyle observed, it is a "chilling artifact of the techniques of political terror."[46]

After carefully analyzing the document, Ms. Doyle "concluded that the presidential military intelligence unit known as the Archivo was responsible for the abductions in this document and the writing of this document." In a hearing before the Inter-American Commission on Human Rights, Ms. Doyle explained how she determined the document was authentic and how she determined it was created by the Archivo. First, she compared the names of the disappeared and the dates of abduction in the Diario with U.S. Department of Defense and Department of State communiqués. The names and dates in

[44] Kate Doyle, "The Guatemalan Military: What the U.S. Files Reveal," National Security Archives Electronic Briefing Book, http://www.gwu.edu/~nsarchiv/NSAEBB/NSAEBB32/index.html (Last accessed May 17, 2012).
[45] Ibid.
[46] Kate Doyle, "Remains of Two of Guatemala's Death Squad Diary Victims Found in Mass Grave," National Security Archive Electronic Briefing Book No. 363 (November 22, 2011). http://www.gwu.edu/~nsarchiv/NSAEBB/NSAEBB363/index.htm; The Diario Militar is available at http://www.gwu.edu/~nsarchiv/guatemala/logbook/index.htm.

the Diario matched disappearances reported in the U.S. documents. Her first clue that the Archivo was responsible was that the Diario itself "describes the unit's function as investigating and acting against the insurgency." A 1986 CIA document had identified the Archivo as a secret force inside the president's office to "investigate and act against the insurgency." Ms. Doyle explained that the Diario describes "coordination between the unit responsible for these abductions and many other units within the security services of the Guatemalan security and police apparatus." In her opinion, the Archivo was the unit most capable of commanding this level of coordination. Ms. Doyle pointed out that the "information gathered on suspects could only have been collected by the Archivo." The Diario shows that the unit responsible had "reports from the national police or internal reports from the detective corps ... [that] include[d] personal identification details such as the victims' height or color of their eyes, the names of their parents ... their personal identification numbers. This is the kind of information that only the Archivo could have access to in a universal way." Finally, Ms. Doyle explained that "the Archivo is not a unit named in this document, rather the unit that created this document coordinated with almost every other known intelligence and police unit that existed in Guatemala at the time."[47] In 2009, the Guatemalan government admitted the Diario was an authentic government document.

The Diario lists the abductions and disappearances the Archivo conducted, and in doing so it displays the methods and motives of a brutal death squad. The Archivo sought to find and eliminate anyone believed to be an internal enemy, and it used "torture to extract information from prisoners about their colleagues, friends and family members."[48] The Diario Militar "was created precisely to report and classify that information so that security forces could then move against additional targets."[49] Because it was a document created by the Guatemalan state itself, it could be used to prove conclusively the

---

[47] Kate Doyle, Testimony before the Inter-American Commission for Human Rights, *José Miguel Gudiel Álvarez and others v. Guatemala* ("Diario Militar"), Referral No. 116/10, Case No. 12.590, transcribed by the author.

[48] Doyle, "Remains of Two of Guatemala's Death Squad Diary Victims Found in Mass Grave."

[49] Ibid.

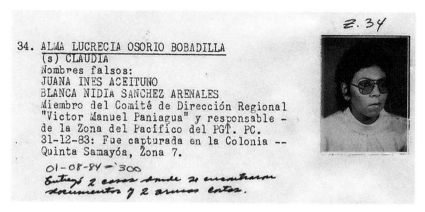

34. ALMA LUCRECIA OSORIO BOBADILLA
(s) CLAUDIA
Nombres falsos:
JUANA INES ACEITUNO
BLANCA NIDIA SANCHEZ ARENALES
Miembro del Comité de Dirección Regional
"Victor Manuel Paniagua" y responsable -
de la Zona del Pacífico del PGT. PC.
31-12-83: Fue capturada en la Colonia --
Quinta Samayóa, Zona 7.

01-08-84 - 300

Figure 5.2. Diario Militar, Alma Lucrecia Osorio Bobadilla.

state's responsibility for abducting and killing the victims identified inside. It lists in detail the allegations against each victim, the date and time when the victims were abducted, where they were abducted, and their ultimate fates.

As Ms. Doyle explained, "In many of the entries we see reference to victims who were captured, held for a long period of time and then executed. Many of these same victims were used as informants to point out other suspected subversives on the street so that the Archivo could then go after them." One such abductee was Alma Lucrecia Osorio Bobadilla. She was held for eight months in 1983 and 1984 and we learn from the Diario that "she both turned over houses that contained propaganda and weapons but also named other suspects who the Archivo then went and picked up – and those people are also in the Diario Militar" (see Figure 5.2).

The entry for Osorio Bobadilla lists her alias as "Claudia" and states that she identified someone on the street as Sergio Vinicio Samayoa Morales. According to the Diario, when she pointed him out, Samayoa Morales ran. Guatemalan death squads had abducted his mother, his two sisters, and his brother in the preceding years, and he had not seen any of them since. Daylight was no defense. The Archivo and other government security forces frequently attacked their victims in broad daylight. As Ms. Doyle stated, "It is a known fact ... that the Archivo and other Guatemalan military units used vehicles with polarized [windows] and operated openly in broad daylight in Guatemala City to kidnap their victims."[50] The Archivo men came after Mr. Morales. He turned down First Avenue and the men opened fire. He was hit and down he went. The Archivo men were seconds from throwing him in the back of their van and taking him to a prison, where, like his mother, sisters, and brother, he would probably have been tortured for so long that he would beg to be executed. Then he heard the ambulance and saw the paramedics.

The Diario shows that after the ambulance left, the Archivo worked with a unit of the Guatemalan army to track Samayoa Morales down. As Ms. Doyle explained, "the Archivo coordinated with the Direccion de Inteligencia or the D2 which is the principle branch of intelligence in the Guatemalan military to recover Samayoa Morales while he was in the hospital – and they re-kidnapped him and disappeared him."[51] The entry in the Diario shows an identification photo of Samayoa Morales, and a photo of him after he was abducted from the hospital (see Figure 5.3).

The Archivo later executed Osorio Bobadilla according to the Diario, and Samayoa Morales was never seen again. Ms. Doyle corroborated the account of his fate using secret State Department documents. A memo from the embassy in Guatemala to U.S. Secretary of State George Schultz stated: "The victim was carried out on a stretcher from a hospital by ten armed men with a bottle of intravenous fluid still dripping into his arm. He was in the emergency room about to undergo surgery for the removal of bullets received earlier in the day from an assassination attempt. He was the one remaining member of a family of four"[52] (see Figure 5.4).

[50] Doyle, interview with author.

[51] Kate Doyle, Testimony, Hearing before the Inter-American Commission for Human Rights, *José Miguel Gudiel Álvarez and others v. Guatemala* ("Diario Militar"), Referral No. 116/10, Case No. 12.590, reported in "Update: The Guatemalan Death Squad Diary and the Right to Truth National Security Archive Expert Testifies before International Court," *National Security Archive Electronic Briefing Book* No. 378, May 3, 2012, http://www.gwu.edu/~nsarchiv/NSAEBB/NSAEBB378/ (Last accessed June 1, 2012).

[52] Document obtained by the National Security Archive, "Guatemalan Death Squad Dossier, Internal Military Log Reveals Fate of 183 'Disappeared,'" National Security Archive Electronic Briefing Book No. 15, May 20, 1999. http://www.gwu.edu/~nsarchiv/NSAEBB/NSAEBB15/.

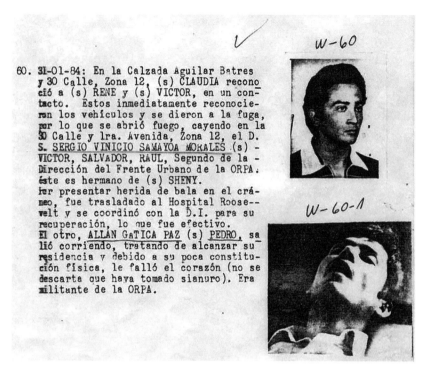

60. 31-01-84: En la Calzada Aguilar Batres
    y 30 Calle, Zona 12, (s) CLAUDIA recono
    ció a (s) RENE y (s) VICTOR, en un con-
    tacto. Éstos inmediatamente reconocie-
    ron los vehículos y se dieron a la fuga,
    por lo que se abrió fuego, cayendo en la
    30 Calle y 1ra. Avenida, Zona 12, el D.
    S. SERGIO VINICIO SAMAYOA MORALES (s) -
    VICTOR, SALVADOR, RAUL, Segundo de la -
    Dirección del Frente Urbano de la ORPA.
    Éste es hermano de (s) SHENY.
    Por presentar herida de bala en el crá-
    neo, fue trasladado al Hospital Roose--
    velt y se coordinó con la D.I. para su
    recuperación, lo que fue efectivo.
    El otro, ALLÁN GaTICA PAZ (s) PEDRO, sa
    lió corriendo, tratando de alcanzar su
    residencia y debido a su poca constitu-
    ción física, le falló el corazón (no se
    descarta que haya tomado sianuro). Era
    militante de la ORPA.

Figure 5.3. Diario Militar, Sergio Vinicio Samayoa Morales.

The Archivo tortured "Claudia" into naming Julio César Pereira Vasquez as well. He is listed at number seventy-three in the Diario, and the entry states that Claudia turned him in (see Figure 5.5). He was captured on February 22, 1984, in Guatemala City's Zone 12. Unlike most captives in the Diario's entries, however, Mr. Pereira was released by the Archivo and he immediately sought asylum from Venezuela and later Canada.[53] The entry states that Mr. Pereira was released for his contacts, meaning he was tortured into giving the Archivo names of other insurgents. He has since returned to Guatemala to testify and help others find their missing loved ones, and in doing so he acknowledged naming Sergio Saúl Linares

---

[53] The Diario's statement that he sought asylum at the French Embassy is an error. See Catherine Nolin, *Transnational Ruptures: Gender and Forced Migration* (Surrey, UK: Ashgate Publishing, Ltd., 2006), 72.

```
O 022216Z FEB 84
FM AMEMBASSY GUATEMALA                            DECAPTIONED
TO SECSTATE WASHDC IMMEDIATE 9568
                                                      DECAPTIONED
C O N F I D E N T I A L SECTION 01 OF 02 GUATEMALA 01154

PXILS

DEPARTMENT PLEASE PASS TO SECRETARY SHULTZ AND
ASSISTANT SECRETARY ARA MOTLEY FROM AMBASSADOR CHAPIN

E.O.12356: DECL: 2/2/90
TAGS: PGOV, PINS, GT, SHUM
SUBJECT: RECENT KIDNAPPINGS:  SIGNS POINT TO
-        GOVERNMENT SECURITY FORCES

REF: GUATEMALA 1155

(C) SUMMARY:  THE CIRCUMSTANCES OF TWO RECENT
GUATEMALA CITY KIDNAPPINGS CLEARLY SUGGEST THEY
WERE PERPETRATED BY GOVERNMENT SECURITY FORCES.
IN ONE CASE THE YOUNG VICTIM WAS SEIZED BY AN
ARMED GROUP IN TWO CARS FROM ONE OF THE CITY'S
MAIN SHOPPING CENTERS, WHILE NATIONAL POLICE
STOOD IDLY BY.  IN THE SECOND, MORE FLAGRANT
CASE, THE VICTIM WAS CARRIED OUT ON A STRETCHER
FROM A HOSPITAL BY TEN ARMED MEN WITH A BOTTLE
OF INTRAVENOUS FLUID STILL DRIPPING INTO HIS ARM.
HE WAS IN THE EMERGENCY ROOM ABOUT TO UNDERGO
SURGERY FOR THE REMOVAL OF BULLETS RECEIVED
EARLIER IN THE DAY FROM AN ASSASSINATION ATTEMPT.
HE WAS THE ONE REMAINING MEMBER OF A FAMILY OF FOUR.
HIS MOTHER AND TWO SIBLINGS HAD PREVIOUSLY BEEN
CONFIDENTIAL

CONFIDENTIAL

PAGE 02        GUATEM 01154  01 OF 02  022226Z

ABDUCTED FROM THEIR HOME BY ARMED MEN OVER A
YEAR AGO IN A CASE UNIVERSALLY ATTRIBUTED TO
GOVERNMENT SECURITY FORCES.  HIS MOTHER WAS AN

                    Page - 1
```

Figure 5.4. Cable from U.S. Embassy in Guatemala to U.S. Secretary of State Regarding Samayoa Morales.

Morales after being tortured. Linares Morales is number seventy-four in the Diario (discussed further later in this chapter).[54]

Among the 183 victims in the dossier was Wendy Méndez's mother, Luz Haydee Méndez, listed as number eighty-three (see Figure 5.6). Wendy Méndez explained that the Diario "has meant the privilege to push forward the cases of forced disappearances in Guatemala."[55] She

[54] *José Miguel Gudiel Álvarez and Others ("Diario Militar") v. Guatemala*, Int. Am. Comm. H.R., Report No. 116/10, Case 12.590 (October 22, 2010), at para. 203; Nolin at 72.
[55] Méndez Interview.

ate Printed: 12/12/1997   DOC_NUMBER: UNCLASSIFIED 1154   CHANNEL: n/a   5

EMPLOYEE OF THE NATIONAL UNIVERSITY OF SAN CARLOS,
A SUSPECTED HOTBED OF SUBVERSIVE ACTIVITY. THESE NEW
SHOCKING ABDUCTIONS INDICATE THAT THE GOG SECURITY
FORCES WILL STRIKE WHENEVER THERE IS A TARGET OF
IMPORTANCE. THE SEPARATE MESSAGE ON ABDUCTIONS IN
HUEHUETENANGO INDICATES THAT THE GOG ARMY WILL DO
LIKEWISE. WE MUST COME TO SOME RESOLUTION IN POLICY
TERMS. EITHER WE CAN OVERLOOK THE RECORD AND
EMPHASIZE THE STRATEGIC CONCEPT OR WE CAN PURSUE A
HIGHER MORAL PATH. WE SIMPLY CANNOT FLIP FLOP BACK
AND FORTH BETWEEN THE TWO POSSIBLE POSITIONS.
MUDDLING THROUGH WILL SIMPLY GO NOWHERE. END SUMMARY.

1. (U) TEN MEN ARMED WITH SUBMACHINE GUNS AND
AUTOMATIC RIFLES ENTERED THE ROOSEVELT
EMERGENCY HOSPITAL IN GUATEMALA CITY ON
JANUARY 31 AND KIDNAPPED SERGIO VINICIO SAMAYOA
MORALES, AGE 29. SAMAYOA WAS SEIZED AS HE WAS
ABOUT TO BE TAKEN INTO SURGERY TWO HOURS AFTER
BEING ADMITTED TO THE HOSPITAL SUFFERING
FROM BULLET WOUNDS. HE WAS TAKEN AWAY IN A
WHITE PANEL TRUCK BY THE KIDNAPPERS.

2. (U) SAMAYOA WAS WOUNDED BY TWO ARMED MEN
ABOUT 4:30 IN THE AFTERNOON OF JANUARY 31,
ACCORDING TO NEWSPAPER REPORTS, AT HIS PLACE
OF WORK. HE WAS SHOT FIVE TIMES BY HIS
ATTACKERS. HOWEVER, THEY FAILED TO KILL HIM
AND AFTER THEY FLED HE WAS TAKEN BY AMBULANCE
TO THE EMERGENCY HOSPITAL IN GRAVE CONDITION.
CONFIDENTIAL

CONFIDENTIAL

PAGE 03   GUATEM 01154 01 OF 02 022226Z

3. (U) TWO HOURS LATER, A GROUP OF ARMED MEN
ENTERED THE HOSPITAL'S EMERGENCY WARD, DISARMED
THE TWO POLICEMEN ON DUTY AND QUESTIONED THE
DUTY PHYSICIAN ABOUT THE WHEREABOUTS OF THE
GUNSHOT VICTIM. AFTER HE WAS LOCATED IN THE
PREP ROOM FOR SURGERY, HE WAS TAKEN OUT TO
THE WAITING VEHICLES, ON A STRETCHER ALONG WITH
THE BOTTLE OF INTRAVENOUS FLUID WHICH WAS STILL
DRIPPING INTO HIS ARM.

4. (U) THE SAMAYOA MORALES FAMILY HAS SUFFERED
FROM SIMILAR VIOLENCE IN THE PAST. ON

Page - 2

Figure 5.4. (*continued*)

pointed out that in "all of Latin America, there have been government
files that have been declassified, but there is no other like it, there is
no other until today that has been done by military officials as part of
their day to day work." Her reaction to the Diario demonstrates the
importance of the truth and government documents in the process
of justice.

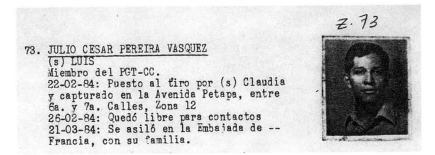

Figure 5.5. Diario Militar, Julio César Pereira Vasquez.

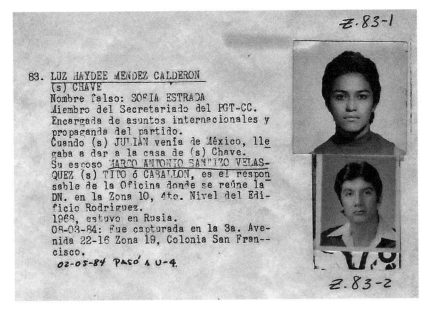

Figure 5.6. Diario Militar, Luz Haydee Méndez.

Secret Documents – The Edgar Fernando García Case

Through GAM, Ms. Montenegro and Fernando García's daughter, Alejandra García, worked to expose the truth and pursue justice. For fifteen years, the state denied any knowledge of Fernando's whereabouts or any involvement in his disappearance. Then the discovery of the Diario Militar provided hard documentary evidence that Guatemalan state officials carried out the capture and interrogation of Fernando

EDGAR FERNANDO GARCIA: **

Hijo de María Emilia García, ojos cafés, cabello negro,
tez morena, 1.72 de estatura, soltero, maestro de educa
ción primaria, nació en la ciudad capital de Guatemala
el 25 de noviembre de 1,957. Posteriormente contrajo ma
trimonio con la señora NINETH MONTENEGRO. reside en la
13 calle "B" 29-78 Zona 7.

29-07-77   Propuesto para ocupar plaza en el Instituto Nacional de
            Sismología, Vulcanología, Meteorología é Hidrología ----
            -INSIVUMEH-.

19-07-79   Se le extendió el pasaporte No. 606929.

00-04-84   Miembro activo del Sindicato de CAVISA, perteneciente a
            la Junta Negociadora de Condiciones de Trabajo.

18-04-84   Fué secuestrado a inmediaciones de la 3ra. avenida y 7a.
            calle de la Zona 11, por hombres desconocidos, sin que -
            hasta la fecha se conozca de su paradero.

Figure 5.7. Diario Militar, Edgar Fernando García.

García. The Diario reports that he was captured on February 18, 1984, in Zone 11 of Guatemala City. Unlike most entries, however, his does not have a picture and does not report any final disposition. It merely states that "so far his whereabouts are unknown" (see Figure 5.7).

On August 22, 2000, GAM filed a complaint against Guatemala in the Inter-American Commission on Human Rights for the shooting and disappearance of Fernando García. In an interview, Nineth Montenegro explained that, "With the failure of the internal process we went to the international courts but it takes many years … too many."[56] Ms. Montenegro and Ms. García would have to wait six years before the commission ruled that the case was admissible on October 21, 2006, and four more for a decision on the merits. During that time, GAM and the state submitted evidence to the commission, but the state continued to refuse to reveal any information on Fernando García's capture and whereabouts. In October 2010, the commission issued its report finding that Guatemala violated numerous provisions

---

[56] Nineth Montenegro, Radio Interview, "Corte IDH podría dictar sentencia en Caso de Desaparición de Fernando García en Ocho Meses," Emisoras Unidas 89.7, Guatemala City, May 2, 2012, http://noticias.emisorasunidas.com/noticias/primera-hora/corte-idh-podria-dictar-sentencia-caso-desaparicion-fernando-García-ocho-meses (Last accessed May 27, 2012).

of the American Human Rights Convention, and four months later the commission brought the case to the Inter-American Court of Human Rights.

Some of the most important evidence in this and countless other cases in Guatemala came from a deserted arms depot in Guatemala City. Residents complained to the government's human rights department that the depot contained unexploded ordnance in July 2005. When human rights officials entered the rat-infested building, however, they found seventy-five million pages of documents belonging to the National Police – the institution responsible for countless atrocities during, before, and after the war. Kate Doyle was called in to advise the officials on how to preserve and process the documents. While there she saw filing cabinets labeled "assassinations" and "disappeared" as well as folders with the names of known victims. After painstakingly pouring over these documents, Velia Muralles Bautista and her colleagues in the Police Archives found several documents that referred to Fernando García. They discovered documents in which the high command of the National Police ordered a "cleansing operation" to go after the communists, insurgents, and other internal enemy groups.[57] The operation began on the day Fernando García was captured. As Nineth Montenegro later told the Inter-American Court, the documents prove "exactly what we have been saying all along – that Fernando was captured in Zone 11 of the city by officers of the Fourth Corps of the National Police."[58]

Ms. Muralles and her associates found documents showing that National Police officers monitored García's actions as early as 1978, believing that the trade union he helped run was a subversive organization – an internal enemy. In an amazing discovery, they found one document that identified the officers who actually shot and captured Fernando García and Danilo Chinchillo. Senior officers at the National Police drafted this document in which they recommended

<hr>

[57] Kate Doyle, "'I wanted him back alive.' An Account of Edgar Fernando García's Case from Inside 'Tribunals Tower,'" Unredacted: the National Security Archive, October 26, 2010, http://nsarchive.wordpress.com/2010/10/26/i-wanted-him-back-alive-"-an-account-of-edgar-Fernando-Garcias-case-from-inside-tribunals-tower/ (Last accessed June 2, 2012).
[58] Montenegro Testimony, Inter-Am. Ct.

commendations, medals, and awards for officers who had distinguished themselves. Among the officers singled out for this honor were Ramírez Ríos, Lancerio Gómez, and two other police agents who are still in hiding. Ríos and Gómez were recommended for their "heroic actions" in capturing "subversives" on "February 18, 1984, at 11:00 a.m., while carrying out an Operation in the Guard's Market, Zone 11" (see Figure 5.8).[59]

Nineth Montenegro and Alejandra García had concrete documentary proof that Ríos, Gómez, and their two associates were the men who shot and captured Fernando García. Yet Guatemalan officials still refused to issue criminal charges against these police officers. In addition to the documents uncovered in the police archives, the Inter-American process pressured Guatemalan officials to move the domestic case. Finally, state officials charged Ríos and Gómez within weeks of an Inter-American Commission's visit to Guatemala in which commission officials met with Guatemalan representatives for one last try at convincing the state to agree to a settlement in the case. Within days of the commission releasing its report on the merits of the case in October 2010, Guatemalan courts finally began criminal proceedings against the police officers, Ríos and Gómez.

Nineth Montenegro stated that it was through litigating the case in the Inter-American system that the truth came out. "It is with strong disgust that we now find that what we have always said is what happened," Ms. Montenegro commented.[60] She stressed the importance of discovering the Diario Militar and the police archives. "The archive is marvelous," she said. "In it are the day, time, police district ... how many days Fernando was inside ... and who were the ones who captured him and who gave the order ... there is a lot of proof." According to Ms. Montenegro, "through the international process it has come out."[61]

"While it is true that Fernando García cannot be present, I am here, his daughter who has become his clamoring voice to demand justice for him, and I will do so until the day I can see him again,

[59] Doyle, "'I Wanted him Back Alive.'"
[60] Nineth Montenegro, Radio Interview.
[61] Ibid.

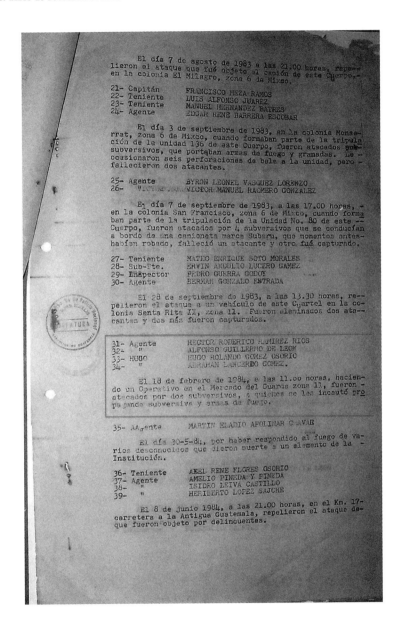

El día 7 de agosto de 1983 a las 21.00 horas, repelieron el ataque que fué objeto el camión de este Cuerpo,-
en la colonia El Milagro, zona 6 de Mixco.

21- Capitán   FRANCISCO MEZA RAMOS
22- Teniente   LUIS ALFONSO JUAREZ
23- Teniente   MANUEL HERNANDEZ BATRES
24- Agente   EDGAR RENE BARRERA ESCOBAR

El día 3 de septiembre de 1983, en la colonia Monse-
rrat, zona 6 de Mixco, cuando formaban parte de la tripula
ción de la unidad 136 de este Cuerpo, fueron atacados por
suversivos, que portaban armas de fuego y granadas. Se -
ocasionaron seis perforaciones de bala a la unidad, pero -
fallecieron dos atacantes.

25- Agente   BYRON LEONEL VASQUEZ LORENZO
26-   VICTOR MANUEL RAOMERO GONZALEZ

El día 7 de septiembre de 1983, a las 17.00 horas, -
en la colonia San Francisco, zona 6 de Mixco, cuando forma
ban parte de la tripulación de la Unidad No. 80 de este --
Cuerpo, fueron atacados por 4 subversivos que se conducían
a bordo de una camioneta marca Subaru, que momentos antes-
habían robado, falleció un atacante y otro fué capturado,

27- Teniente   MATEO ENRIQUE SOTO MORALES
28- Sub-Tte.   ERVIN ARNULFO LUCERO GAMEZ
29- Inspector   PEDRO GUERRA GODOY
30- Agente   GERMAN GONZALO ESTRADA

El 28 de septiembre de 1983, a las 13.30 horas, repelieron el ataque a un vehiculo de este Cuartel en la colonia Santa Rita II, zona 11. Fueron eliminados dos ata--
cantes y dos más fueron capturados.

31- Agente   HECTOR RODERICO RAMIREZ RIOS
32- "   ALFONSO GUILLERMO DE LEON
33- HUGO   HUGO ROLANDO GOMEZ OSORIO
34- "   ABRAHAN LANCERDO GOMEZ.

El 18 de febrero de 1984, a las 11.00 horas, hacien-
do un Operativo en el Mercado del Guarda zona 11, fueron -
atacados por dos subversivos, a quienes se les incautó pro
paganda subversiva y armas de fuego.

35- AAgente   MARTIN ELADIO APOLINAR CHAVAR

El día 30-5-84, por haber respondido al fuego de va-
rios desconocidos que dieron muerte a un elemento de la -
Institución.

36- Teniente   ABEL RENE FLORES OSORIO
37- Agente   AMELIO PINEDA Y PINEDA
38- "   ISIDRO LEIVA CASTILLO
39- "   HERIBERTO LOPEZ SAJCHE

El 8 de junio 1984, a las 21.00 horas, en el Km. 17-
carretera a la Antigua Guatemala, repelieron el ataque de-
que fueron objeto por delincuentes.

Figure 5.8. Document recommending Ríos and Gómez for
commendation.

dead or alive."[62] During the trial of Ríos and Gómez, Alejandra García told a court in the Tribunals Tower in Guatemala City that her father "was a simple man of clear convictions, who believed that if each of us added our grain of sand we could make Guatemala a better country."[63] Ms. Muralles's testimony about the Police Archives was crucial. Using documents from the archives, she proved the chain of command leading from Ríos and Gómez to senior officers in the National Police and the Guatemalan army. She introduced documents from the army ordering preparations for the cleansing operations and designating units to carry out the operation. She even introduced a hand-drawn map of Guatemala City, demonstrating which unit would be responsible for which part of the city. As Nineth Montenegro has been saying for twenty-eight years, the Fourth Corps of the National Police was given Zone 11, where García and Chinchillo were shot and captured (see Figure 5.9).[64]

Alejandra García articulated the purpose of justice clearly – to restore human dignity. "I wonder, what was the crime committed by my dad that would allow those who stand here accused to take upon themselves the right to decide on the life and fate of my father, as if they had the right to completely change the fate of my family."[65] "If my father is dead," she told the trial court, "he deserves to be buried like the beloved man that he was and still is, his name deserves dignity, he was not a sewer rat that can be killed with impunity, he was a human being."[66] "I do not seek revenge neither would my dad have," she testified, "but I do seek the truth, I want to know where he was taken, I want to know why he wasn't formally charged, I want to know who gave the order, I want to know where he was taken and who he was handed over to, I want to know what happened to him."[67] In an open

---

[62] Alejandra García, Statement to the Court, Trial of Héctor Roderico Ramírez Ríos and Abraham Lancerio Gómez, Guatemala City, Guatemala, November 1, 2010, http://casofernandoGarcía.org/post/1454795096/statement-from-alejandra-García-at-the-close-of-her (Last accessed May 29, 2012).

[63] Ibid.

[64] Kate Doyle and Emily Willard, "27 Years Later, Justice for Fernando García," The National Security Archive, February 18, 2011, http://www.gwu.edu/~nsarchiv/NSAEBB/NSAEBB337/index.htm (Last accessed June 2, 2012).

[65] Alejandra García, Statement to the Court.

[66] Ibid.

[67] Ibid.

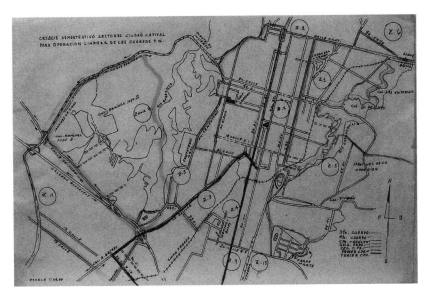

Figure 5.9 Guatemala police archives map of Guatemala City delegating "cleansing operation" authority to various police corps. The Fourth Corps, outlined in gray, was given the western area of the city where García was captured.

letter to her father published before the trial, Alejandra wrote, "With the trial, I hope to restore the dignity your soul deserves."[68] Kate Doyle also testified at the trial in Guatemala City and also emphasized the importance of revealing the truth. "The worst crime is the silence for years," she told the court.[69] Ríos and Gómez were convicted and sentenced to forty years in prison.

During the hearing before the Inter-American Court, Nineth Montenegro rejected the notion that these convictions amounted to justice for her and her family. "Justice that is so late, is not justice," she told the court. She explained that it was just coincidence that the case happened at all. "When we had the concrete proof from the archives, we continued with the internal process, but was it justice? No – it was

[68] Alejandra García, Letter to Fernando García, 2010, http://casofernandoGarcía.org/ Carta_a_Fernando_García (Last accessed May 30, 2012).
[69] Kate Doyle, Testimony to the Court, Trial of Héctor Roderico Ramírez Ríos and Abraham Lancerio Gómez, Guatemala City, Guatemala, November 1, 2010, http://casofernandoGarcía.org/page/2 (Last accessed May 30, 2012).

just happenstance that the archives were found." Ms. Montenegro's view supports the conceptualization of justice as a process. Because the state had blocked every attempt to move the process along, and because the only reason it finally moved was "happenstance," the convictions themselves did not amount to justice for her. "Because we are people with a lot of strength … and because we know that the state has a moral obligation and a political obligation to us, we will continue to resist."[70] For her, the process of justice would not culminate with the Inter-American Court, or even with domestic convictions. She told the court that she would continue until her husband or his remains were found and returned to her family. "Many times I was offered the chance to leave Guatemala, but I never accepted. I stayed to wage this battle until the end, and that's what I'm going to do." She explained that her idea of justice is not vengeance and it is not compensation. "They robbed me of our family … the anguish we feel knowing he was tortured, that he didn't sleep or eat, that he was martyred … nothing can compensate for that – nothing." Her "hope for justice" is "without vengeance, without hate." She explained further, "It's easy to say 28 years later 'that is passed.' No, there are things that don't pass – things that hurt, that affect your life, the life of your family … we hope for justice not for Fernando … but [for the fact] that he was a husband, a father and a son." She stressed the importance of having Fernando's remains returned to the family. "If they returned his body for us to bury," she explained, "that could give us the peace they've kept from us for 28 years." She went on, "We hope to know what happened after he was taken, we hope to find his remains – for me, for my family, for Fernando's mother who is still alive, that is fundamental."[71]

Uncovering Secret Documents around the World

Advocates all over the world are digging up old documents to prove human rights cases. In Chapter 3, I discussed the efforts by Polish

[70] Nineth Montenegro Testimony.
[71] Ibid.

survivors to use Soviet documents to expose the truth about Soviet culpability for the Katyn Massacre in 1939. Kate Doyle testified in Peru's criminal trial of former President Alberto Fujimori, introducing U.S. intelligence documents into evidence. In 1998, the archives of Argentina's police were discovered buried behind a wall. The government released the documents in 2003, and, like the Guatemalan police archives, they document an elaborate system of surveillance, oppression, disappearance, and death. These documents have been used in a series of criminal trials against high-level officials.

In another example, in 2012, after secret documents were exposed, a British high court ruled that survivors of alleged atrocities in Kenya during the Mau Mau uprising against the British colonial authorities could sue the British government. Five Kenyan survivors, Ndiku Mutua, Paulo Mzili, Wambugu Nyingi, Jane Muthoni Mara, and Susan Ngondi, had initially filed the suit in 2009, alleging they suffered torture and maltreatment in British detention camps.[72] In response, the government argued that the case should be dismissed because the alleged offenses had taken place more than fifty years beforehand.

Kenyans rebelled against British colonial rule from 1952 until 1956. In 2005 and 2006, the British government responded to Freedom of Information requests for documents related to this period by claiming that no documents existed. Then three scholars, David Anderson of Oxford University, Caroline Elkins of Harvard University, and Huw Bennett of Kings College of London, discovered evidence in the Kenyan National Archives that proved that an enormous set of documents had indeed been transferred to London.[73] These three scholars presented significant historical

---

[72] *Ndiku Mutua and 4 Others and the Foreign and Commonwealth Office:* Approved Judgment, Case No: HQ09X02666. London: Royal Court of Justice, 2011.
[73] Richard Drayton, "Britain's Secret Archive of Decolonisation," Histories of the Present (April 19, 2012). http://www.historyworkshop.org.uk/britains-secret-archive-of-decolonisation/; Caroline Elkins, *Imperial Reckoning: The Untold Story of Britain's Gulag in Kenya* (New York: Macmillan, 2005); David Anderson, *Histories of the Hanged: Britain's Dirty War in Kenya and the End of Empire* (New York: W. W. Norton, 2005); Huw Bennett, *British Army Counterinsurgency and the Use of Force in Kenya, 1952–56*, Ph.D. diss, University of Wales, Aberystwyth, 2007.

evidence of atrocities committed during the decolonization process in Africa. As Elkins observed, this "historical research provided the much-needed historical documentation to get the ball rolling in the British High Court."[74]

The British High Court process forced the government to admit that it possessed thousands of relevant documents at its storage facility in Hanslope Park, and Justice Richard McCombe ordered them released. Like the Guatemalan police archives, the Hanslope documents contain gruesome accounts of atrocities among the routine records of bureaucracy. For example, one document recorded charges against an officer for "beating up and burning two Africans" and another for "beating up and roasting alive of one African" (see Figure 5.10).[75] As a result of these and other documents, Justice McCombe refused to dismiss the case because he concluded there was sufficient documentary and other evidence on which to base a case. "There is ample evidence even in the few papers that I have seen suggesting that there may have been systematic torture of detainees during the emergency."[76]

The revelation of these documents has been instrumental in moving the process of justice forward for the survivors. During a hearing in the summer of 2012, three of the original plaintiffs testified about their suffering in colonial prison camps. In a surprising turn of events, the government admitted for the first time that prisoners in these camps were tortured. Before beginning his cross-examination of one of the plaintiffs, the Foreign Office's lawyer, Guy Mansfield, QC, stated, "I wish to make it clear that the British Government does not dispute that each of you suffered torture and other ill-treatment at the hands of the colonial administration." He then addressed one plaintiff, Paulo Nzili, and said, "I do not dispute with Mr Nzili that terrible things happened to him."[77]

---

[74] Caroline Elkins, "Alchemy of Evidence: Mau Mau, the British Empire, and the High Court of Justice," *The Journal of Imperial and Commonwealth History* 39(5) (December): 731–48, 732–33.

[75] Dominic Casciani, "British Mau Mau abuse Papers Revealed," BBC, April 11, 2011. http://www.bbc.co.uk/news/uk-13044974.

[76] *Ndiku Mutua and 4 Others.*

[77] Sam Greenhill, "Lawyer's Admission as Three Mau Mau Survivors Tell of Horror," *Daily Mail* (July 18, 2012).

EMERGENCY

DECYPHER OF TELEGRAM TO THE SECRETARY OF STATE.

Despatched: 17th January, 1955.

No. 58. TOP SECRET. Your telegram No. 48. Information required is as follows:-

(a) All accused in cases which are to proceed are Africans. Charge in every case is murder as a result of beating up or shooting of prisoners.

(b) There are eight Europeans who are the subject of the following allegations which are already to some extent public knowledge and who will be given immunity from prosecution under the new policy:-

     (i) One District Officer, accessory after the fact to murder in which Chief Mundia is charged as principal;

     (ii) One District Officer and one K.P.R. Officer, accessories after the fact to murder of two Africans in screening camp on 13th September, 1954;

     (iii) One Kenya Regiment Sergeant and one Field Intelligence Assistant, assault by beating up and burning of two Africans during screening operations on 19th September 1954;

     (iv) One District Officer, murder by beating up and roasting alive of one African in Home Guard Post on 17th November, 1954;

     (v) One District Officer, murder by shooting of African after interrogation on 12th December, 1954;

     (vi) One District Officer, murder by shooting of African after interrogation on 23rd December, 1954.

2. Previous paragraph is full information received from the Attorney General's Office this morning in reply to your enquiry. All the persons described as "District Officers" are temporarily employed District Officers (Kikuyu Guard) and

/not ....

19

Figure 5.10. Telegram Regarding British Treatment of Kenyan Rebels.

Using Secret Documents to Excavate the Truth

Amancio Samuel Villatoro was a labor union leader at the Chiclets Adams chewing gum factory in Guatemala City. He went to work on January 30, 1984, and never returned. Later that day, eight armed men forcibly entered his family home, searched it, and took documents, belongings, and money.[78] They went directly to a secret compartment in the master bedroom ceiling, which they could only have known about by interrogating Mr. Villatoro. One of Amancio's sons, Néstor Amílcar Villatoro Bran, remembered that, "My 17-year old brother … tried to defend my mother, but they put a machine-gun to his chest, and when I left my room to see what was going on, they put a pistol to my head and pushed me to the floor."[79]

In an all too similar story, Sergio Linares Morales was abducted as he left his work at the Municipal Development Institute on February 23, 1984. He was the head of the Data Processing and Systems Department office and was a leading member of the Association of University Students. Guatemalan security forces targeted university students and faculty for disappearances – especially those involved in student or faculty unions and organizations.[80] In the first three months of Óscar Humberto Mejía Víctores's presidency in 1984, security forces disappeared 635 people, including seven leaders of the University Student Association.[81] One of these was Sergio Linares Morales. As with the Villatoro family, the Linares home was invaded by armed men shortly after the disappearance. Despite continuous efforts by both families, neither man has been seen again. Amancio Villatoro is number fifty-five in the Diario and Sergio Linares is number seventy-four (see Figures 5.11 and 5.12).

The Guatemalan Police Archives contained information on each victim showing the efforts by family members to get the investigations moving but reporting no information on their whereabouts (see Figures 5.13 and 5.14). Then, on November 22, 2011, twenty-seven

---

[78] La Fundación de Antropología Forense de Guatemala (FAFG), "Amancio Samuel Villatoro" (November 22, 2011). http://www.fafg.org/BoletinExterno/Boletin_de_prensa_Amancio_Villatoro_Ingles.pdf.

[79] *José Miguel Gudiel Álvarez and Others ("Diario Militar") v. Guatemala*, Int. Am. Comm. H.R., Report No. 116/10, Case 12.590 (October 22, 2010), at para. 165.

[80] Guatemala: Memoria in Silencio: Caso Ilustrativo 48.

[81] Ibid.

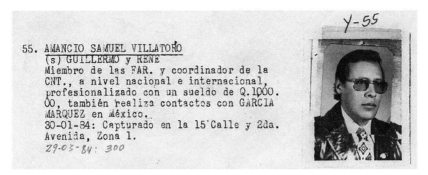

Figure 5.11. Diario Militar, Amancio Samuel Villatoro.

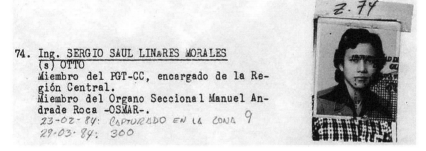

Figure 5.12. Diario Militar, Sergio Saul Linares Morales.

years after their disappearances, the Guatemalan Forensic Anthropology Foundation (FAFG) announced it had positively identified the remains of both men. The FAFG had begun excavating a mass grave near a military base in Comalpa, a town about forty miles from Guatemala City, in 2003. Archaeologists recovered the remains of 220 people and collected bone samples from 212 skeletons to conduct DNA analysis. They found what turned out to be the bodies of Sergio Linares and Amancio Villatoro in a grave with four other bodies. FAFG archeologists concluded from the position of the bodies that they were thrown in. This, according to FAFG, shows that the "persons who buried the bodies were also the perpetrators, and that the six victims were killed at the same time."[82] Eight

---

[82] La Fundación de Antropología Forense de Guatemala (FAFG), "Amancio Samuel Villatoro" and "Sergio Linares Morales" (November 22, 2011). http://www.fafg.org/BoletinExterno/Boletin_de_prensa_Amancio_Villatoro_Ingles.pdf; http://www.fafg.org/BoletinExterno/Boletin_de_prensa_Linares_Morales_Ingles.pdf.

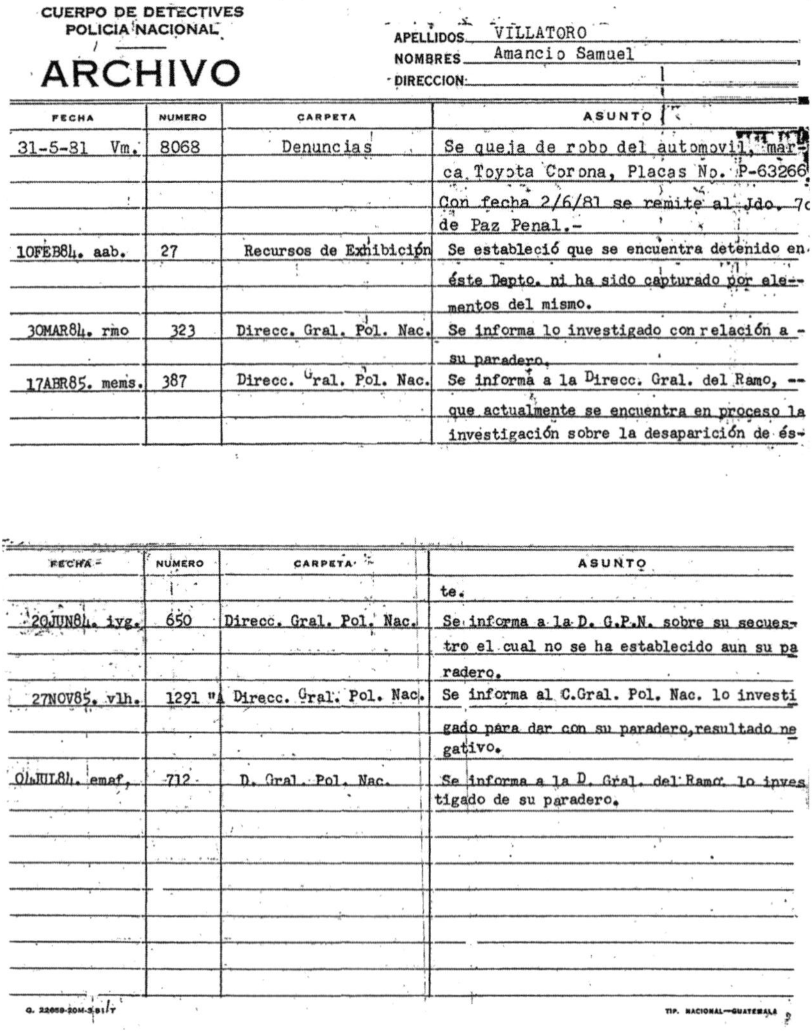

CUERPO DE DETECTIVES
POLICIA NACIONAL

ARCHIVO

APELLIDOS VILLATORO
NOMBRES Amancio Samuel
DIRECCION:

FECHA	NUMERO	CARPETA	ASUNTO
31-5-81 Vm.	8068	Denuncias	Se queja de robo del automovil, mar-
			ca Toyota Corona, Placas No. P-63266
			Con fecha 2/6/81 se remite al Jdo. 7o
			de Paz Penal.-
10FEB84. aab.	27	Recursos de Exhibición	Se estableció que se encuentra detenido en
			éste Depto. ni ha sido capturado por ele-
			mentos del mismo.
30MAR84. rmo	323	Direcc. Gral. Pol. Nac.	Se informa lo investigado con relación a -
			su paradero.
17ABR85. mems.	387	Direcc. Gral. Pol. Nac.	Se informa a la Direcc. Gral. del Ramo, --
			que actualmente se encuentra en proceso la
			investigación sobre la desaparición de és-

FECHA	NUMERO	CARPETA	ASUNTO
			te.
20JUN84. ivg.	650	Direcc. Gral. Pol. Nac.	Se informa a la D. G.P.N. sobre su secues-
			tro el cual no se ha establecido aun su pa
			radero.
27NOV85. vlh.	1291 "A	Direcc. Gral. Pol. Nac.	Se informa al C.Gral. Pol. Nac. lo investi
			gado para dar con su paradero, resultado ne
			gativo.
04JUL84. emaf.	712	D. Gral. Pol. Nac.	Se informa a la D. Gral. del Ramo lo inves
			tigado de su paradero.

TIP. NACIONAL—GUATEMALA

Figure 5.13. Guatemalan Police Archives Records, Amancio Samuel Villatoro.

years after beginning the excavation, the FAFG positively identified the two men by matching their DNA with samples from family members. They also considered factors like dental work, size, age, and clothes. For example, Amancio was wearing Levis at the time of his disappearance and these were found on his body. After all these

Figure 5.14. Guatemalan Police Archives Records, Sergio Saul Linares Morales.

years, their families finally had the remains of their loved ones to bury and a place to honor their lives. Without the Diario, the police archives, and the subsequent work by the FAFG, these men would still be disappeared.

CONCLUSION

Documents like secret U.S. diplomatic cables, the Diario Militar, and old police archives have given families and victims the answers they have demanded for decades. They have armed advocates to conclusively impeach repeated state denials and formed the basis of legal actions at home and abroad. These records have allowed victims and their loved ones to prove what happened to them and their missing family members. They have led to more discoveries, more revelations, and a more complete truth. The case studies in this chapter demonstrate clearly the importance of revealing the truth through original records in activating, and on occasion fulfilling, the process of justice. Kate Doyle and the National Security Archive have revolutionized the discovery and use of these documents. Ms. Doyle observed, "First and foremost what I see in the documents are lives – I see human lives." "I see patterns, I see planning, and I see orders," she said.[83] In the next chapter, I examine how courts in nations far from the human rights violations have empowered these advocates, victims, and families to reveal and prove the truth and kick-start the process of justice at home.

---

[83] Kate Doyle, *Granito: How to Nail a Dictator.*

6 EXPOSING THE TRUTH AND JUMP-STARTING THE PROCESS IN EXTRA-TERRITORIAL COURTS

UNLOCKING THE PROCESS

On October 12, 2007, Mirthala Elizabeth Linares Morales testified about the disappearance of her brother, Sergio, before the Inter-American Commission on Human Rights in Washington, DC. She told the commission that she learned of her brother's disappearance from "witnesses who were present in Zone 9 of the Capital who indicated emphatically that he was forcefully taken by two heavily armed men who put him in a white paneled van."[1] The witnesses "feared reprisals from the state." After capturing Sergio, security forces invaded the Linares family home, beating and torturing Mirthala and removing all of Sergio's personal belongings. The family went to the police and the army, but they treated the reported disappearance with "complete indifference." Mirthala Linares told the commission how she went to the head of state, Óscar Mejía Victores, and his officials told her that the state did not have her brother "and that maybe he had moved to the United States." "Obviously, this was a tremendous frustration," she recalled. Her mother helped start GAM, and, because of their work to obtain information about Sergio's whereabouts, "armed men in civilian clothes" often attacked them in their homes and workplaces. They told Mirthala she "would suffer the same fate as her brother." Through all this, though, she told the commission, "Those people never intimidated me."[2]

---

[1] Mirthala Linares Morales, Testimony before the Inter-American Commission for Human Rights, *José Miguel Gudiel Álvarez and others v. Guatemala* ("Diario Militar"), Referral No. 116/10, Case No. 12.590, October 12, 2007, transcribed and translated by the author.
[2] Ibid.

After the National Security Archive released the Diario Militar, the Linares family knew that their account of what happened to Sergio was true and that any state investigation into his whereabouts had been a sham. "There is no desire to investigate," Mirthala told the commission, "there is complete impunity, not just in the case of my brother Sergio but in the thousands of Guatemalans who were disappeared." "I have completely lost faith in the system of justice," she testified. When asked what she wanted from the commission, she responded that she wanted the case brought before the Inter-American Court and she wanted the court to "condemn those responsible for the disappearance of my brother Sergio … the men who captured, tortured and assassinated my brother because they know the truth."[3]

When states successfully arrest the process of legal justice at home, advocates and victims can keep the process going by litigating cases outside their home nations. In so doing, they actually start a process that can overcome entrenched impunity at home. Victims, survivors, and witnesses can construct an historical truth before an official tribunal and subject it to rigorous evidentiary standards, which is crucial. Human rights nongovernmental organizations (NGOs) have been instrumental in using extra-territorial legal action to overturn entrenched impunity. They are weaving a vast web of accountability that stretches well beyond the affected nations to international tribunals and foreign courts. It is weak in places, and those accused of violations may escape it in those spots. The hope, however, is that when they do they find themselves ensnared by yet another part of the web. Scholars acknowledge the importance of international judicial action. International courts can "put pressure on governments to comply with their international obligations (including their duties to prosecute offenders)," according to Steven Ratner and Jason Abrams.[4] Naomi Rhot-Arriaza observed that, with extra-territorial legal action, "one of the things you're trying to do here is to make the domestic system respond – to jump-start it. Sometimes if you start outside, you can jump-start the processes in the country that move you towards justice."[5] With respect to cases like

[3] Ibid.

[4] Steven R. Ratner and Jason S. Abrams, *Accountability for Human Rights Atrocities in International Law – Beyond the Nuremberg Legacy* (New York: Oxford, 2001), 226.

[5] Amnesty International, "Rios Montt – Justice Without Borders," Film, May 10, 2013, http://www.amnestyusa.org/news/multimedia/rios-montt-justice-without-borders.

Sergio Linares's, Pancho Soto of the Center for Human Rights Legal Action agreed. "If there isn't any outside pressure it is very unlikely that the Guatemalan system will respond."[6]

In addition to jumpstarting the domestic process, extra-territorial legal action is also crucial in revealing the truth. Ratner and Abrams found that these cases "establish an authoritative factual record" and "serve the cause of developing human rights and humanitarian law."[7] Martha Minow supports this view of extra-territorial justice. She argued that when human rights crimes are "prosecuted outside the affected territory, in the absence of regime change, it is perhaps the purest illustration of the potential of law to effect normative transition … indeed, the very response to the crime against humanity instantiates its core value of transcendent justice."[8] Minow further concluded that "especially when framed in terms of universality, the language of rights and the vision of trials following their violation equip people to call for accountability even where it is not achievable."[9]

Courts in oppressive regimes have historically afforded citizens little to no protection against the repressive state, and are typically complicit in the state's violence against its people. As Sieder writes of El Salvador, "the judicial system consummately failed to challenge the impunity of the military which refused to submit to the rule of law."[10] The courts in El Salvador "actively promoted impunity by shielding the armed forces from investigations into egregious cases of human rights violations," according to J. Michael Dodson and Donald Jackson.[11] Similarly, in their study of Guatemala and El Salvador, these scholars find that, during the authoritarian regimes, the military "was so heavily involved in the investigation and punishment of crime that the distinction between executive and judicial functions became blurred beyond recognition."[12] As Anthony Pereira illustrates, "Because they have

---

[6] Amnesty International, "Rios Montt – Justice Without Borders," Film, May 10, 2013, http://www.amnestyusa.org/news/multimedia/rios-montt-justice-without-borders.

[7] Ibid.

[8] Ibid.

[9] Martha Minow, *Between Vengeance and Forgiveness* (Boston, MA: Beacon Press, 1998), 48.

[10] Rachel Sieder, *Central America: Fragile Transition* (New York: St. Martin's Press, 1996).

[11] J. Michael Dodson and Donald W. Jackson, "Judicial Independence in Central America," in *Judicial Independence in the Age of Democracy*, Peter H. Russell and David M. O'Brien, eds. (Charlottesville: University of Virginia Press, 2001), 254.

[12] Ibid., 255.

often been purged, manipulated, and reorganized by prior authoritarian regimes, courts frequently embody authoritarian legacies."[13] The
only way around these institutions of impunity, therefore, is through
extra-territorial courts.

THE INTER-AMERICAN HUMAN RIGHTS SYSTEM

In 1959, the Organization of American States (OAS) established the
Inter-American Commission on Human Rights (Commission) and
charged it with monitoring compliance with the American Declaration
of the Rights and Duties of Man. Then, in 1965, the OAS empowered
the Commission to hear individual human rights cases and to recommend resolutions. In 1969, the OAS adopted the American Convention
on Human Rights (Convention), which not only set out basic human
rights law for member states, but created the Inter-American Court
of Human Rights (IACtHR). Of the thirty-five OAS member nations,
twenty-five have signed and ratified the Convention and twenty-four
have accepted the binding jurisdiction of the IACtHR.[14] For example,
Guatemala signed the Convention on May 25, 1978, and accepted the
jurisdiction of the Court on March 9, 1987.

The Convention charges the Commission with hearing individual complaints to impose conciliatory remedies, monitoring compliance with the Convention, conducting on-site studies of human rights
conditions, and imposing precautionary measures to prevent human
rights violations. Victims of human rights violations wishing to pursue
a case in the Inter-American system must first file a complaint with the
Commission. The Commission then asks the state accused of the violation to respond. Once a response is received, the Commission decides
if the case is admissible or within the Commission's jurisdiction. The
complaint is admissible if it alleges violations of rights protected by one
of the several instruments recognized by the OAS and the petitioners

---

[13] Anthony W. Pereira, "Virtual Legality: Authoritarian Legacies and the Reform of Military
Justice in Brazil, the Southern Cone, and Mexico," *Comparative Political Studies* 34(5):
555–74, 556.
[14] Jo M. Pasqualucci, *The Practice and Procedure of the Inter-American Court of Human Rights*
(Cambridge: Cambridge University Press, 2003).

have exhausted their domestic remedies.[15] The Commission can hear complaints against any member nation of the OAS.[16]

Once the Commission decides the case is admissible, it considers evidence presented by each of the parties, holds hearings, and frequently encourages a negotiated settlement. If these negotiations fail, the Commission can hand down a ruling on culpability. If the Commission decides that the accused nation is responsible for violations, it issues recommendations and prescribes remedies. Such rulings are confidential at this stage, which is supposed to encourage nations to comply with the recommendations to save face. If a nation refuses to comply with the remedies and recommendations, the Commission can bring the case before the IACtHR. Here the Commission changes its role from adjudicator to prosecutor. It is responsible for litigating the case against the accused nation. Commission lawyers file written pleadings and submit evidence, and the accused nation responds. The IACtHR then holds a formal hearing in which witnesses for both parties may testify. It then issues a written decision on admissibility, culpability, and, if applicable, remedies. The victims and surviving families may be represented by outside counsel in proceedings before the Commission and IACtHR.[17]

The Diario Militar Case, *Gudiel v. Guatemala,* in the Inter-American System

Kate Doyle testified as an expert witness during the Inter-American Court of Human Rights hearing in the Diario Militar Case (*Gudiel v. Guatemala*), in which Wendy Méndez, Mirthala Linares, and many others were petitioners. She explained in detail how the state built its wall of impunity and the step-by-step process of justice that has been dismantling it. Ms. Doyle has worked with those in Guatemala to obtain information about wartime human rights violations since

---

[15] Rules of Procedure of the Inter-American Commission on Human Rights, Ch. II, Art. 30–34.

[16] Ibid., Art. 27.

[17] See Jeffrey Davis and Edward H. Warner, "Reaching beyond the State: Judicial Independence, the Inter-American Court of Human Rights and Accountability in Guatemala," *Journal of Human Rights* 6(2): 233–55.

before the peace accords were signed in 1996. She testified that "The State of Guatemala has systematically hidden the information in its power about the internal armed conflict." Moreover, the "policy of silence has survived the peace accords; it has survived the Historical Clarification Commission; and it continues today – despite the discovery of archives, the exhumations of clandestine cemeteries, the criminal convictions of perpetrators of human rights violations, and the unceasing demand for information by families of the disappeared."[18]

As a consultant to the Historical Clarification Commission (Guatemala's truth commission), established after the peace accords, Ms. Doyle saw firsthand how the government stonewalled commissioners when they requested information and records. The state's answer then, as it is now, was "No. There were no documents, documents did not exist, they had been destroyed, they had been lost, or they remained under the seal of national security." During her testimony, Ms. Doyle referred to one of many letters the commissioners received in which government officials denied the existence of any documents that would reveal the fates of the disappeared (see Figure 6.1).[19] The letter stated that "after an exhaustive search," no documents could be found.

One year later, just weeks after the Historical Clarification Report was released, Ms. Doyle was handed the Diario Militar – exactly the type of documentation the existence of which the Guatemalan government had denied. She also told the court of the importance of the police archives discovered in 2005 explaining that, to date, "2,530 documents have been found inside the [archives] with a direct relation to the captures registered in the Military Logbook" (the Diario Militar). However, according to Ms. Doyle, the state and the army still refuse to reveal any information or disclose any documents. As she concluded in her testimony,

"The Army's posture – and the legacy of silence about historic repression on the part of the State – has left survivors of the conflict

---

[18] Kate Doyle, Testimony, Hearing before the Inter-American Commission on Human Rights, *José Miguel Gudiel Álvarez and others v. Guatemala* ("Diario Militar"), Referral No. 116/10, Case No. 12.590, reported in "Update: The Guatemalan Death Squad Diary and the Right to Truth National Security Archive Expert Testifies before International Court," *National Security Archive Electronic Briefing Book* No. 378, May 3, 2012, http://www.gwu.edu/~nsarchiv/NSAEBB/NSAEBB378/ (Last accessed June 1, 2012).

[19] National Security Archive, "Update: The Guatemalan Death Squad Diary."

MINISTERIO DE LA DEFENSA NACIONAL
REPUBLICA DE GUATEMALA, C. A.

No. 092-MDN-98

GUATEMALA, 11 DE MAYO DE 1998

SEÑOR
CHRISTIAN TOMUSCHAT
COORDINADOR DE LA COMISION
PARA EL ESCLARECIMIENTO HISTORICO
PRESENTE.

SEÑOR COORDINADOR:

    TENGO EL AGRADO DE DIRIGIRME A USTED; CON EL OBJETO DE INFORMARLE QUE, EN RESPUESTA A SU OFICIO No. CT/071-98/LG, SE REALIZO UNA BUSQUEDA EXHAUSTIVA EN LOS ARCHIVOS DEL MINISTERIO DE LA DEFENSA NACIONAL, NO HABIENDOSE ENCONTRADO NINGUNA DOCUMENTACION QUE SE REFIERA AL MENCIONADO DECRETO LEY EN DONDE SE ENCUENTREN "LA PERSONAS AFILIADAS A PARTIDOS O ENTIDADES COMUNISTAS Y PERSONAS CONDENADAS EN SENTENCIA FIRME DE CONFORMIDAD CON ESTA LEY", SUPONIENDO QUE ESTA NUNCA FUE APLICADA POR LO QUE NO SE LLEVO EL CITADO REGISTRO.

    SIN OTRO PARTICULAR, APROVECHO LA OPORTUNIDAD PARA SUSCRIBIRME DE USTED, CON LAS MUESTRAS DE CONSIDERACION Y ESTIMA.

EL GENERAL DE BRIGADA
MINISTRO DE LA DEFENSA NACIONAL

HECTOR MARIO BARRIOS CELADA

Figure 6.1. Defense ministry document (claiming that "after an exhaustive search" no documents related to the massacres could be found).

and the family members of victims with less than nothing, with expectations raised by a peace process that to date has not resulted with the fundamental information they require: What happened and why? Who is responsible? And where are the disappeared?"[20]

When Wendy Méndez testified, she told the judges how soldiers came for her mother when she was just nine years old. "They made my [eleven-year-old] brother and I watch as they tortured her, while they pulled out her fingernails one by one with pliers."[21] "The last time I saw my mother I saw her being tortured," she said, and the last thing her mother said to Wendy and her brother was "Be strong." She told the Inter-American Court about the countless ways she has missed her mother through the years – not having someone to help her grow up, not having a mother with whom to share her successes or to teach her how to be a mother to her own son. "I missed my mother's embrace ... something so simple." The Diario Militar motivated her to fight for justice in her mother's case. She founded HIJOS (as discussed earlier) with other children of the disappeared. "It was important to me and to the others to be organized, and to explain to society the need to find the remains of their loved ones and to have justice so that no one will ever again suffer these things."[22]

Once again in this case we see the absolute importance of the international system in advancing the process of justice. While to date, the Diario Militar case has not resulted in criminal convictions in Guatemala, it has had an indispensible impact in other ways. First, the remains of five victims listed in the Diario have been discovered and turned over to their families. Ms. Mendez stated that, "All of these successes these discoveries of remains of the disappeared have happened thanks to the organizations and the testimony of survivors," and the international process has been crucial to that aim. Her words clarify the role the Inter-American Court plays in the process of justice:

I want to tell the court, that when I was nine years old, when I was violated ... I could not scream, and there was no one there

[20] Doyle, Testimony, IACtHR.
[21] Wendy Méndez, Testimony, Hearing before the Inter-American Court on Human Rights, *José Miguel Gudiel Álvarez and others v. Guatemala* ("Diario Militar"), No. 116/10, Case No. 12.590, April 25, 2012, transcribed and translated by the author.
[22] Ibid.

to defend me.... That girl, who still lives inside me, had a hope of today, to say these things to the court, and that this tribunal would condemn them because then, at that moment, I could not defend myself, but now after that time has passed maybe this court will defend me.

Ms. Mendez was clear, however, that the process has also given her strength. "I don't want you to be confused," she told the court, "I am not here as a victim, passive and weak. I am here as a woman, a survivor, who is very proud of my mother." And she emphatically articulated her case. "I am proud of her political work ... she had that right," she explained. "And the army did not have the right to capture her, to torture her or to disappear her, and they don't have the right today to deny us justice and to deny us a final resting place for her remains."[23]

The Decision of the Inter-American Court

On November 20, 2012, nearly thirty years after the disappearance of Luz Haydee Méndez, Sergio Linares Morales, Amancio Villatoro, José Gudiel, and twenty-two others, the IACtHR handed down its decision in the case brought by surviving family members. It ruled that Guatemala violated the rights protected by the American Convention on Human Rights and other instruments by disappearing the twenty-six victims and then by preserving systematic denial and impunity. The judges explained that forcible disappearance is an offense that violates several human rights protections, beginning with the victim's right to personal liberty, continuing with the denial of the rights to truth and information, and often culminating with the denial of the right to life.[24] They held forced disappearance perpetrates a lengthy attack on the rights that protect the fundamental dignity of the victims and families. "Analysis of forced disappearance must realize that the deprivation of liberty is just the beginning of a complex set of violations that persist until the families know the fate and whereabouts of the victim," the court explained. Each rights violation "should not only be considered in isolation, divided and fragmented in detention, or possible torture,

---

[23] Ibid.
[24] *José Miguel Gudiel Álvarez and others v. Guatemala* ("Diario Militar"), Inter-Am. Ct. H.R., Sentencia, November 20, 2012, at para. 191 (translated by the author).

or the risk of death," it held, "but rather the focus should be on all the facts presented in the case under consideration before the Court."[25]

The court detailed the lengths to which Guatemalan officials went to hide the truth and preserve impunity. For example, in the case of Sergio Linares, the court pointed to repeated denials by the Fourth Corps (Cuatro Cuerpo) and other units of the police of any knowledge of Linares's detention – some of these denials were made in domestic court. Time and time again Guatemalan security officials told local courts that Linares "was not detained and was not being held by elements of its departments."[26] In the case of Luz Haydee Méndez, the court pointed to a three-year investigation by the human rights ombudsman for the Guatemalan government. At the end of this investigation, it announced that "there was no precise evidence that would permit the Ombudsman to make a substantive declaration about the disappearance of the person mentioned."[27]

Then, in May 1999, the National Security Archive released the Diario Militar, proving that the government disappeared all twenty-six of the petitioners in this case, as well as many others. Even then the government blocked nearly all attempts to discover the details of the disappearances, those responsible, and the final resting place of the many who were never seen again. For example, when the public prosecutor sought the names of those in the military who were in command of various units implicated in the Diario, the army refused because the "form" of the request "did not meet the requirements of the Code of Criminal Procedure."[28]

The IACtHR found that the Diario was conclusive evidence that Guatemala violated the rights to life, to personal integrity, to be free from torture, and rights protected in the Convention against Forced Disappearances. "The Diario Militar demonstrates that 17 of the 26 disappeared victims in the case were executed and this confirms the violation of the right to life."[29] It also "could not fail to mention that in cases of forced disappearance … the authorities must quickly

[25] Ibid., para. 196.
[26] Ibid., para. 109.
[27] Ibid., para. 117.
[28] Ibid., para. 167.
[29] Ibid., para. 206.

exhume and examine the remains for identification. As long as the remains remain hidden or unidentified the forcible disappearance continues."[30]

The court also stressed the importance of the Diario Militar, not just for proving state responsibility for the disappearances, but because it is evidence of the many rights violations involved in the actions of the Guatemalan state. The court held that the prohibition against forced disappearance is a jus cogens rule of international law, and the state acknowledged its responsibility for this violation. The Diario helps prove the full extent of this rights violation. First of all, for many of the victims listed, the Diario designated their date of execution. The length of time between capture and execution was, to the court, evidence of torture. As the court pointed out, "twelve victims were captured for between 15 and 60 days" before execution. "Otto René Estrada Illescas was detained 79 days and Orencio Calderón Sosa was detained 106 days while Rubén Amílcar Farfán was executed the same day he was captured, and none of their remains have been found or identified."[31] Furthermore, the court observed that the Diario shows that many of the victims were transferred to different prisons during their detention. It held that "frequent transfers of detainees was not a common practice during the armed conflict" and was clearly "intended to erase all traces of the victim, preventing any action that might avail the victim to justice or return them to the care of their families."[32]

Moreover, the victims were transferred "to specialized interrogation centers." The court held that "operating and maintaining clandestine detention centers is a per se violation of … the rights to personal liberty, personal integrity, life and to juridical personhood."[33] The Inter-American Court recognized that the target of the state's attack against these victims was their human dignity – their personhood. It held that "using forced disappearance, especially considering the number and complexity of this grave violation of human rights, constituted a direct violation of the right to recognition as a person before the law."[34] The

[30] Ibid., para. 207.
[31] Ibid., para. 199.
[32] Ibid.
[33] Ibid., para. 200.
[34] Ibid., para. 208.

judges explained that, "because the state refused to acknowledge the deprivation of liberty or reveal the whereabouts of the person, in conjunction with the other elements of the disappearance, it deprived victims of the protection of the law and of their personal and legal security thereby directly preventing the recognition of legal personality."[35] Disappearances are especially destructive of human dignity. It is "one of the most serious forms of theft of a person" and "also denies the victim's existence and leaves them in a kind of limbo."[36] The court concluded "that such violations can also be characterized or classified as crimes against humanity."[37]

The Inter-American Court also ruled that Guatemala violated its obligation to investigate these violations and prosecute those responsible for carrying them out. It held that, because "the prohibition against forced disappearance is a jus cogens norm, the correlating obligation to investigate and when appropriate prosecute those responsible, takes on particular intensity and importance."[38] Impunity was "particularly evident in this case," according to the court, and even after the release of the Diario Militar the investigation "remained at the same level of uncertainty and paralysis."[39] In the twenty-nine years since the disappearances in this case began there has been a "systematic pattern of denial of justice and impunity."[40] For example, the court pointed out that the Guatemalan government "gave various reasons for not submitting documents" related to these and other human rights violations and that it then claimed "the required documents never existed or had been lost or destroyed." However, "the documents whose existence had been repeatedly denied by the Executive actually existed and were stored in units of the national army."[41]

The court pointed out that "victims of gross human rights violations and the public have the right to know the truth" and that "in cases of forced disappearance … the right to know the truth includes the right of the relatives to know what happened to the victim and the

---

[35] Ibid.
[36] Ibid., para. 209.
[37] Ibid., para. 215.
[38] Ibid., para. 232.
[39] Ibid., para. 243.
[40] Ibid., para. 265.
[41] Ibid., para. 296.

location of his or her remains." The judges recognized the impact of continued state denials on the victims. They held that "deprivation of the truth about the whereabouts of a victim of forced disappearance is a form of cruel and inhuman treatment for close relatives, so the violation of the right to personal integrity can be linked to a violation of their right to know the truth."[42] It was clear to the court that the state violated the families' rights to truth and to humane treatment.

With regard to Wendy Méndez, in addition to the holdings discussed earlier in this chapter, the court also ruled that Guatemala violated its obligation to investigate the sexual attack against her when she was nine. Though the rape itself was not alleged in this case, the court could rule on the state's obligations to investigate and punish those responsible. This obligation to investigate and punish arises from the substantive violation itself – the sexual attack by an agent of the state. Among the several instruments such an attack violated, the court cited Article 11 of the American Convention and held that the rape would be a violation of the obligation by Guatemala to protect a person's "honor and dignity."[43] The court pointed out that Wendy Méndez has been providing specific facts regarding her rape and her mother's capture for years, and "the Public Prosecutor has failed to follow up appropriately in its investigation."[44] Ms. Méndez "provided specific information on the police station where she was detained, along with her brother and their mother."[45] Nevertheless, the state has completely failed to investigate these leads or any other aspect of the crimes against Ms. Méndez and her mother. This was a clear violation of the state's obligation to investigate these serious violations.

The court found additional violations of numerous rights protected by the American Convention and other instruments incorporated by the Inter-American system. It concluded the state violated the rights of victims and families to residence and circulation (Article 22) by displacing families and depriving them of economic support. As I described previously, Makrina Gudiel, Florentín Gudiel, and other family members moved to Mexico and later the United States after

---

[42] Ibid., para. 301.
[43] Ibid., para. 276.
[44] Ibid., para. 280.
[45] Ibid.

José Gudiel was abducted. These victims left their homes because they feared for their safety after being attacked by state officials, and the court recognized this to be a violation of their rights to residency and circulation. The court held that they were able to prove it was impossible for them to return to Guatemala after that country accepted the jurisdiction of the court in 1987. The state listed Gudiel family members as insurgents until it signed the peace accords in 1996.

The court also found that the forced disappearances "destroyed, in some cases, the structure of the family." Article 19 protects the right to participate in family life. After the state forcibly disappeared parents, several children had to move and live with extended family. This violated the state's obligation to protect the right to participate in family life. Guatemala also violated the rights to freedom of association by attacking people for their membership in groups. Many of the disappeared were union members, students, or academics. The court realized that fifteen of the family members were part of GAM. It found that during the civil war, Guatemala considered many of its citizens "internal enemies," including "those who for whatever reason were not in favor of the regime established." Clearly, "organizations seeking justice were considered to be 'internal enemies' so their members were subjected to acts of intimidation, threats and human rights violations." GAM was one of the organizations "most affected" by this government strategy.[46]

As in similar cases from Guatemala and other nations in the region, the court ruled that "the State must remove all obstacles, de facto and de jure, that maintain impunity in this case, and initiate, continue, promote, reopen, conduct and complete investigations necessary to determine and, if necessary, punish those responsible for the forced disappearance of the victims in this case."[47] The judges also required Guatemala to investigate the torture of Wendy Méndez and her brother and, if appropriate, prosecute those responsible. The court set out criteria for these investigations. For example, it instructed the state to refrain from applying amnesty laws or any other doctrine to preclude investigations and culpability. It also ordered the state to reveal the full

---

[46] Ibid., para. 315.
[47] Ibid., para. 327.

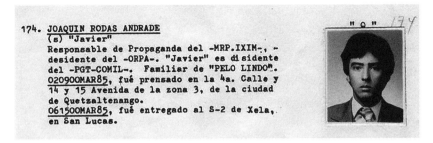

174. JOAQUIN RODAS ANDRADE
(a) "Javier"
Responsable de Propaganda del -MRP.IXIM-, -
desidente del -ORPA-. "Javier" es disidente
del -PGT-COMIL-. Familiar de "PELO LINDO".
020900MAR85, fué prensado en la 4a. Calle y
14 y 15 Avenida de la zona 3, de la ciudad
de Quetzaltenango.
061500MAR85, fué entregado al S-2 de Xela,
en San Lucas.

" Q "

Figure 6.2. Diario Militar, Joaquin Rodas Andrade.

truth "avoiding omissions" and taking logical steps in light of the existence of the Diario Militar.[48]

The judges stressed the right to information as well. "The State must ensure victims or their families full access to all aspects of the investigation and prosecution."[49] In addition to victims and families, society also possesses the right to truth, according to this court. "The results of the investigation should be published so that Guatemalan society knows the facts of this case and those responsible."[50] The Inter-American Court recognized "that the most important demand of the family is to know the truth of what happened, the fate of their loved ones and to find their remains."[51] To that end, it ordered the state to find and produce the remains of the disappeared victims. "Receiving the bodies of the missing persons is paramount to the families, allowing them to bury them according to their beliefs, as well as close the grieving process that they have been living over the years."[52]

Josefa Elizabeth Andrade testified early in the Diario case about the disappearance of her son, Joaqin Rodas Andrade. He appears as number 174 in the Diario Militar (see Figure 6.2). After Joaqin Andrade did not come home one night, Josefa Andrade recalled that she and her husband "were going around asking people if they had seen anything and one person said yes, he saw these vehicles with

---

[48] Ibid., para. 327(a).
[49] Ibid., para. 328.
[50] Ibid.
[51] Ibid., para. 332.
[52] Ibid., para. 333.

the security personnel come in and forcibly capture my son."[53] Like Nineth Montenegro and countless others, Josefa Andrade met with military commanders and even the head of state, Óscar Mejía Victores. Without exception, they denied that state officials had captured Joaqin. She testified about learning about the Diario Militar, hoping "that even though this Diario had the photo of my son with the exact dates and the seal it wouldn't have the code showing he was dead." It does not have Code 300 listed under Joaqin's entry. "I felt very distressed," she recalled. "Once again it awakened the cruelty in our hearts." She told the judges that she believes "that somewhere in this world my son is alive. I don't know why, perhaps it is my faith in god, or maybe because we never received any news of him and it is with this idea, this strength, this faith that I come to you so that you will force a full investigation." She declared, "I accuse the state of Guatemala, I accuse the army, I accuse the public ministry."

Ms. Andrade described the experience of testifying in the Inter-American system. "I'm not here for me, I'm here for all the mothers," she stated, "and I am here for my sisters and brothers in suffering … who tell me go, go and represent us please, that your voice will be our voice, and that you will carry us in your heart. Even if it's necessary to suffer, and even if it's necessary to beg, tell them to give us justice." It was an enormous step in the process of justice for Ms. Andrade to testify. She reflected, "It gives me very powerful emotion in my heart and soul to be in this place where never in my life I imagined I would be – I am very grateful and very emotional because you are listening to me."[54]

The Decision of the Inter-American Court in *Fernando García and Family v. Guatemala*

On the same day the Inter-American Court of Human Rights delivered its decision in the Diario Militar case, it also issued its ruling in the Edgar Fernando García case. I described his disappearance and the

---

[53] Josefa Elizabeth Andrade, Testimony before the Inter-American Commission for Human Rights, *José Miguel Gudiel Álvarez and others v. Guatemala* ("Diario Militar"), Referral No. 116/10, Case No. 12.590, October 12, 2007, transcribed and translated by the author.
[54] Ibid.

tireless work for justice by his wife, Nineth Montenegro, and daughter, Alejandra, in the previous chapter. Once again the court found that Guatemala had violated numerous provisions of the American Convention on Human Rights not only by disappearing Mr. García, but also through its aggressive campaign of denial and impunity. It also echoed its holdings that the rights to truth and information were violated. Its overall analysis of the violations of rights encompassed by the forcible disappearance was identical to that of the Diario case.

The court held that the state's disappearance of Fernando García violated his rights to free expression and association because he was targeted as a result of his leadership of a trade union. Marco Tulio Álvarez Bobadilla, an expert witness, testified that he found documents in the Guatemalan police archives that indicated García had been targeted because of his union activities. He directed the court to a 1980 application by Fernando García for permission to have a parade. Security officials wrote instructions on the application to "exercise control" over the parade and "to take note of all the bodies" present.[55] The court concluded that, like so many others, Fernando García's union activity marked him as an "internal enemy" in the eyes of the state.

The judges recognized the enormous destructive effect of the disappearance on Fernando García's family members and on the integrity of the family itself. The disappearance was a "violation of the right to physical and moral integrity of the family ... which is increased by the constant refusal of state authorities to provide information on the whereabouts of the victim or conduct an effective investigation in order to clarify what happened."[56] The court held that "the deprivation of the truth about the whereabouts of a victim of enforced disappearance entails a form of cruel and inhuman treatment to close relatives, which presumes harm to the mental and moral condition of the family."[57] The judges acknowledged that Nineth Montenegro, Alejandra García, and Maria Emilia García "have suffered great uncertainty and profound suffering and anguish to the detriment of their physical, mental and moral condition because of the forced disappearance of their loved

---

[55] *García y Familiares v. Guatemala*, Inter-Am. Ct. H.R., Sentencia, November 20, 2012, at para. 118–19, translated by the author.
[56] Ibid., para. 161.
[57] Ibid.

one and the action of the state authorities regarding the investigation of what happened."[58]

As I described in Chapter 5, Ms. Montenegro was threatened and attacked because of her involvement in GAM. The court held that the state violated her rights to freedom of association by launching these attacks. It held that Guatemala conducted "a systematic campaign to discredit and disqualify" Ms. Montenegro and portray her and GAM as "seditious, liars, crazy ... as the plague of society."[59] The judges recognized that this oppressive campaign injured Alejandra García as well. Even though she was just a child and too young to have her association rights hindered, the effect on her was relevant to the rights of her mother, Nineth. Alejandra testified that the state "generated fear in many people close to her, who chose to stay away." The court cited Alejandra's testimony that she was an outcast as the "daughter of a guerrilla."[60] Nineth and later Alejandra García were doing "the work of promoting and defending human rights [and] ... states have a duty to allow human rights defenders to freely conduct their activities; protect them when they are threatened; prevent attacks on their lives and refrain from imposing obstacles to their work."[61] It was clear to the court that Guatemala failed in these obligations. It cited documents found in the police archives that showed that the police and army considered GAM and its members "real enemies of the military government and its Security Forces in general," which required it to "neutralize or eliminate them."[62]

The Diario Militar and García cases were monumental steps in the process of legal justice for the families involved and for Guatemala. To comply with the orders of the court, the state will have to investigate the disappearances fully, release all information to the families, and perhaps establish a commission to search for the whereabouts of the disappeared. Of course, the state can choose not to comply with any or all of the remedies prescribed by the court. As I show in the next chapter, however, the ruling is a potent tool for victims and advocates

[58] Ibid., para. 162.
[59] Ibid., para. 165.
[60] Ibid.
[61] Ibid., para. 179.
[62] Ibid., para. 180.

to advance the process of legal justice at home. These decisions by the court represent an official recognition of the truth in each of the disappearances and in the campaign of impunity and oppression that followed. The facts that the families alleged for years – decades – have been proven true. More than this, though, the court linked these facts to specific violations of human rights law. The truths recognized by the court were not simply the facts – the tragic stories of the disappeared – but that these facts reflected specific violations of human rights law.

BRINGING HUMAN RIGHTS CASES FROM LATIN AMERICA IN THE UNITED STATES

Teófila Ochoa and Cirila Pulido were twelve years old when Peruvian soldiers occupied their village near the town of Accomarca and massacred their families and neighbors (see Chapter 1). On July 11, 2007, these women filed suit against Telmo Hurtado, the commander of the army unit who led the troops who carried out the massacre, in the U.S. Federal District Court for the Southern District of Florida in Miami. On the same day, these women filed suit against Juan Manuel Rondón, a former lieutenant in Hurtado's "Lince" Company, in the Southern District of Maryland. Hurtado was living in Miami and Rondón was in Maryland at the time, and this allowed Ms. Ochoa and Ms. Pulido to file claims against the men. In both cases, CJA represented Ms. Ochoa and Ms. Pulido, demonstrating yet again the importance of human rights advocacy groups.

Even though the United States is more than three thousand miles from Accomarca, its courts had jurisdiction over the alleged violations under two federal laws, the Alien Tort Statute and the Torture Victims Protection Act. The Alien Tort Statute of 1789 (ATS) grants federal courts the authority to hear cases in tort brought by aliens for violations of international law. This law lay nearly dormant for almost 200 years until the Filártigas, a Paraguayan family, successfully sued the Paraguayan police chief who tortured and killed their son and brother, Joelito Filártiga, in Asuncion, Paraguay. The Second Circuit Court of Appeals held that the ATS gave federal courts the authority to hear the Filártigas case because torture was a clear violation of international law.[63] Writing for the court, Judge Kaufman explained that

> In light of the universal condemnation of torture in numerous international agreements, and the renunciation of torture as an instrument of official policy by virtually all of the nations of the world (in principle if not in practice), we find that an act of torture committed by a state official against one held in detention violates established norms of the international law of human rights, and hence the law of nations.[64]

Therefore, the court ruled, "whenever an alleged torturer is found and served with process by an alien within our borders, [the law] provides federal jurisdiction."[65] In 2004, the U.S. Supreme Court upheld the Second Circuit's interpretation of the ATS, holding that the law allowed federal courts to recognize causes of action based on international law as long as the international law norms were "specific, universal and obligatory."[66] There is consensus that torture and extrajudicial killing meet this standard.

However, On April 17, 2013, in *Kiobel v. Royal Dutch Petroleum*, the U.S. Supreme Court held that the presumption against the extra-territorial application of federal law applied to the ATS. In a 5–4 decision, the court ruled that the presence of a multinational corporation in the United States was insufficient to rebut this presumption. The majority explained that "where the claims touch and concern the territory of the United States, they must do so with sufficient force to displace the presumption against extraterritorial application."[67] While this decision significantly limited the reach of the ATS, it in all likelihood does not impact the *Hurtado* and *Rondon* cases or the other ATS cases discussed in this book. The *Kiobel* majority declined to rule on whether individuals who move to the United States seeking safe haven would still be liable under the ATS. More important, Ms. Ochoa and Ms. Pulido also

---

[63] *Filartiga v. Peña-Irala*, 630 F.2d 876, 878 (2nd Cir. 1980).
[64] Ibid., citing *United States v. Smith*, 18 U.S. (5 Wheat.) 153, 160–61, 5 L. Ed. 57 (1820).
[65] Ibid., 878.
[66] *Sosa v. Alvarez-Machain*, 542 U.S. 692, 124 S.Ct. 2739, 2761, 159 L.Ed.2d 718 (2004), at 2765; See also Jeffrey Davis, *Justice across Borders* (New York: Cambridge University Press, 2008), chapter 2.
[67] *Kiobel v. Royal Dutch Petroleum*, Case No. 10–1491, p. 14, 569 US ___, (2013).

filed their lawsuits under the Torture Victim Protection Act of 1992 (TVPA) and the *Kiobel* decision does not affect that law.[68] Congress passed the TVPA endorsing the Second Circuit's interpretation of the ATS and allowing citizens to sue under its provisions in addition to aliens. The law states that:

> An individual who, under actual or apparent authority, or color of law, of any foreign nation – (1) subjects an individual to torture shall, in a civil action, be liable for damages to that individual; or (2) subjects an individual to extrajudicial killing shall, in a civil action, be liable for damages to the individual's legal representative, or to any person who may be a claimant in an action for wrongful death.[69]

Ms. Ochoa and Ms. Pulido alleged Hurtado committed the human rights violations directly and that he was also liable for violations committed by his troops under the doctrine of command responsibility. He failed to answer the suit and the court granted the plaintiffs' motion for a default judgment. Even though the issue of Hurtado's liability was decided, the court held a trial to determine damages. This is a crucial step in the process of legal justice – proving the truth and allowing the victims to testify in a court of law with strict evidentiary rules. On March 4, 2008, District Court Judge Adalberto Jordan ordered Hurtado to pay $37 million in compensatory and punitive damages to Ms. Ochoa and Ms. Pulido and to the estates of their family members. In his order on damages Judge Jordan acknowledged, "As a general matter, a human life is not subject to intrinsic monetary valuation. Indeed, any arbitrary value placed on a life threatens to demean it or cheapen it because of its obvious inadequacy. The same goes for human suffering. But placing values, for purposes of assessing damages, is all that a court can do."[70] This routine statement demonstrated clearly that the verdict and assessment of damages is just a part of the process of legal justice in which testifying and proving the truth were crucial elements.

---

[68] See Justice Kennedy's concurrence, *Kiobel* at p. 15.
[69] Public Law No. 102–256 (1992).
[70] *Ochoa v. Hurtado*, Order on Damages, Case No. 07–21783-CIV-JORDAN (S.D.Fl. 2008), 5.

The Rondón Case and Obstacles to Extra-Territorial Legal Justice

In his case, Rondón filed a motion to dismiss Ms. Ochoa and Ms. Pulido's complaint. He argued the case was filed after the ten-year statute of limitations and was therefore barred. He also claimed he was entitled to sovereign immunity, that the case was barred by the political question doctrine, and that the case should be dismissed because the plaintiffs did not exhaust their remedies in Peru. He also argued the act of state doctrine barred the suit. All of these legal arguments serve valuable purposes in appropriate cases, but they can also be misused to block the revelation of the truth and preserve impunity. Overcoming defenses like these is an important step in the process of legal justice. The district court in Maryland denied the motion and Rondón appealed to the Fourth Circuit Court of Appeals. On February 26, 2009, the Fourth Circuit agreed with the district court and rejected all of Mr. Rondón's grounds for dismissal.

The TVPA has a ten-year statute of limitations, and courts have ruled that this limitation applies to the ATS as well. Peru's soldiers attacked Accomarca on August 14, 1985, and the lawsuit was not filed until 2007. In postconflict human rights cases, victims and survivors frequently cannot bring cases against those responsible until long after the violations occurred. The oppressive regimes under which the violations occurred are not typically receptive to accusations of wrongdoing. Those who complain often suffer violent reprisals, evidence disappears, or the courts are controlled by the oppressive regime in question. These difficulties often persist long after the transition to democratic governance as evidence is difficult to uncover and military officials often retain a great deal of power. My case studies of the Guatemalan disappearances, the murder of Myrna Mack, and the Jesuits case are examples of these phenomena. Statutes of limitations, therefore, are often formidable barriers to the process of legal justice.

In the *Rondón* case, the Plaintiffs argued that the statute of limitations should be equitably tolled, or frozen, because they could not pursue a case against Rondón until 2000. Writing for the Fourth Circuit, Judge Messitte explained that equitable tolling is justified when "due to circumstances external to the party's own conduct ... it would be unconscionable to enforce the limitations period against the party and gross injustice would result."[71] He recognized that the "political climate in Peru was unremittingly hostile to any effort on their part to pursue remedies against Rivera Rondón" before 2001. Moreover, he agreed that the plaintiffs would have subjected themselves to violent retribution if they made their accusations against Rondón before that year.[72] Therefore, the Fourth Circuit held that the statute of limitations was tolled until at least 2000 and that the plaintiffs' suit was filed well within the ten-year limitations period.

Rondón also argued he was entitled to immunity because at the time of the attack he was acting in his official capacity as an officer of Peru. Sovereign and official immunity are additional doctrines that can in some cases play a valuable role in protecting sovereign states and their officials from unlawful intrusion by another state's courts. However, in many cases the doctrine is just a tool to preserve impunity. In the Rondón case, he claimed the Foreign Sovereign Immunities Act (FSIA) blocked the plaintiffs' suit. Judge Messitte ruled "that 'based on the language and structure of the statute, … the FSIA does not apply to individual foreign government agents."[73] Rondón was not entitled to immunity, therefore. One year after this case was decided, the U.S. Supreme Court upheld this interpretation of the FSIA in an ATS case accusing a former Somali head of the military of human rights violations.[74]

Rondón next argued the case should be dismissed because Ms. Ochoa and Ms. Pulido failed to exhaust their legal remedies in Peru. As I pointed out earlier, the Inter-American system also enforces an exhaustion requirement. Indeed most international courts require parties to exhaust their remedies at home before seeking redress internationally. For example, the International Criminal Court's jurisdiction is based on the principle of complementarity, meaning it will only try a case if the nation or nations that have jurisdiction over the crime will not or cannot try it. These requirements express the principle that extra-territorial jurisdiction should only be exercised if the state with

---

[71] *Ochoa v. Rondón*, 642 F. Supp. 2d 473, 480 (4th Cir. 2009).
[72] Ibid., 482.
[73] Ibid., 483, quoting *Yousuf v. Samantar*, 552 F.3d 371, 381 (4th Cir. 2009).
[74] *Samantar v. Yousuf*, 560 U.S. 305 (2010).

territorial jurisdiction is unable or unwilling to facilitate the cases. They give victims and families a way to circumvent impunity at home but not a way to merely circumvent undesirable outcomes.

In the United States, the TVPA expressly requires plaintiffs to exhaust their local remedies before bringing a case. However, the ATS has no such requirement, and no court has ruled that ATS plaintiffs need to exhaust their local remedies. On the other hand, courts have used other legal doctrines to protect the interests that the exhaustion requirement protects, such as the forum non conveniens doctrine. Under this doctrine a defendant may assert that the extra-territorial court is an inappropriate forum to hear the case. In *Mujica v. Occidental*, an ATS case arising from Colombia, the District Court for the Central District of California explained that the "standard governing a motion to dismiss on the basis of forum non conveniens is whether 'defendants have made a clear showing of facts which establish such oppression and vexation of a defendant as to be out of proportion to plaintiff's convenience.'"[75] Unlike the exhaustion requirement, the defendant has the burden of proof in forum non conveniens disputes and the plaintiffs' convenience is a factor in the analysis. In many ATS cases, the defendants are unable to show that it would be safe for plaintiffs to bring their case in their country of origin. In *Mujica*, Judge Rea pointed out that the plaintiffs' efforts to obtain justice in Colombia "resulted in the dangerous conditions precluding their ability to bring a suit against these defendants in Colombia."[76] He held "an alternative forum is inadequate if the claimants cannot pursue their case without fearing retaliation."[77]

In the *Rondón* case, Judge Messitte explained that with an exhaustion of local remedies issue the "question is whether Rivera Rondón has shown that the remedies in Peru are 'effective, obtainable, not unduly prolonged, adequate and not otherwise futile.'"[78] He pointed out that the plaintiffs would not be able to bring their civil case in Peru until criminal charges against Rondón were resolved. (The criminal case is discussed later in this chapter). Judge Messitte held that

---

[75] *Mujica v. Occidental*, 381 F. Supp. 1134, 1140 (C.D.Cal. 2005) quoting *Dole Food Co., Inc. v. Watts*, 303 F.3d 1104, 1118 (9th Cir. 2002).
[76] Ibid. at 1142.
[77] Ibid. at 1143.
[78] *Rondón* at 484–85, quoting S. Rep. No. 102–249, at 10.

the "record is barren of any evidence that the criminal case against him is proceeding apace or that there is any reasonably foreseeable date for its conclusion" and therefore domestic remedies in Peru are unobtainable.[79]

Rondón also claimed the case should be dismissed because it presented a non-justiciable political question. The political question doctrine requires courts to dismiss cases if the Constitution delegates the issue presented to Congress or the president for resolution. For example, in *Nixon v. U.S.* the Supreme Court refused to review the impeachment trial of a federal judge because the Constitution delegates the power to try impeachments to the U.S. Senate.[80] Courts occasionally use the doctrine to dismiss challenges to U.S. foreign policy decisions holding that these issues are delegated to the president. The doctrine is an important mechanism preserving separation of powers and keeping courts from intruding on nonjudicial matters. However, it is occasionally misused to prevent judicial scrutiny of unlawful or embarrassing foreign policy actions.[81] Rondón argued that because members of his "Lince" battalion were trained by the United States, and because the U.S. administration supported Peru's war against Sendero Luminoso, the case against him should be dismissed. The Fourth Circuit refused to accept Rondón's arguments. Judge Messitte explained that, "Although Rivera Rondón argues that the U.S. provided training to Peru to assist in fighting the terrorists … there is no basis for connecting his individual role in the alleged massacre to any policy decision of the U.S. or to any conduct of the U.S. armed forces." The cases in which the political question doctrine required dismissal "called into question the propriety of specific decisions made by the U.S. officials in conducting defense operations – issues unquestionably committed to the executive branch." "Nothing of the kind is at issue here."[82]

Rondón also asked the court to dismiss the action based on the act of state doctrine. As the Fourth Circuit explained, the "act of state doctrine prevents courts from adjudicating a dispute if the matter

---

[79] Ibid. at 485.
[80] *Nixon v. U.S.*, 506 U.S. 224 (1993).
[81] See Davis, *Justice across Borders*, 99–101.
[82] *Rondón* at 487.

involves assessing official actions of a foreign sovereign."[83] The doctrine plays an important role in ensuring that extra-territorial adjudication does not improperly intrude on the legitimate official actions of another country. Along with sovereign and official immunity, this defense is designed to protect national sovereignty and comity. When used to perpetrate impunity they can present formidable obstacles to the process of legal justice.

The Supreme Court set out three factors courts should consider in adjudicating the act of state doctrine: whether there is consensus regarding the area of international law at issue in the case, whether the issue "touch[es] ... sharply on national nerves," and whether the government accused of the violations is still in power.[84] In applying these standards, Judge Messitte pointed out that the "act of state doctrine does not call for abstention merely because a case may require the acts of a former foreign government official to be judged."[85] The plaintiffs alleged extrajudicial killing, torture, and war crimes, and these are clearly established violations of international law. Moreover, as Judge Messitte explained, "torture and similar human rights abuses can never be 'public acts' for the purpose of the acts of state doctrine."[86] The Fourth Circuit also held that there was no risk that the case would touch on the nerves of the Peruvian government. "All the acts complained of here are illegal under Peruvian law," Judge Messitte pointed out, "and, most importantly, the Peruvian Government has presented a letter to the Court in effect denying the alleged acts were Peruvian acts of state."[87] This last point also resolved the third factor in considering the act of state doctrine – whether the accused government was still in power. As the court held, because "the Peruvian Government is today firmly on record as condemning the acts purportedly committed at Accomarca, the act of state doctrine in no way stands as a bar to prosecution of Plaintiffs' claims in this forum."[88]

The Fourth Circuit rejected Rondón's demands for dismissal and the case was sent back to the trial court. In the next chapter, I pick

---

[83] Ibid.
[84] *Banco Nacional de Cuba v. Sabbatino*, 376 U.S. 398, 428 (1964).
[85] *Rondón* at 488.
[86] Ibid. at 488–89, quoting S. Rep. No. 102–249, pt. 4, at 8 (1991).
[87] Ibid. at 489.
[88] Ibid.

up on this case study and explain how these cases against Hurtado and Rondón advanced the process of legal justice for Ms. Ochoa and Ms. Pulido and for Peru. It is clear from the analysis presented in this chapter that overcoming the legal obstacles in Rondón's motion to dismiss was an important element of the process of legal justice. As Minow argued, "once each individual is understood to be a rights bearer of equal dignity, the rationales of state sovereignty and privacy can no longer shield violations of individual rights from view. Instead, such shields begin to look like governmental complicity with the perpetrators of violence."[89]

CJA and its partners have tracked down dozens of military, intelligence, and political figures in the United States who were responsible for human rights violations in their home nations.[90] Dozens of these cases come from Latin America. In Chapter 4, I discussed the Manfredo Velásquez case that established the right to truth before the Inter-American Court of Human Rights. With CJA's help, Mr. Velásquez's sister Zenaida Velásquez tracked down the Honduran commander living in the United States who detained Mr. Velásquez before he was killed. They sued him under the ATS and TVPA with other Honduran plaintiffs.[91] Before the trial began, Ms. Velásquez explained that the suit "will enable us to hold a high-ranking official responsible and thereby begin to pierce the culture of impunity."[92] CJA represented a surviving family member of Salvadoran Archbishop Óscar Romero in a suit against Captain Alvaro Saravia under the ATS and TVPA. They won the case, proving Saravia was responsible for helping to orchestrate the assassination of one of the most powerful voices for peace and justice in the region. The case in the United States was the only time anyone has ever been held accountable for one of the most notorious crimes in Latin American history.[93]

One of CJA's partners, the Center for Constitutional Rights (CCR), represented eight Guatemalan plaintiffs and an American nun

---

[89] Minow, *Between Vengeance and Forgiveness*, 58.
[90] See Davis, *Justice across Borders*.
[91] *Reyes v. Grijalba*, Case No. 02–22046 (S.D.Fla. 2006).
[92] CJA, *Reyes v. Grijalba*, Plaintiff Profile. http://cja.org/article.php?id=469 (Last accessed February 10, 2012).
[93] *Doe v. Saravia*, 348 F.Supp.2d 1112 (E.D.Cal. 2004).

in their ATS and TVPA suit against former Guatemalan Minister of Defense Hector Gramajo. Dianna Ortiz, the American nun, accused Mr. Gramajo of ordering his forces to carry out horrific acts of rape and torture to which she fell victim in 1989. Sister Ortiz was held, tortured, and raped for twenty-four hours before an American working with the Guatemalan security forces recognized her as an American who had been reported missing. The Guatemalan survivors alleged that Mr. Gramajo's troops "ransacked their villages and engaged in brutal and barbarous practices."[94] They presented evidence that they "were themselves subjected to torture and arbitrary detention [or] were forced to watch as their family members were tortured to death or summarily executed."[95] Many of the cases brought by CJA and CCR reveal the truth of U.S. involvement in the atrocities committed in Latin America, and this case was no exception. In addition to Sister Ortiz's evidence that an American was working with the Guatemalan soldiers who tortured and raped her, Mr. Gramajo was trained at the School of the Americas at Fort Benning, Georgia. He gave the commencement address at that school shortly before the suit was filed. Mr. Gramajo was seen as a favorite to lead postwar Guatemala, and to that end he earned a masters degree at the Kennedy School of Government at Harvard University. As he stood waiting for his diploma, an agent for the victims served him with the ATS and TVPA lawsuit.[96]

The plaintiffs' complaint alleged that Mr. Gramajo was "personally responsible for ordering and directing the implementation of the program of persecution and oppression that resulted in the terrors visited upon the plaintiffs and their families."[97] The District Court of Massachusetts ruled that "Gramajo was aware of and supported widespread acts of brutality committed by personnel under his command resulting in thousands of civilian deaths [and] refused to act to prevent such atrocities [and i]n the face of public outcry, 'the massacres continued and indeed got worse.'"[98] This case is a tragic example

---

[94] *Xuncax v. Gramajo*, 886 F.Supp. 162, 169 (D.Ma. 1995).
[95] Ibid.
[96] See J. Patrice McSherry and Raul Molina Mejia, "Confronting the Question of Justice in Guatemala," *Social Justice*, September 22, 1992.
[97] *Xuncax v. Gramajo* at 171.
[98] Ibid. at 173.

of how human rights atrocities are a fundamental denial of human dignity. After the war, Mr. Gramajo spoke openly about replacing the national security doctrine that existed during the war with the "thesis of national stability." In an interview with U.S. scholar and journalist Jennifer Schirmer, Mr. Gramajo stated, "You needn't kill everyone to complete the job.... We aren't going to return to the large-scale massacres.... We have created a more humanitarian, less costly strategy, to be more compatible with the democratic system. We instituted Civil Affairs, which provides development for 70% of the population while we kill 30%. Before, the strategy was to kill 100%."[99] The court awarded more than $47 million in damages to the nine plaintiffs in the *Gramajo* case.

BRINGING LATIN AMERICAN CASES BEFORE SPANISH NATIONAL COURTS

The Guatemala Genocide Case

Nobel Laureate Rigoberta Menchú and other survivors of several massacres inflicted against Mayan villages in the 1980s filed charges of genocide, extrajudicial killing, torture, and unlawful detention in criminal court in Spain. Guatemalan forces tortured and killed Ms. Menchú's mother and brother. Her father died with thirty-eight other people when the army set fire to the Spanish Embassy in 1980. In their complaint, filed in December 1999, they accused five generals, a colonel, and two police chiefs of ordering and planning the crimes. Three of these defendants were former heads of state, Efrain Rios Montt, Óscar Humberto Mejía Victores, and Romeo Lucas García, although Lucas García died in 2006. The Guatemalan Historical Clarification Commission found that of the two hundred thousand people killed in Guatemala's civil war, 83 percent were Mayan. Ms. Menchú and the other victims claimed the Spanish national court had jurisdiction under Spain's universal jurisdiction law, Article 23.4 of the Organic Law of

---

[99] Jennifer Schirmer, "The Guatemalan Military Project: An Interview with Gen. Hector Gramajo," *Harvard International Review* 10(Summer): 11.

the Judicial Branch. Spain enacted the law in 1985 to give its courts the power to adjudicate prosecutions of the most serious international crimes such as genocide, terrorism, and other crimes recognized in international treaties ratified by Spain, regardless of who committed the crimes or where they were committed. When, pursuant to the universal jurisdiction law, Spanish Judge Baltasar Garzón won extradition of former Chilean president Augusto Pinochet from the United Kingdom in 1998, human rights advocates realized that Spain's courts could significantly advance the cause of justice.[100]

Three months after receiving Ms. Menchú's complaint, Judge Guillermo Ruiz Polanco agreed to open an investigation. He ruled that the Spanish court had jurisdiction because several of the victims were Spanish, because some had been killed at the Spanish Embassy in Guatemala, and because officials in Guatemala were unwilling to pursue the case. Judge Ruiz made Spain's universal jurisdiction contingent on the unavailability of justice in the country of origin and on ties between the case and Spain. However, a few months later the full court reversed this decision and ruled that it could not assert jurisdiction over the case. It held that, at that time, it could not make the necessary conclusion that trials in Guatemala were impossible. The Spanish Supreme Tribunal partially reversed this decision two years later, when it ruled the cases that included Spanish victims or that stemmed from the embassy attack could proceed.[101] It ruled that its courts should not examine whether Guatemala's courts were unwilling or unable to try these cases because the courts of one nation should not be in the business of evaluating the effectiveness of courts in another. It narrowed the scope of Spain's universal jurisdiction law to allow only cases with strong ties to Spain because it found this interpretation to be consistent with the preeminence of national sovereignty in international law.

Again Ms. Menchú and the other victims appealed. On September 26, 2005, the Spanish Constitutional Tribunal ruled that the universal jurisdiction law allowed cases to be brought in Spanish courts for certain international law crimes regardless of any connection with Spain

---

[100] Naomi Roht-Arriaza, *The Pinochet Effect: Transitional Justice in the Age of Human Rights* (Philadelphia: University of Pennsylvania Press, 2005).

[101] Judgment No. 327/2003, Tribunal Supremo, S.P., February 25, 2003.

and regardless of any showing of inability to prosecute in the home state.[102] It ruled that, in passing the law, parliament meant to make Spain a country that embraces the principle of universal jurisdiction. The tribunal explained that requiring victims to be Spanish conflicted directly with the very notion of universal jurisdiction. It held that the injuries inflicted by the crimes for which Spain has universal jurisdiction "transcend the harm to specific victims and affect the international community as a whole." "Therefore, prosecution and punishment are not only a shared commitment, but are in the shared interest of all states." Jurisdiction in these cases, the tribunal explained, "cannot depend on the interests of each state."[103] The tribunal then sent the case back to the trial court.[104]

Judge Santiago Pedraz presided over the investigation. In July 2006, he issued arrest warrants for the eight defendants in the original complaint, including Ríos Montt and Óscar Humberto Mejía Victores. Ms. Menchú and the other victims asked CJA to serve as lead counsel in the case, and CJA lawyers began working to serve the warrants and track down a missing defendant. To litigate the case, CJA established a team of lawyers from several countries and several human rights organizations. Its work on this case is another clear example of the vital importance of human rights NGOs in moving the process of human rights justice.

Despite appeals by the defendants, the Guatemalan Constitutional Court upheld the Spanish arrest warrants, the last such order coming in October 2007. CJA and its partners had already begun extradition proceedings and had amended the Spanish complaint to include new clients who were survivors of massacres in the Baja Verapaz area in 1982. However, in December 2007, the Guatemalan Constitutional Court suddenly reversed its earlier holdings and ruled that the Spanish arrest warrants and extradition petitions were void in Guatemala. The process of legal justice in Guatemala ground to a halt. Once again

---

[102] Judgment in the Guatemala Genocide Case, No. STC 237/2005, Tribunal Constitucional, September 26, 2005

[103] Ibid. at Sec. II, para. 9.

[104] In 2009, the Spanish government amended its universal jurisdiction law to require the defendants to be present in Spain, for them to be Spanish, or for the case to be related to Spanish interests. The law does not apply retroactively, so existing cases were not affected.

Guatemalan officials had deployed the mechanisms of impunity. In response to the ruling, a Spanish lawyer working on the case, Antonio García, observed that, "This is one of the few cases in which a state has given its seal of approval to a genocide."[105]

However, because the case was in Spanish courts, CJA and Judge Pedraz circumvented the Guatemalan obstacles and kept the process moving. They did so by revealing and enshrining the truth. Judge Pedraz invited witnesses, survivors, and victims to come to his chambers in Madrid and testify. CJA orchestrated visits by four delegations of witnesses, the first of which testified before Judge Pedraz in January 2008. Fifteen Mayan survivors of massacres and three expert witnesses testified in that first group, "a historic moment for the Mayan survivors as it represented the first time a national court had allowed them to present evidence of the campaign of torture, rape and killing perpetrated against their communities in the early 1980's."[106]

The genocide case in Spain has facilitated significant advancement in the process of legal justice for the survivors and victims of the brutal massacres and torture that security officials inflicted during the civil war. It has allowed dozens of witnesses to testify and produce evidence. After watching Mayan survivors testify in Spanish court, Ms. Doyle observed, "The catharsis of being able to come and give testimony before an official, a judge, in a real court room is extraordinary."[107] "These survivors in Madrid said that over and over, independent of each other, to the judge, in his chambers, during and after their testimony."[108]

In the thirty years since the massacres at the heart of the genocide case occurred, survivors and advocates have made countless attempts to uncover records, documents, and evidence related to the attacks. Once again, however, the military tried to block every effort to reveal and prove the truth. When faced with a demand for documents on

---

[105] Ivan Briscoe, "Guatemala's Court Wars and the Silenced Genocide," North American Congress on Latin America (February 4, 2008), http://www.nacla.org/news/guatemala's-court-wars-and-silenced-genocide (Last accessed December 12, 2012).

[106] Center for Justice and Accountability, "The Guatemala Genocide Case before the Spanish National Court." http://cja.org/article.php?list=type&type=83 (Last accessed February 8, 2012).

[107] Kate Doyle, senior analyst, National Security Archive, interview with the author, January 28, 2010.

[108] Ibid.

the massacres in the genocide case, it replied that no such documents existed. One set of documents specifically requested were those related to a counterinsurgency operation called "Operation Sofia." One month after the military denied the existence of any documents related to the operation, Kate Doyle was secretly handed a package containing the very documents they requested (see Figure 6.3).[109] As Ms. Doyle commented, "the petitioners did receive a Guatemalan document containing critical evidence – not from the institutions of the State that created it, but through my organization, a non-governmental group based in the United States."[110]

Ms. Doyle testified that the "fragile telegrams, planning documents, orders, hand-drawn maps, and reports from patrol units" included among the Operation Sofia documents proved the "strict chain of command that functioned during the scorched earth operations." She told Judge Pedraz the documents included "orders issued by senior officers in the Army General Staff flowing down through commanders to patrol units in the field, and subsequent handwritten reports flowing back up to commanders and then the Army General Staff chronicling the killings, captures, and interrogations of unarmed Mayan residents of the Ixil region."[111] This proceeding was the first time a court of any kind had access to records created by Guatemala's security forces. Fredy Peccerelli, executive director of the Forensic Anthropology Foundation of Guatemala (FAFG), also testified in Madrid. FAFG exhumed dozens of gravesites and discovered the remains of hundreds of victims of forced disappearance and of Guatemala's massacres. Mr. Peccerelli testified that "of the 1,884 victims exhumed, more than 25 percent were infants or children [and] 78 percent exhibited gunshot wounds to the head."[112] In the next chapter I explain further how the testimony and evidence put forth in Madrid kept the process of justice moving in the genocide case.

---

[109] Kate Doyle, "Operation Sofia: Documenting Genocide in Guatemala," National Security Archive Electronic Briefing Book No. 297, December 2, 2009. http://www.gwu.edu/~nsarchiv/NSAEBB/NSAEBB297/index.htm.

[110] Doyle, Testimony, IACtHR.

[111] Kate Doyle, "A Personal Account of Testifying at a Guatemalan Genocide Trial," December 10, 2009. https://nsarchive.wordpress.com/2009/12/10/a-personal-account-of-testifying-at-a-guatemalan-genocide-trial-by-kate-doyle/.

[112] Ibid.

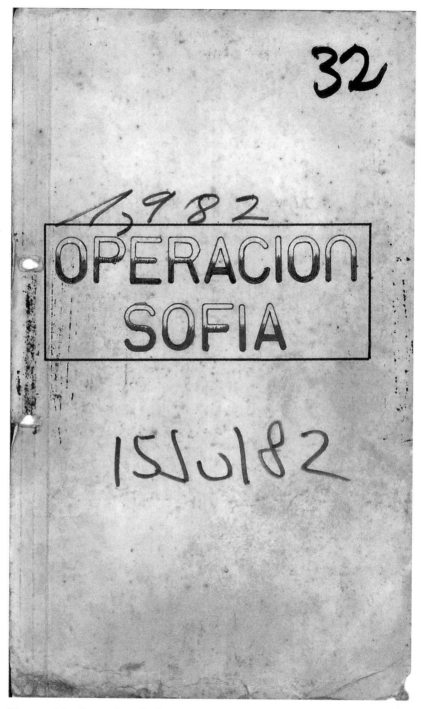

Figure 6.3. Operation Sofia Documents from the Guatemalan Police
Archives.

S E C R E T O

Copia No. 6 de 15 copias
Base Militar de Tropas Paracaidistas
"General Felipe Cruz".
Puerto San José, Escuintla.
150800JUL82
A-009.

PLAN DE OPERACIONES "SOFIA"

REFERENCIAS: Mapa de la República de GUATEMALA, Escála 1:250,000
y Escála 1:50,000.

    I. ESCALA 1:250,000, Hojas:

        PUERTO SAN JOSE   ND 15-12
        GUATEMALA   ND 15-8
        COBAN   ND 15-4
        CUILCO   ND 15-3

    II. ESCALA 1:50,000, Hojas:

        BARILLAS   1963   III
        SOLOMA   1962   IV
        CHIANTLA   1962   III
        SAN LUIS IXCAN   1963   II
        ILOM   1962   I
        NEBAJ   1962   II
        SAN ANTONIO EL BALDIO   2063   III
        IZTAJA   2062   IV
        USPANTAN   2062   III

    III. DOCUMENTOS:

        Mensaje No. 3-M-00792 de la Jefatura del Esta----
        do Mayor General del Ejército de fecha 8 de ju---
        lio de 1,982.

ORGANIZACION PARA EL COMBATE.

Primera Cía. Parac.   Segunda Cía. Parac.   Tercera Cía.Parac.

Primer Pelotón   Primer Pelotón   Primer Pelotón
Segundo Pelotón   Segundo Pelotón   Segundo Pelotón
Tercer Pelotón   Tercer Pelotón   Tercer Pelotón
Cuarto Pelotón   Cuarto Pelotón   Cuarto Pelotón

Control del Batallón:

Compañía de Apoyo de Servicios del Batallón (-).

Un Pelotón de Morteros Calibre 120 mm.

    I. SITUACION:

        A. Fuerzas Enemigas:

        Anexo "A" Resumen de Inteligencia.

        B. Fuerzas Amigas:

        La Base Militar de Tropas Paracaidistas "General Felipe-
        Cruz", con sus Tres Compañías del Primer Batallón de Pa-
        racaidistas, ejecutará Operaciones Contrasubversivas y -
        Operaciones Psicológicas en el área de Operaciones de la
        Fuerza de Tarea "Gumarcaj". en coordinación con dicha ---
        Fuerza de Tarea, quedando el resto de Unidades organicas
        y agregadas a orden en la sede de la BMTPGFC, Pto. San -
        José, Escuintla.

S E C R E T O

Figure 6.3. (*continued*)

The Jesuits Case

On January 13, 2009, Spanish Judge Eloy Velasco charged fourteen former officers of El Salvador's army, including Colonel Ponce, with murder, crimes against humanity, and state terrorism for orchestrating the massacre of the Jesuit priests, their housekeeper, and her daughter. Once again CJA represented the victims' families. Judge Velasco declined to charge President Cristiani but reserved the right to do so later. He has held four hearings in the case. In the first, several Spanish diplomats and politicians testified about their work monitoring the botched investigation of the crimes in El Salvador. Then in November 2009, CJA put on four witnesses. Two of these were former prosecutors in El Salvador who worked on the Jesuits case, Henry Campos and Sidney Blanco. Both resigned in protest over the government's manipulation of the investigation and its refusal to allow the investigation of those truly responsible. Kate Doyle also testified, explaining how U.S. intelligence documents, like those I used in Chapter 1, demonstrated the military's culpability for the murders. El Salvador expert Professor Terry Karl took the stand to put the Jesuits massacre in the context of El Salvador's oppressive counterinsurgency.[113]

CJA's participation in the case was again indispensible. A person who was complicit in the killing approached Aludena Bernabeu and asked if he could testify confidentially as a protected witness. Because at this stage of the proceedings the testimony is kept secret, CJA was able to make this happen. This witness gave Judge Velasco a first-hand account of how the murders were carried out, describing how the orders were given and executed and how the officers covered up their culpability. Several months later, another insider witness met with CJA and agreed to be deposed by the court. According to CJA, this witness provided "details unknown until this date." Through this testimony, CJA was able to "present as complete a picture of the background to, the ordering of, and the carrying out of the assassinations" as has ever been given. As it asserted, the "goal was not only to give Judge Velasco evidence of the involvement of high ranking officials but

---

[113] Center for Justice and Accountability, "The Jesuits Massacre Case." http://cja.org/article. php?list=type&type=84 (Last accessed February 10, 2013).

to create an accurate historical record of the crime."[114] To CJA and its clients, revealing and enshrining the truth was a crucial part of the process of legal justice.

In May 2011, Judge Velasco issued indictments against twenty former Salvadoran military officials for their involvement in the Jesuits massacre. Then in August, the judge issued arrest warrants for fourteen of the defendants. When it became clear that the Salvadoran National Police would honor the arrest warrants, nine of the defendants met on August 7 at a country club outside of San Salvador to plan their next steps. That very night all nine turned themselves into military authorities. This step was presumed to be yet another attempt to frustrate civilian authority over international arrest warrants. The military has protected those involved in the assassination since it occurred more than twenty years ago. However, in an unprecedented development, the Salvadoran minister of defense endorsed the validity of the international arrest warrants and turned the defendants over to civilian authorities.[115]

However, once again Salvadoran authorities stepped in to slow down the process of justice. The supreme court invalidated the arrest warrants, claiming they were void because Spain had not requested extradition. Then, when Judge Velasco issued his extradition requests, the court ruled them invalid as well. This is a clear violation of the bilateral extradition treaty between the two nations. CJA and its partners in El Salvador are still working to extradite the defendants to Spain.[116]

Judge Velasco's rulings in the Jesuits case have restarted efforts for justice in El Salvador, and as I show in the next chapter, in the United States as well. The hearings in Spain revealed new evidence on the massacre and, for the first time, participants in the crime told a court what happened. Similarly, Judge Pedraz's hearings in the Guatemalan genocide case tested and enshrined the evidence presented by Ms. Doyle, Mr. Peccerelli, and the dozens and dozens of victims and survivors who testified. As I demonstrate in the next chapter, the truth revealed in Madrid and Judge Pedraz's warrants and extradition orders have energized the process of legal justice in Guatemala.

---

[114] Ibid.
[115] Ibid.
[116] Ibid.

7 THE EFFECT OF EXTRA-TERRITORIAL COURTS ON THE PROCESS OF JUSTICE AND CONCLUSION

EFFECT OF EXTRA-TERRITORIAL LEGAL ACTION ON THE PROCESS

Effect of the Cases in Spain

Of course one of the most powerful effects of the Spanish hearings was the revealing and documenting of the truth. Kate Doyle testified about the secret documents she obtained and about the volumes of evidence supporting the charges found in the police archives. The documents describe the killing of civilians with cold military precision. For example, one document stated, "A woman was found hiding in a ditch and realizing her presence, the point man fired, killing her and two 'chocolates.'" The "two 'chocolates'" referred to two children the woman was trying to protect.[1] Again in this passage we see a direct connection between the atrocity committed and the way the military perceived its victims as lacking equal human dignity. Another document stated, "The point man indicated an individual who on seeing the patrol tried to flee, but he was eliminated. He was carrying only supplies (juice, rice and salt)."[2] Ms. Doyle explained that the documents and the Spanish proceedings have forced the military to respond. She stated, "For years I have listened to the survivors tell their stories but the military has always been allowed to remain mute."[3] The Spanish case has forced the military to respond.

---

[1] Elisabeth Malkin, "Court Papers Detail Killings by the Military in Guatemala," *New York Times*, December 4, 2009.
[2] Ibid.
[3] Ibid.

Moving the Process in Guatemala

As Ivan Briscoe, a researcher at a Spanish nongovernmental organization (NGO), argued, one reason to bring Guatemalan cases in foreign courts "is the possibility that chipping away at Guatemala's criminal fortress might one day spark life into the country's silent courtrooms."[4] CJA lawyer Almudena Bernabeu argued, "The Spanish case has the ability to push the case forward in Guatemala."[5] She is working with Guatemalan human rights lawyer Francisco Soto from the Center for Human Rights and Legal Action (CALDH). Ms. Bernabeu suggested they "present here in Guatemala the same expert testimonies Judge Pedraz heard in Spain." She believed that "for some, the Spanish case is an embarrassment, that in Guatemala genocide can't be prosecuted."[6]

The Spanish case has indeed spurred Guatemalan authorities to pursue criminal investigations on the massacres at home. On January 26, 2012, Judge Carol Patricia Flores Blanco ordered General Ríos Montt to stand trial for charges of genocide and crimes against humanity along with his chief of army intelligence, José Mauricio Rodríguez Sánchez. Both men were charged with orchestrating a brutal scorched-earth offensive against the Guatemalan insurgency in 1982–83. The indictment accused them of presiding over fifteen massacres of civilians in Guatemala's Ixil region. Victims and survivors testified for several hours in open court, a rare occurrence in the search for justice in Guatemala, before Judge Flores issued her order.[7] Then, after a similar hearing on May 21, 2012, Judge Flores added a charge alleging Montt's criminal responsibility for the Dos Erres Massacre in 1982. The process of justice, spurred on by the Spanish case, had gathered speed in Guatemala.

One year after the indictment, Judge Miguel Ángel Gálvez presided over a hearing in the Tribunals Tower in Guatemala City to determine whether Ríos Montt could be tried for genocide and other human rights

---

[4] Ivan Briscoe, "Guatemala's Court Wars and the Silenced Genocide," North American Congress on Latin America (February 4, 2008), http://www.nacla.org/news/guatemala's-court-wars-and-silenced-genocide (Last accessed December 12, 2012). Briscoe is a senior researcher at the Fundación para las Relaciones Internacionales y el Diálogo Exterior.

[5] Malkin, "Court Papers Detail Killings by the Military in Guatemala."

[6] *Granito: How to Nail a Dictator*, Skylight Pictures, 2011.

[7] Elisabeth Malkin, "Accused of Atrocities, Guatemala's Ex-Dictator Chooses Silence," *New York Times*, January 26, 2012.

crimes. The parties submitted their proposed witnesses and documentary evidence so the court could assess their admissibility. Defense lawyers objected to the introduction of the military's Operation Sofía documents (discussed in Chapter 6) that detailed the attack on Mayan villages in the Ixil region in 1982. Judge Gálvez ruled that the documents were admissible, explaining that the Inter-American Court had held states could not exclude evidence from human rights trials because they were state secrets. This ruling by Judge Gálvez is evidence of two central arguments in this book. First, it shows the increased importance of truth and of proving the truth with original documents. Second, it demonstrates the impact of extra-territorial legal action – in this case the Spanish courts and the Inter-American Court.[8]

On March 19, 2013, Judge Yassmín Barrios began the trial of Rios Montt and José Mauricio Rodríguez Sánchez for genocide and crimes against humanity in Guatemala City's High Impact Court "A". Over the next eight weeks, more than ninety Ixil Guatemalans testified about the massacres, attacks, rapes, torture, and displacements that took place during the military's scorched earth campaign. On the first day of the trial two survivors of the March 25, 1982 massacre in the village of Canaquil testified. One of these witnesses, Bernardo Bernal, was only nine years old when soldiers attacked his village. He told the court how soldiers shot at him as he ran to escape and how he survived by hiding in a creek nearby. When he returned to his village after the attack, he discovered that soldiers had killed his parents and two younger siblings.[9]

Almudena Bernabeu, CJA lawyer bringing the genocide case in Spain, reflected on the beginning of the trial in Guatemala: "Today may be, finally, the day that the former general, dictator and president of Guatemala, Efrain Rios Montt, is tried for genocide in Guatemala. Today, after more than 13 years, is the day that all the investigative and legal efforts led by the victims and carried out by lawyers in Guatemala, Spain, and again in Guatemala converge in a court, with a demand

---

[8] Kate Doyle, "A Day of Reckoning for Guatemalan Genocide?" Counterpunch, Feb. 8–10, 2013. http://www.counterpunch.org/2013/02/08/a-day-of-reckoning-for-guatemalan-genocide/print (Last accessed February 13, 2013).

[9] Emi MacLean, "Trial Opens with Statements, Prosecution Witnesses, after Defense Challenges Rejected," *The Trial of Efrain Rios Montt & Mauricio Rodriguez Sanchez*, March 20, 2013, http://www.riosmontt-trial.org/2013/03/trial-opens-with-prosecution-witnesses-after-defense-challenges-rejected.

for – this time without divisions or any mincing of words – the truth and a fair trial."[10]

During the first week of the trial, thirty-seven witnesses testified. Juan Raimundo Maton described how soldiers came into his village several times in October 1982. They killed more than sixteen people, burned people's houses, destroyed their crops, and killed and stole animals. Mr. Raimundo's testimony shows the soldiers' utter disregard for the victims' human dignity: "they viewed us as if we were not people."[11] Other witnesses described soldiers drowning their family members, smashing their heads with rocks, burning them alive in their homes, and shooting them. They described the destruction of entire villages and being forced to flee into the mountains and live in fear. Juan Raimundo told the court that the military's attacks "ended our culture."[12] On the eighth day of the trial, thirteen witnesses testified about the rapes and sexual assaults committed by the soldiers. Judge Barrios told the press not to publish the names or photographs of the witnesses. Most covered their faces on the witness stand. They described horrific sexual crimes committed against themselves and their daughters, some as young as twelve years old.[13]

On the last day of the trial, Rios Montt ended his silence and addressed the court. "I never authorized, I never proposed, I never ordered acts against any ethnic or religious group," he stated.[14] Though he blamed regional commanders for the atrocities committed against

[10] Almudena Bernabeu, "El Día en que se va a Juzgar a Efraín Ríos Montt," *Al Reves y al Derecho*, March 19, 2013, http://alrevesyalderecho.infolibre.es/?p=348; translated by Carolyn O'Neil, "Almudena Bernabeu: The 13-Year Struggle to Bring Rios Montt to Court," *The Trial of Efrain Rios Montt & Mauricio Rodriguez Sanchez*, March 25, 2013, http://www.riosmontt-trial.org/2013/03/the-13-year-struggle-to-bring-rios-montt-to-court.

[11] Emi MacLean, "'They Viewed us as if we Were not People': Witness Testimony Continues for a Fourth Day in Rios Montt Trial," *The Trial of Efrain Rios Montt & Mauricio Rodriguez Sanchez*, March 23, 2013, http://www.riosmontt-trial.org/2013/03/they-viewed-us-as-if-we-were-not-people-witness-testimony-continues-for-a-fourth-day-in-rios-montt-trial/.

[12] Ibid.

[13] Shawn Roberts, "Witnesses Testify to Rape in Rios Montt Genocide Trial; Defense also Objects to Documents," *The Trial of Efrain Rios Montt & Mauricio Rodriguez Sanchez*, April 3, 2013, http://www.riosmontt-trial.org/2013/04/witnesses-testify-to-rape-in-rios-montt-genocide-trial-defense-also-objects-to-documents/.

[14] Jo-Marie Burt, "Historic Genocide Trial Nears End; Rios Montt Addresses the Court, Declares Innocence," *The Trial of Efrain Rios Montt & Mauricio Rodriguez Sanchez*, May 10, 2013, http://www.riosmontt-trial.org/2013/05/historic-genocide-trial-nears-end-rios-montt-addresses-the-court-declares-innocence/.

the Ixil, he acknowledged that he "was the head of state. What is the job of head of state and commander in chief? Command and control and administration of the Army."[15]

On May 10, 2013, the three-judge panel led by Judge Barrios found Montt guilty of genocide and crimes against humanity. They sentenced him to fifty years in prison for genocide and thirty years for crimes against humanity. The ruling came thirty years after the crimes were committed and thirteen years after the case was filed. Rios Montt was eighty-six years old. Reading a summary of the judgment from the bench, Judge Barrios stated: "We are completely convinced of the intent to destroy the Ixil ethnic group."[16] The court held that Montt had "full knowledge of what was happening and did nothing to stop it – having the knowledge of the events, and the power and the capacity to do so."[17] The Court emphasized the testimony of the fact witnesses as well as the testimony from countless expert witnesses as the basis for its decision. It found that the prosecution had proved Montt was responsible for the murder of 1,771 Ixil Guatemalans, the forcible displacement of 29,000 more, and several cases of sexual violence and torture. Judge Barrios relied heavily on documents from the police archives to find Montt's responsibility for ordering the operations against the Ixil including "Operation Sofia" discussed in Chapter 5.

The forces of impunity did not go quietly, however. Ten days after Montt's conviction, the Guatemalan Constitutional Court nullified the verdict. This was the second time the Constitutional Court had interfered with the trial, having suspended the case on April 19. This new ruling nullified all the proceedings that occurred since that date. Neither ruling challenged the factual basis of the verdict but instead addressed how the trial court handled an event on the first day of the trial. On March 19, Montt showed up in court having dismissed his defense lawyers. His new lawyer promptly moved to recuse two of the three judges presiding. This type of motion was not permitted at

---

[15] Ibid.
[16] Elisabeth Malkin, "Former Leader of Guatemala Is Guilty of Genocide Against Mayan Group," *New York Times*, May 10, 2013.
[17] Jo-Marie Burt, "Rios Montt Convicted of Genocide and Crimes against Humanity: The Sentence and its Aftermath," *The Trial of Efrain Rios Montt & Mauricio Rodriguez Sanchez*, May 10, 2013, http://www.riosmontt-trial.org/2013/05/rios-montt-convicted-of-genocide-and-crimes-against-humanity-the-sentence-and-its-aftermath.

that stage of the case, so the judges denied the request and dismissed the lawyer from the case. The trial court's decision left Montt with only his codefendant's lawyer until the next morning when he again appeared with his original defense lawyers. The Constitutional Court suggested that the trial court's actions prejudiced Montt's defense, even though the trial judges excluded evidence from the first day of trial. In the 3–2 decision, Justices Mauricio Chacon and Gloria Patricia Porras dissented. They argued that Montt's tactics on the first day of the trial were obstructionist and the Constitutional Court was rewarding obstructionist behavior. They also criticized the majority for denying the victims their constitutional right to justice.[18] At this writing it is unclear whether the case will be retried at all, and if it is whether it will start from the beginning or from the stage at which it was halted on April 19.

The Montt case demonstrates clearly that the work of human rights NGOs and extra-territorial judicial action are indispensible in moving the process of justice. Ms. Bernabeu stated that working on the case in Spain "generated immediate effects in Guatemala." She explained that exposing the truth was crucial and the coordination of human rights NGOs was essential in doing so. "Part of the strategy was the presentation of witnesses from the many areas that were most affected by the military campaigns, [and] this required close collaboration between several of the country's victims' organizations." Ms. Bernabeu acknowledged that "these organizations played an important role in choosing witnesses, working with them and traveling with them to give evidence in Spain." She sees the work of the domestic and international legal action as an integrated process. "We attorneys on the international legal team were always moved by the need to make a difference in the national situation in Guatemala and by the fact that – for many in Guatemalan civil society – this process and others like it were the only hope for change and for justice for the victims."[19]

---

[18] Emi MacLean, "Guatemala's Constitutional Court Overturns Rios Montt Conviction And Sends Trial Back To April 19," *The Trial of Efrain Rios Montt & Mauricio Rodriguez Sanchez,* May 21, 2013, http://www.riosmontt-trial.org/2013/05/constitutional-court-overturns- rios-montt-conviction-and-sends-trial-back-to-april-19.

[19] Bernabeu, "El Día en que se va a Juzgar a Efraín Ríos Montt."

Kirsten Weld, a Harvard University historian specializing in Latin America, recognized the importance of the network of activists and extra-territorial courts in finally bringing this case to trial in Guatemala. Professor Weld observed that "Most of the credit goes to survivors and victims' families for 30 years of tenacious research and advocacy," and that "international human rights groups, the Inter-American Court of Human Rights, the United Nations and foreign governments helped." She pointed out that the "overarching goal of the Guatemalan counterinsurgency was to destroy all oppositional thinking." The fact that Ríos Montt went to trial, she argued, was proof that a "state's efforts to make its opponents 'disappear in silent anonymity' are doomed to failure." In that sense, she concluded, even though the outcome is uncertain, "the dictator had lost."[20] Anthropologist Victoria Sanford stated, "For Ríos Montt to be tried breaks the wall of impunity.... It says genocide is genocide and it is punishable by law."[21] Anita Isaacs made the connection between this attempt at legal justice and peace. "There was a hope that if he could be brought to trial, this could be the end of the armed conflict."[22] While the truth of these assessments depends somewhat on the outcome of the appeals process in Guatemala, the trial itself – with its power to reveal the truth and demonstrate legal violations – is an enormous step forward.

In April 2011, Spanish Judge Pedraz added another defendant to the genocide case when he issued an arrest warrant and an extradition request for Jorge Sosa Orantes. Judge Pedraz accused Mr. Sosa of genocide, torture, and extrajudicial killing for his role in the massacre of more than 200 men, women and children at Dos Erres in 1982. According to CJA, "Sosa Orantes and troops under his command surrounded Dos Erres, preventing anyone from escaping, and searched every home for weapons. They separated the men from the women and children and then in the course of three days, systematically killed the villagers." They alleged that Sosa Orantes and his comrades committed horrific atrocities, including mass rapes and the murder of numerous infants. Pamela Merchant, the executive director

[20] Kirsten Weld, "A Chance at Justice in Guatemala," *New York Times*, February 13, 2013.
[21] Elisabeth Malkin, "Ex-Dictator Is Ordered to Trial in Guatemalan War Crimes Case," *New York Times*, January 28, 2013.
[22] Ibid.

of CJA, commented, "The victims in the Guatemala Genocide case have been working tirelessly for years to find and make sure that Sosa Orantes and many like him are prosecuted for the brutal crimes they committed. Charging Sosa Orantes with genocide and securing his prosecution for the Dos Erres massacre is the beginning of the justice the victims want and deserve."[23] The difference in Mr. Sosa Orantes's case is that he was a U.S. citizen living in Canada.

EFFECT OF U.S. CASES

As a result of Judge Pedraz's warrant, U.S. officials charged Mr. Sosa Orantes with lying on his U.S. citizenship application. Canadian officials arrested him pursuant to the U.S. warrant and are holding him pending extradition.[24] This case is an example of a new approach in the process of legal justice developed by CJA lawyers in conjunction with U.S. government lawyers. When CJA lawyers uncover evidence that their defendants are responsible for human rights violations in their home countries, they turn this evidence over to U.S. government lawyers. They then pull up the suspect's immigration documents to see if he or she denied participation in these activities. As Mr. Sosa Orantes's case demonstrates, to gain admittance and citizenship, those responsible for human rights violations must hide their involvement. Once CJA uncovers the evidence, the U.S. government lawyers can bring a deportation action or a criminal case for making false statements as they did with Mr. Sosa Orantes.

This new avenue has three effects that echo arguments I have made throughout the book. First, this approach demonstrates once again the importance of truth and the effect revealing the truth can have in advancing the process of justice. Officials who have left their countries to escape legal justice find themselves ensnared in their new homes once the truth is exposed. Second, these cases demonstrate the importance

---

[23] Center for Justice and Accountability, "Spanish Court Issues Arrest Warrant for Guatemalan Lieutenant Responsible for Dos Erres Massacre." http://www.cja.org/article. php?id=981 (Last accessed February 14, 2013).

[24] See the Center for Justice and Accountability Case Summary, http://cja.org/article. php?list=type&type=83 (Last accessed June 2, 2012).

of NGOs like CJA in exposing the truth and moving the process of legal justice. CJA works with NGOs in Spain and in Latin America to track down evidence, find defendants in hiding, and bring innovative cases in courts worldwide. Through these immigration cases, CJA has managed to make sure the United States and Canada are not safe havens for some human rights violators. Third, this approach demonstrates the importance of seeing legal justice as a process, not a result. If our view of legal justice is narrowed to a dichotomous question of guilt or innocence, we miss the importance of cases like that of Sosa Orantes. The process of legal justice is varied, and each element has a meaningful effect on justice for victims, survivors, and perpetrators, and for the countries from which these cases arise.

On September 16, 2010, U.S. Federal District Court Judge William Zloch sentenced Gilberto Jordán to ten years in federal prison. Mr. Jordán was a special forces soldier in Guatemala who participated in the Dos Erres massacre. After Kate Doyle and the National Security Archive uncovered evidence of his culpability, the federal court convicted Mr. Jordán of lying on his citizenship application to hide his crimes. One of only two known survivors of the massacre testified at the sentencing hearing. Ramiro Osorio Cristales told the court about watching soldiers kill his parents and six brothers and sisters. According to Kate Doyle, who served as an expert witness in the case, Mr. Jordán "confessed to throwing a baby down the well at the start of the massacre and bringing dozens of other men, women and children to the well to be killed."[25]

Judge Zloch's sentence was far greater than the six months typically called for in the Federal Sentencing Guidelines. He justified the lengthy sentence in part by arguing "those who commit egregious human rights violations abroad" will not find "safe haven from prosecution" in the United States.[26] Moreover, he explained that Jordán's offense was "well beyond the heartland of the applicable guidelines," because his case "is virtually unprecedented."[27] Judge Zloch reasoned

---

[25] Kate Doyle, "Wrenching Testimony and a Historic Sentence: US Court Convicts Dos Erres Perpetrator for Lying about Role in Massacre," *Unredacted*, September 17, 2010. https://nsarchive.wordpress.com/2010/09/17/wrenching-testimony-and-a-historic-sentence-us-court-convicts-dos-erres-perpetrator-for-lying-about-role-in-massacre/.
[26] Ibid.
[27] *U.S. v. Jordan*, 432 Fed. Appx. 950, 952; 2011 U.S. App. LEXIS 13518, quoting *U.S. v. Jordan*, Docket No. 9:10-cr-80069-WJZ-1 (S.D.FL. 2010).

that he was not aware of "any more serious basis for immigration fraud than an individual's concealment of his prior participation in a mass murder of innocent civilians."[28] With this sentence, Mr. Jordán was the first person held accountable for the Dos Erres massacre in the more than twenty-eight years since the last shot was fired.

He appealed, claiming Judge Zloch's sentence in excess of six months was unreasonable. The Eleventh Circuit Court of Appeals upheld the ten-year sentence. In a per curium opinion, the court pointed out that a departure from the Sentencing Guidelines may "be warranted in the exceptional case in which there is present a circumstance that the [Sentencing] Commission has not identified in the guidelines but that nevertheless is relevant to determining the appropriate sentence."[29] It held "nothing in the guidelines contemplated the particular factor relied on by the district court – concealment of Jordán's member-ship in the military and his participation in a massacre to fraudulently obtain United States citizenship."[30] The Eleventh Circuit agreed with Judge Zloch: "By concealing his role in the murders, Jordán was able to fraudulently obtain United States citizenship and a virtual safe-haven," and therefore "the upward departure was reasonable."[31]

CJA uncovered new evidence about the Jesuits massacre during the hearings in Spain and as a result discovered that Salvadoran Vice Minister of Public Safety Inocente Orlando Montano was involved in the conspiracy. Mr. Montano was living in Everett, Massachusetts at the time, so CJA turned its evidence over to federal immigration authorities. On September 11, 2012, Mr. Montano stood in federal district court in Boston and pled guilty to six counts of immigration fraud and perjury.[32] Prosecutors have urged the court to hold that Mr. Montano lied on his immigration forms to conceal his involve-ment in war crimes. If the court made this ruling, it could sentence Mr. Montano to more than ten years in prison, although standard immigration fraud convictions can only result in sentences of up to two years in prison. The conviction also raises the possibility that U.S.

---

[28] Ibid. at 952, quoting *U.S. v. Jordan*, Docket No. 9:10-cr-80069-WJZ-1 (S.D.FL. 2010).

[29] Ibid. at 951, citing U.S.S.G. § 5K2.0(a)(2)(B).

[30] Ibid. at 951–52.

[31] Ibid.

[32] See Milton J. Valencia, "Salvadoran Convicted of Immigration Fraud: Ex-military Commander Sought by Spain in 1989 Killing of Priests," *Boston Globe*, September 11, 2012.

officials would extradite Mr. Montano to Spain, where he would face criminal charges arising from the Jesuits massacre and up to thirty years in prison. At this writing, the court is still deliberating his sentence.[33] Due to El Salvador's amnesty law, this is the first time anyone anywhere has been held legally accountable for crimes connected to the Jesuits massacre. The process continues.

Represented by CJA lawyers, Dr. Juan Romagoza, Neris González, and Carlos Mauricio won an ATS and TVPA case against General José Guillermo García and General and Minister of Defense Eugenio Vides Casanova of El Salvador in 2002 (discussed in previous chapters).[34] After winning these cases, CJA asked U.S. immigration officials to deport the two generals. Pamela Merchant, CJA's executive director, and Dr. Juan Romagoza testified before the Senate Judiciary Subcommittee on Human Rights and the Law in 2007, and told the senators that Generals García and Vides Casanova "continued to enjoy safe haven in Florida."[35] Senator Richard Durbin and Senator Tom Coburn sent several letters to the Department of Justice and the Department of Homeland Security demanding that officials explain why these Salvadoran generals continued to enjoy safe haven in the United States.

CJA's efforts had an effect. Lawyers for the Department of Homeland Security filed removal actions against both men under a 2004 federal law that allows deportation of those who committed human rights violations in their country of origin.[36] On February 23, 2012, Judge James Grim ruled that General Vides Casanova could be deported because he assisted in carrying out widespread killings and torture during his command. Federal prosecutors have mounted a similar effort against General García. In December 2012, Dr. Romagoza and former U.S. ambassador to El Salvador Robert White testified about the widespread killings and torture carried out under General

---

[33] For further developments, see http://www.cja.org/article.php?list=type&type=518.

[34] *Romagoza v. García*, 434 F.3d 1254 (11th Cir. 2006); See Jeffrey Davis, *Justice across Borders* (New York: Cambridge University Press, 2008) for a detailed analysis of this case.

[35] Center for Justice and Accountability, "CJA Reporting from Vides Casanova Removal Hearing." http://www.cja.org/article.php?id=1000 (Last accessed February 13, 2013).

[36] 8 U.S.C. § 1227(a)(4)(D) (2006), 8 U.S.C. § 1182(a)(3)(E)(iii)(I).

García's command. Stanford University Professor Terry Karl walked Judge Michael Horn through the volumes of U.S. intelligence documents introduced to link General García to the widespread atrocities carried out during his tenure. Again, these cases represent significant advances in the process of legal justice, not just for the victims who testified, but for the populations of victims whose dignity had been degraded by the atrocities these men ordered. As Dr. Romagoza explained after the Vides Casanova removal judgment, "This victory is not just my own. It is a victory for the entire country of El Salvador.... The torture I suffered was not unique to me. It was the suffering of many innocent Salvadorans."[37] These cases make clear the importance of extra-territorial courts in exposing the truth and moving the process of justice. CJA stated, "the removal of Vides Casanova from the U.S. would represent the successful use of one more tool in the accountability arena and brings us one step closer towards justice for Salvadorans."[38] These cases are still pending at this writing.

The removal cases are an important innovation, supplementing the human rights cases filed under the ATS and TVPA described in Chapter 6. The ATS and TVPA cases are the foundation through which the truth is revealed, victims and survivors testify, and the accused are sometimes confronted. The experience of testifying in these cases can be a pivotal experience in the process of justice for victims and survivors. CJA lawyer Almudena Bernabeu observed, "For the specific plaintiff, with the specific son who was disappeared, the only remedy – the only opportunity to say 'judge my son is disappeared' ... the only remedy is the [ATS and TVPA] in federal courts and universal jurisdiction in other countries."[39] Pamela Merchant said, "there's no question that it is an extraordinarily therapeutic process for our clients." She explained that for CJA's clients, "to walk into a U.S. courtroom, where you're being taken seriously, and there's a judge sitting there,

---

[37] Center for Justice and Accountability, "Ex-Salvadoran Defense Minister Vides Casanova Ruled Deportable for Human Rights Abuses." http://cja.org/article.php?id=1078 (Last accessed February 15, 2013).

[38] Center for Justice and Accountability, "CJA Reporting from Vides Casanova Removal Hearing."

[39] Almudena Bernabeu, interview with the author, July 18, 2006, from Davis, *Justice across Borders*, 284.

and there's a jury sitting there, and you're trying someone who was the vice-minister of defense for your country ... that day in court is very powerful for people."[40]

Cecilia Moran Santos, another victim of torture at the hands of El Salvador's military, successfully sued Colonel Nicolás Carranza in U.S. court under the ATS and TVPA. She remembered that, "During the trial I relived the pain and suffering I had endured during my imprisonment and torture, my nightmares continued, but during those days they began falling into the past as less painful memories."[41] "My nightmares ended the day the jury gave its verdict and sentence for Colonel Carranza." "I was able to feel how my spirit was released from the enormous weight that I carried for over 25 years without being able to reconcile the need for justice and live with the weight of such impunity," Ms. Santos recalled.[42] She is now the director of Centro Salvadoreño, a New York organization that helps Latino immigrant communities.

Óscar Reyes, who along with his wife was detained and tortured by Honduran forces, testified in his ATS and TVPA case against Colonel Grijalba. Mr. Reyes recalled, "I was able to confront [Colonel Grijalba], before the judge, and see how he put his head down to hear the charges I presented against him." He also was moved "to hear that the judge who took our case declared him culpable of all allegations made against him."[43]

Of course, it is almost always extremely difficult for victims and survivors to testify about violations committed against them or their loved ones. Frequently for victims telling the story of their violations is the same as reliving the horrors. Dr. Romagoza recalled, "Before the trial started, I couldn't sleep. I felt fear knowing that the generals would confront me."[44] Of testifying, he stated, "it was the first time someone from the other side was listening to me, they were right there in front of me – the ones that caused all this pain were right there before

---

[40] Pamela Merchant, interview with the author, July 18, 2006, from Davis, *Justice across Borders*, 285–86.

[41] Cecilia Moran Santos, interview with the author, December 8, 2011. See *Chavez v. Carranza*, 413 F. Supp. 2d 891, 897 (W.D.Tenn. 2005).

[42] Ibid.

[43] Óscar Reyes, interview with the author, November 7, 2011. See *Reyes v. Grijalba*, Case No. 02–22046 (S.D.Fla. 2006).

[44] Juan Romagoza Arce, "Reflections on the Verdict." http://www.cja.org/forSurvivors/reflect.doc (Last accessed September 12, 2007).

me." Dr. Romagoza's experience is exemplary of the effect of extra-territorial judicial action. "I felt that they had stolen my voice from me and that my body was the body of thousands of other people right then," he remembered. "It was such a heavy moment, but also so beautiful." "I think the very fact of speaking out and taking the case to this level, I believe that now the wounds are truly beginning to heal."[45]

EFFECT OF CASES BEFORE THE INTER-AMERICAN COURT

The Inter-American human rights system affects the process of legal justice in five ways. First, it provides victims and survivors a forum to testify and present evidence, and second, it establishes an historical record of the truth.[46] Third, the IACtHR's rulings "equip people to call for accountability" and win that accountability.[47] Fourth, it facilitates the legal and moral condemnation of human rights violations.[48] Finally, its jurisprudence transcends the individuals in the case and extends the normative value of justice, equality, and human dignity to broad classes of victims.[49]

Receiving Testimony and Enshrining the Truth

As I have shown throughout this book, human rights violations are nearly always accompanied by denial, obfuscation, and impunity. The Inter-American system is an exceptional vehicle for allowing the victims' story to come out through testimony, for enshrining it in the judicial record, for testing and admitting evidence, and for establishing the truth. Makrina Gudiel Álvarez, whose brother was disappeared and whose father was assassinated in Guatemala, described the effect of

---

[45] Ibid.
[46] See Ruti Teitel, "Transitional Jurisprudence: The Role of Law in Political Transformation," *Yale L.J.* 106 (2009): 2050–51.
[47] See Martha Minow, *Between Vengeance and Forgiveness* (Boston, MA: Beacon Press, 1998), 48.
[48] Jamie Mayerfeld, "Who Shall Be Judge?: The United States, the International Criminal Court, and the Global Enforcement of Human Rights." *Human Rights Quarterly* 25:93–129, 100 (2002).
[49] See Minow, *Between Vengeance and Forgiveness*.

testifying in the Inter-American system. "It hurts to speak about those events," she said, "but at the same time it is a form of healing."[50] Soraya Long, a lawyer for CEJIL who frequently represents victims before the IACtHR, pointed out in an interview that for the people she has represented "it was very significant to come here to [the Inter-American Court] because with the internal proceeding they felt thwarted ... and to come to this court and say what occurred, to establish a record and to demonstrate that they had overcome."[51] The IACtHR enshrines the truth in the *hechos probados* (proven facts) sections of its opinions, which are often extensive and memorialize the victims' lives as well as the state's violations and resulting impunity.

This function was especially important in the *Plan de Sanchez* case. On July 18, 1982, Guatemalan soldiers and civil patrol members slaughtered 268 civilians in Plan de Sanchez and the surrounding communities. "Soldiers randomly picked their victims, raping and torturing young women before rounding up villagers in a house, throwing in hand grenades and firing machine guns."[52] Almost all of the victims were Mayan. In the 2004 case before the IACtHR, the judges stressed the injury inflicted on the victims and survivors by the state's repeated denials and obstruction. It held that "the impunity in this case keeps the memory of these acts fresh and impedes social reconciliation."[53] Augusto Willemsen-Diaz, an expert on the rights of indigenous peoples, connected revealing the truth to restoring the human dignity of Guatemalan Mayans. "To end the discrimination and racism of the indigenous people in Guatemala," he told the court, "I recommend that the most important things are the acknowledgment of what occurred and that the people take notice of the enormous amount of abuses that have occurred."[54] The anguish in the victims' stories was

---

[50] *José Miguel Gudiel Álvarez and Others ("Diario Militar") v. Guatemala*, Int. Am. Comm. H.R., Report No. 116/10, Case 12.590 (October 22, 2010), at para. 104.

[51] Soraya Long, Counsel for the Center for Justice and Accountability, interview with the author, July 5, 2004.

[52] Guatemala Human Rights Commission, "Ruling against Government in Plan de Sanchez Massacre," *Guatemala Human Rights Update* 16(4): December 15, 2004. See also Guatemalan Historical Clarification Commission Report, 1998. http://shr.aaas.org/guatemala/ceh/report/english/toc.html.

[53] *Plan de Sanchez v. Guatemala*, Judgment of April 29, 2004, Inter-Am. Ct.H.R. (Ser. C) No. 105 (2004), para. 49.18.

[54] Ibid., para. 38.

memorialized in the court's opinion. Through the survivors' testimony and the court's opinion, this episode in Guatemala's violent past was established as an historical truth.[55]

Equipping Advocates to Advance the Process at Home

The Inter-American system helps victims, survivors, and advocates move the process of legal justice at home. In Chapter 5 I discussed the Fernando García case in Guatemala in which García's wife, Nineth Montenegro, won her case in the IACtHR as well as guilty verdicts against officials in Guatemala. Ms. Montenegro argued that "through the international process [the truth] has come out."[56] International or regional rulings against the state can shatter the view that the state is untouchable or immune from legal accountability and can inspire domestic attempts to overcome impunity.[57] Steven Ratner and Jason Abrams pointed out that international and regional courts "put pressure on governments to comply with their international obligations including their duties to prosecute offenders."[58]

The *Myrna Mack* case is an excellent example of this. After all, the IACtHR revived the domestic case on at least two occasions. After Guatemalan security forces killed Myrna Mack on September 11, 1990, the Myrna Mack Foundation tried for more than ten years to convict those who carried out and planned the murder. Guatemala had an interest in keeping the domestic legal case alive to preserve its argument that domestic remedies had not been exhausted, and that therefore the Inter-American case was inadmissible. Then, in March 2000, as the IACtHR hearing was set to begin, the government offered to take international responsibility for the murder. Domestic courts suddenly revived the stalled trial of senior officers accused in the

---

[55] Edward H. Warner, Esq. and Sebastian Amar, Esq. assisted with the research for this section.

[56] Nineth Montenegro, Radio Interview, "Corte IDH podría dictar sentencia en Caso de Desaparición de Fernando García en Ocho Meses," Emisoras Unidas 89.7, Guatemala City, May 2, 2012, http://noticias.emisorasunidas.com/noticias/primera-hora/corte-idh-podria-dictar-sentencia-caso-desaparicion-fernando-garcia-ocho-meses (Last Accessed on May 27, 2012).

[57] Teitel, "Transitional Jurisprudence," 2047–48.

[58] Steven R. Ratner and Jason S. Abrams, *Accountability for Human Rights Atrocities in International Law – Beyond the Nuremberg Legacy* (New York: Oxford, 2001), 226.

case. Armed with IACtHR rulings, prosecutors won guilty verdicts against two officers who planned the murder. As attention faded from the IACtHR proceeding, an appeals court vacated the convictions. Once again the IACtHR stepped in to revive the domestic process. In December 2003, the IACtHR ruled that Guatemala had violated Myrna Mack's right to life and the right to judicial guarantees and protection. The judges ordered Guatemala to, among other things, remove the obstacles to accountability in the case. Only one month later the Guatemalan Supreme Court reinstated the guilty verdicts against the officers who orchestrated Myrna Mack's murder.

The lead CEJIL counsel in the *Mack* case stated that Myrna's sister "Helen [Mack] only brought the case before the IACtHR because the Guatemalan system was not working."[59] She explained that her "principal objective was to force the Guatemalan judicial system to work … she wanted to use the Inter-American system to pressure the Guatemalan judiciary." Through the Mack case, lawyers from CEJIL attacked the systematic impunity in Guatemala and asserted that "perhaps for the first time, that impunity itself was a violation." They brought evidence of improper delays, the government's stalling tactics, "the improper use of national security and legal doctrines," and the intimidation and threats against those involved in the case.[60] Kate Doyle, who worked with CEJIL and the Myrna Mack Foundation on the case, concluded, "One of the lessons we all learned from the *Mack* case … was that the Inter-American case actually prodded and pushed and encouraged the Ministerio Publico [public prosecutor] in Guatemala to have the trial there, finally – and in the end they had the trial before the Inter-American Court did."[61]

It is clear from observations of hearings before the IACtHR that judges see their role as moving the domestic process of justice. They frequently ask victims, advocates, and state representatives what the court could order to remove obstacles and push human rights cases through domestic courts.[62] For example, in one hearing Judge García

[59] Roxanna Altholz, Former attorney for the Center for Justice and Accountability, interview with the author, May 11, 2004.
[60] Ibid.
[61] Doyle interview.
[62] See Jeffrey Davis, "Struggling through the Web of Impunity – The Jorge Carpio Nicolle Case." *Human Rights Review* 8(1): 53–66.

Sayan asked several witnesses "what ingredients might be necessary to conduct an effective investigation" in domestic cases. Similarly, Judge Jackman asked the lawyers, "What formal steps are needed to reopen the [domestic] case in Guatemala?"[63] The Inter-American Commission, of course, plays a crucial role in this process. In an interview, Olger González, a lawyer for the IACtHR, explained that, in cases like the *Mack* case, "the Court was acting the moment it had to act."[64] However, he stressed that, "how and when the case reaches the Court is a decision of the Commission – always." Once before the court, it "has certain forms of participation" to prod the domestic case along, Mr. González explained. For example, the court can always "order the state to produce the case file regarding the situation regarding this victim or this perpetrator." This interaction between the Inter-American system and the state "is dynamic and depends on the political situation in the state."[65]

The court also equips victims and advocates in their pursuit of legal justice at home by protecting their safety. The IACtHR can issue "provisional measures" for litigants and witnesses ordering protection of those the court believes to be in danger.[66] The court will often issue these "provisional measures," ordering, for example, that the defendant state provide armed security to participants in one of its cases. The court also protects the safety of participants indirectly through the international publicity that accompanies these cases.

In *Gudiel v. Guatemala* (the *Diario Militar* case), the court ruled that "when a state is party to international treaties like the American Convention on Human Rights … these treaties are binding on all its bodies, including the judiciary, whose members should ensure that the effects of the provisions of these treaties are not affected by the application of standards or interpretations contrary to its object and purpose."[67] In this holding, the court required "judges and bodies

---

[63] Jeffrey Davis and Edward H. Warner, "Reaching beyond the State: Judicial Independence, the Inter-American Court of Human Rights and Accountability in Guatemala," *Journal of Human Rights* 6(2): 246.

[64] Olger I. González, legal officer, Inter-American Court of Human Rights, interview with the author, May 12, 2010. Mr. González's opinions are his own and do not reflect the position of the IACtHR.

[65] Ibid.

[66] American Convention on Human Rights, November 22, 1969, 9 I.L.M. 673, Art. 63.

[67] *José Miguel Gudiel Álvarez and Others ("Diario Militar") v. Guatemala* at para. 330.

involved in the administration of justice at all levels" to ensure that "domestic norms" are in compliance with "human rights treaties to which the State is a party." In other words, domestic judges may not give legal effect to a state's amnesty laws, immunity laws, and other laws that conflict with the obligations present in the American Convention.

As the *Gudiel* case made clear, the rights to truth and information are formidable tools to facilitate progress in the process of legal justice at home as well as abroad. Truth commission reports, secret documents like the Diario Militar, and U.S. diplomatic documents supported litigation efforts in the *Gudiel* and *García* cases. Similar evidence has been indispensible in many of the other cases I have studied in this book. In the *Mack* case the IACtHR held "in the case of human rights violations, the state authorities cannot resort to mechanisms such as State secrets or the confidentiality of the information, or by virtue of public interest or national security, in order to avoid submitting information required by the judicial or administrative authorities charged with a pending investigation or process."[68] The IACtHR's dismantling of state amnesty laws and other doctrines of impunity has accelerated the process of legal justice in the region.

As I discussed in Chapter 4, the IACtHR issued a landmark ruling striking down Peru's amnesty laws as inconsistent with that nation's treaty obligations in the *Barrios Altos* case. Earlier, in 1992, the commission decided that amnesty laws in Argentina violated the Convention because they prevented justice for serious human rights violations committed by the military in Argentina and Uruguay during their Dirty Wars.[69] In 2005, Argentina's Supreme Court of Justice relied on Inter-American jurisprudence to rule that country's amnesty laws unconstitutional. Similarly, pursuant to IACtHR decisions, Chilean courts ruled that that nation's 1978 amnesty law could not supersede its international law obligations.

As these cases demonstrate, the IACtHR was instrumental in dismantling amnesty laws, and thereby equipped advocates with the enhanced ability to pursue justice domestically. On November 18, 2011, in an effort to comply with the court's ruling in the *Gomes-Lund* case,

---

[68] *Mack* at para 180.
[69] Cases No. 10.147, 10.181, 10.240, 10.262, 10.309 and 10.311, Int.Am.Comm.H.R. Report N° 28/92, October 2, 1992.

Brazil enacted a law creating a truth commission (Lei da Comissão da Verdade). Just one year earlier, the IACtHR had invalidated Brazil's amnesty law, and the truth commission law is an example of how the court's rulings empower advocates to pursue justice domestically. As Victoria Gabois, leader of the human rights advocacy group Torture Never Again, stated, "Without the Inter-American court ruling, there would be no truth commission in Brazil."[70]

Condemning Human Rights Violations

In the previous chapters, I have chronicled more than a dozen cases from Latin America in which states denied responsibility for rights violations for years – sometimes decades – only to be condemned for violating human rights law by the IACtHR. For more than twenty years, Guatemalan officials blocked all attempts to punish those responsible for the Plan de Sanchez massacre. Then, in 2004, the IACtHR ruled that Guatemala was responsible not only for the massacre but for denying justice to the victims and their families. Guatemala was ordered to apologize publicly for the massacre, in addition to providing financial compensation. On July 18, 2005, exactly twenty-three years after the massacre, Vice President Eduardo Stein traveled to Plan de Sanchez and formally apologized to the residents of that scarred community for the killings. In his remarks, Mr. Stein conceded that the army had "unleashed bloodshed and fire to wipe out an entire community." He acknowledged that the "people want moments that commemorate their victims, but more than anything, they don't want what happened to keep being denied officially."[71] As this case demonstrates (in addition to the cases discussed in earlier chapters), the IACtHR does more than simply condemn the violation committed against the initial victim. It goes further and recognizes that denial and impunity are themselves violations of human rights law.

The IACtHR assesses sanctions that go beyond traditional reparations to give effect to its rulings. In one of his first official acts, President

[70] Traci Tong, "Brazil's Truth Commission Under Fire from Military and Torture Victims," Public Radio International, The World, October 30, 2012. http://www.theworld.org/2012/10/brazils-truth-commission-under-fire-from-military-and-torture-victims/.

[71] Associated Press, "Guatemala Acknowledges, Apologizes for Government-Directed Massacre in 1982," July 18, 2005.

Oscar Berger publicly apologized for the murder of Myrna Mack. President Berger apologized to Myrna Mack's sister and daughter and to the Guatemalan people in a ceremony broadcast on national television and held in front of the military and other dignitaries. Thomas Antkowiak, a former lawyer for the IACtHR, explained that the court often orders the construction of monuments to honor the victims of state killings, and often "the Court requires consultation with the survivors as to the design, content and location."[72] "Sensitivity to such factors restores a modicum of dignity to victims and family members and gives them a role in the recording of history."[73]

Using Individual Cases to Address a Broad Class of Victims

Myrna Mack's sister, Helen, testified before the IACtHR in the case arising from her sister's murder. According to Ms. Mack, the "case is a paradigmatic one not only for her family but also for many Guatemalans who see themselves reflected in it" and that by litigating it she was "representing, with dignity, the thousands of victims who had no chance."[74] CEJIL represents most victims and families that appear before the IACtHR, and according to Roxanna Altholz, one of its lawyers, it frequently pursues cases that are "emblematic of a wider set of violations."[75] Similarly, another CEJIL lawyer, Soraya Long, explained that "the court uses its judgments to break systemic and structural failings and solve the macro problems" preventing justice in the region.[76] To that end, Antkowiak found that the court understood the "necessity of non-monetary remedies for victims, such as rehabilitation and the restoration of dignity, in the wake of rights violations.[77] Olger González, an IACtHR lawyer, commented that "the reparations in the Inter-American system are much more developed

---

[72] Thomas M. Antkowiak, "Remedial Approaches to Human Rights Violations: The Inter-American Court of Human Rights and Beyond," *Columbia Journal of Transitional Law* 46, 3 (2008): 366.
[73] Ibid. at 382.
[74] *Mack Chang v. Guatemala*, Judgment of November 25, 2003, Inter-Am. Ct.H.R. (Ser. C) No. 101 (2003).
[75] Altholz, interview with the author.
[76] Long, interview with the author.
[77] Antkowiak, "Remedial Approaches to Human Rights Violations."

than any other system, and they go much beyond the specific case."[78] He argued that the court does this because it "is conscious that those cases that are coming before it are important to the cases the Court will never see." "You have to deal with the bigger problem through a particular case," he explained.[79]

One way the court has made its rulings effective for broader populations is by innovating human rights law. Of course, this also equips victims and advocates to seek accountability at home. Jo Pasqualucci found that the IACtHR has issued crucial legal rulings on several controversial questions of international human rights law, thereby giving advocates legal tools to pursue accountability domestically.[80] In Chapter 4, I described how the IACtHR was indispensible in recognizing the rights to truth and information. In a 1982 advisory opinion, the court rejected the contention that rights are "culturally relative" and instead held them to be universal.[81] According to Pasqualucci, the IACtHR fundamentally altered human rights law in the region when it held that human rights law was part of international law, but that unlike traditional international law, it did not merely grant rights to states. Early in its history, the IACtHR held that international law obligated states and granted to individuals the authority to hold states accountable for breaches.[82] The court has refused to allow the derogation of fundamental human rights even in times of emergency, and it has forbidden states from reserving recognition of fundamental human rights.[83] Pasqualucci also found that the court significantly enhanced rights protections in the region by interpreting the American Convention as a living document with legal protections that develop over time.

[78] González, interview with the author.
[79] Ibid.
[80] Jo M. Pasqualucci, *The Practice and Procedure of the Inter-American Court of Human Rights* (Cambridge: Cambridge University Press, 2003).
[81] *Other Treaties Subject to the Consultive Jurisdiction of the Court*, Inter-Am. Ct HR. Advisory Opinion OC-1/82, of September 24, 1982, Ser. A, No. 1, para 40.
[82] *Effect of Reservations on Entry into Force of the American Convention on Human Rights*, Inter-Am. Ct HR. Advisory Opinion OC-2/82 of September 24, 1982, Ser. A, No. 2, para. 29.
[83] *Habeas Corpus in Emergency Situations*, Inter-Am. Ct HR. Advisory Opinion OC-8/87, of January 30, 1987, Ser. A, No. 8, para 11; *Judicial Guarantees in States of Emergency*, Inter-Am. Ct HR. Advisory Opinion OC-9/87, of October 6, 1987, Ser. A, No. 9, para 35.

The most important area of legal innovation, perhaps, was the IACtHR's jurisprudence on amnesty laws, the right to truth, and the right to information. Victims, survivors, and advocates work through each link in the process of legal justice – the Commission, the IACtHR, and other extra-territorial courts – to weave a web that ensnares those who have eluded accountability at home.

THE PROCESS ESTABLISHES A WEB OF ACCOUNTABILITY

In Chapter 1, I described two notorious human rights atrocities, the massacre of six Jesuit priests, their housekeeper, and her daughter in El Salvador, and the massacre of sixty-nine civilians in Accomarca, Peru. When Judge Zamora finally issued guilty verdicts and prison sentences in the Jesuits case, any legal accountability that may have resulted was wiped away by a legislative decree just two years later. The National Assembly in El Salvador passed a comprehensive amnesty law immediately after the truth commission issued its report detailing the extensive atrocities committed by government forces. Efforts to overturn the law in the courts have failed. In the first such case, the supreme court ruled that it could not void the law because it was a proper product of the political process. More recent cases have limited the amnesty's provisions while upholding most of its applications. Judges, the court ruled, should have the discretion to prosecute cases against military or government officials for violating the constitution between 1989 and 1994, well after most human rights violations occurred.[84]

As I explained in Chapter 6, Spanish Judge Eloy Velasco indicted fourteen Salvadoran officials for the Jesuits massacre and issued extradition requests. Although El Salvador has refused to comply with the extradition requests, the ruling helped set a web of accountability, and one defendant has already been caught. Former Salvadoran Vice Minister of Public Safety Inocente Orlando Montano has been arrested in the United States and, as a result of his involvement in human rights crimes, has pled guilty to six counts of immigration fraud and perjury.[85]

---

[84] Amnesty International, "Annual Report, El Salvador, 2001" http://www.amnestyusa.org/annualreport.php?id=ar&yr=2001&c=SLV (Last accessed March 19, 2011).
[85] Valencia, "Salvadoran Convicted of Immigration Fraud."

Mr. Montano is imprisoned in the United States awaiting sentence and could be extradited to Spain. Even if El Salvador continues to refuse to extradite the remaining defendants, the legal process against Montano and the other defendants puts increasing pressure on El Salvador. It also forces the defendants to live as wanted fugitives. As Kate Doyle observed, "even if it is unlikely that their country will extradite them, if they have to spend the rest of their life worrying about this, that is not a negative outcome in my view."[86]

The web has been even more effective in the Accomarca Massacre case. In the years following the massacre, only Lieutenant Hurtado was convicted of any crime in connection with the killings. Despite being convicted of abuse of authority and sentenced to prison in 1992, he was never incarcerated and was actually promoted by his superiors. Then, fifteen years later, Teófila Ochoa and Cirila Pulido found the two lieutenants, Hurtado and Rondón, who commanded the slaughter of their village living in the United States. With the help of CJA, Ms. Ochoa and Ms. Pulido sued these two former soldiers in U.S. courts under the ATS and TVPA. Lawyers for CJA also notified immigration officials, who in turn started deportation cases against the two men. Ms. Ochoa and Ms. Pulido won their case against Mr. Hurtado in 2008, and while he awaited deportation U.S. officials extradited him to Peru on July 15, 2011. U.S. immigration officials deported Mr. Rondón on August 15, 2008, and he was arrested upon his arrival in Peru.

Because of the IACtHR's ruling in the *Barrios Altos* case that Peru's amnesty laws were unlawful, Mr. Hurtado and Mr. Rondón can be tried and punished there. In fact, since *Barrios Altos*, Peru has tried numerous officials for rights violations and even sentenced President Alberto Fujimori to twenty-five years in prison for orchestrating Peru's death squads. At this writing, at long last, Mr. Hurtado and Mr. Rondón face trial for the Accomarca Massacre in Peruvian courts. The ATS and TVPA case against Mr. Rondón has been postponed pending the outcome of the Peruvian case.[87] As CJA stated, rulings by "the IACtHR and lawsuits brought by CJA on behalf of Teófila Ochoa

---

[86] Doyle interview.
[87] Center for Justice and Accountability, "Criminal Trial Starts in Peru for the Accomarca Massacre," November 18, 2010. http://cja.org/downloads/CJA%20Peru%20ENG.pdf (Last accessed on February 6, 2012).

and Cirila Pulido were instrumental in getting these cases to trial."[88] Ms. Bernabeu commented, "Thanks to the hope and persistence of the survivors of this terrible massacre, the day has finally come to obtain justice ... they are finally getting their day in Peru's court."[89] These cases demonstrate the importance of human rights NGOs in moving the process of legal justice, which can ultimately snare perpetrators all over the world. CJA orchestrated a "combined litigation strategy with the Peruvian Pro Human Rights Organization (APRODEH) ... with a goal of exposing the defendants as human rights abusers and sending them back to Peru to face criminal prosecution."[90] In Peru, victims are entitled to counsel during criminal cases, and CJA and its Peruvian NGO partners, the Institute of Legal Defense (IDL) and APRODEH, are working together to represent Ms. Ochoa and Ms. Pulido as well as other victims.

---

[88] Ibid.
[89] Ibid.
[90] Ibid.

CONCLUSION

LEGAL JUSTICE IS A PROCESS

The experiences of Wendy Méndez, Nineth Montenegro, Alejandra García, Teófila Ochoa, Cirila Pulido, and the others I analyze in this book demonstrate the fact that legal justice is a process in which truth and extra-territorial legal action are crucial elements. For Nineth Montenegro, exposing the facts of her husband's disappearance through the Diario Militar and police archives has been the most important step in that process. According to Ms. Montenegro, it was "through the international process" that this evidence was revealed.[1] For her, the conviction of two former police officials for actually carrying out the abduction was less important – "not justice," she said. Of course, for Ms. Montenegro and her daughter, Alejandra García, finding Fernando's remains and restoring his and their family's dignity is the real goal of the process.

I have described Wendy Méndez's journey along the process of justice throughout this book, culminating in the Inter-American Court decision in her favor on December 21, 2012. In an interview after this decision, Ms. Mendez told me "There is a feeling of having achieved an important part of justice … but also having done right by the disappeared, sort of like finally seeing an important result in the struggle of

---

[1] Nineth Montenegro, Radio Interview, "Corte IDH podría dictar sentencia en Caso de Desaparición de Fernando García en Ocho Meses," Emisoras Unidas 89.7, Guatemala City, May 2, 2012, http://noticias.emisorasunidas.com/noticias/primera-hora/corte-idh-podria-dictar-sentencia-caso-desaparicion-fernando-garcia-ocho-meses (Last Accessed on May 27, 2012).

decades."[2] She sees justice as a process and recognizes that her fellow HIJOS members and fellow petitioners are also part of the process of legal justice. "We are all living a different part of the process," she observed, "some people have been in this struggle since the first 28 disappeared and some only now have broken silence around what happened, but we are all in the same process and have something to give and support."

Some scholars and advocates have argued that, for transitional justice to achieve its purposes, it must be understood as a multifaceted system with social, political, economic, cultural, and legal aspects. The power of the legal element must not be overemphasized, they have argued. In this book, I have endorsed this view of transitional justice, and have argued that legal justice for human rights violations should also be conceptualized as a multifaceted process. For legal justice to achieve its full effect, and for it to contribute fully to transitional justice, it must be understood for what it is – a process. While there are important goals along the way, such as punishment and deterrence, the ultimate goal of the process is to rebuild or establish an equilibrium of human dignity in order to prevent future violence.

W. James Booth analyzed how justice efforts acknowledge the absent deceased victims and argued, "Doing justice is in part the struggle to overcome, to invert those absences by showing that what seems nonexistent and distant in fact retains a presence, one demanding a response."[3] Wendy Méndez told me that the process of justice for her is "not just about punishing the people responsible for these crimes but also about the way that we live our relationship with the dead and the disappeared."[4] "They are always present although they are absent," she explained. "We are always remembering them and some even name them in places, events and objects even though we don't know where they are."[5]

She went on to describe how the disappearance of a loved one creates a void in a family that affects everyone in that family for generations.

---

[2] Wendy Méndez, interview with the author, February 14, 2013.
[3] W. James Booth, "'From This Far Place': On Justice and Absence," *American Political Science Review* 105(4): 750–64, 756.
[4] Méndez, interview with the author, February 14, 2013.
[5] Ibid.

The granddaughters and grandsons of the disappeared are included in HIJOS meetings and in meetings dealing with the Inter-American case, and the parties to the *Gudiel* case argued that their rights were violated as well. "We have even seen them grow up in this space and struggle during at least the past seven years since we presented the case before the Commission," Ms. Méndez recalled. "The absence of the grandparents in their lives, of that generation in relation to them that could speak of the history, family stories even medical history, community, legacy, traditions, wisdom and how their absence affects them." The court recognized the impact of the disappearance on the granddaughters and grandsons. While "there's still so much we don't know, to have that recognition from the court made some of us cry and others smile."[6] Dr. Juan Romagoza, who sued the Salvadoran generals who ordered his torture in U.S. courts, also talked about finding justice for the dead and disappeared. "We've tried to solve this trauma with our silence, but, by not speaking out, we just bury our victims and the ones whom we love deeper inside. So I think it's important to start speaking out. What happened? What happened to us? How did it affect us?"[7]

TRUTH THROUGH TESTIMONY

The case studies in this book have shown clearly how important testifying is as an element of the process of legal justice. After years – sometimes decades – of state denial, the act of telling one's account to a tribunal can be somewhat liberating. It can chip away at the stubborn impunity the state has maintained. When Wendy Méndez was preparing to testify before the Inter-American Court, her lawyers cautioned her that the court might not be willing to hear her testimony regarding her rape. If the court did hear it, the lawyers warned, it might not consider it in its ruling. In the Inter-American system, the commission brings the case to the court, and in the *Gudiel* case the commission had brought the case based on the disappearances and related rights

---

[6] Ibid.
[7] Juan Romagoza Arce, "Reflections on the Verdict," http://www.cja.org/forSurvivors/reflect. doc (Last accessed September 12, 2007).

violations. Ms. Méndez's lawyers were concerned that the court would not see the rape as relevant to the case. As I described in Chapter 6, she did testify in full about the night her mother was captured, including her ordeal as she was raped by one of the soldiers. "I was quite satisfied with the fact that the judges heard my testimony and the fact that representatives of the government had to sit quietly and listen to what had happened to me," Ms. Méndez stated. She told me that days later, after she returned home, "I felt as if there was a liberation of thought, imagine my head is a house and a whole room just cleared up, walls painted light and no furniture or trace of anything that was there. It was incredible."[8]

The court ruled that the state had violated Ms. Méndez's rights by using sexual violence as a form of torture and that it also violated her rights by failing to investigate those responsible. Ms. Méndez felt vindicated by the court's ruling "because I was not expecting it to happen and because I know that this was not an isolated case, that it wasn't a mistake made by one of the soldiers, or that he just took advantage of the situation but rather a form of torture and part of the protocol during the kidnappings." Her testimony and the court's ruling helped establish the truth that sexual violence was part of the Guatemalan state's arsenal of terror.

The power of testimony as a part of the process of justice is not lost on those who would preserve impunity. As we have seen in the preceding chapters, states like Peru, El Salvador, Guatemala, and others have tried everything to silence those who would speak out. This is true, apparently, even up to moments before they are due to testify. According to Ms. Méndez, the day before the hearing before the IACtHR in the *Gudiel* case, representatives for the state of Guatemala confronted Helen Mack in the hallway at the court. They "fought and argued with Helen in the halls with a cheque in hand saying there was no need to appear in court the next day, that everyone had a price."[9]

Dr. Romagoza discussed what it meant for him to testify. "I've exposed the generals, and was able to look them in the face when the truth was being told about all the crimes that were committed," he

---

[8] Méndez, interview with the author, February 14, 2013.
[9] Ibid.

recalled. "The feeling of having done the right thing has helped me a lot to overcome that previous fear," he commented. "The whole process – especially the trial – has been crucial for my healing." Dr. Romagoza found that confronting the generals face to face was especially powerful. "Most of all, that I was there and pointed them out – that's the best possible therapy a torture survivor could have."[10]

TRUTH THROUGH DOCUMENTS

Groups like the National Security Archive have armed victims and survivors to prove the truth with secret government documents. My case studies have shown the power of documentary evidence in cases from all over the region. The Diario Militar and Guatemalan police archives have been revolutionary in transforming the process of justice in Guatemala. Kate Doyle, who has been the leader in obtaining, authenticating, and using these documents, pointed out that in the Diario case "the state has been saying from the day that each of these people was disappeared that they didn't know anything about it." However, through the Diario and archives, "now there is this terrific paper trail documenting how many times the state lied about that on paper with official signatures and stamps."[11] Though the state has denied knowledge for decades and tried to discredit the families by calling them insane, liars, leftists, and insurgents, with these documents the victims, their families, and their advocates have proof. "You suddenly have official confirmation," Ms. Doyle observed, "despite their silence, despite their obstructionism, despite their stonewalling … you have managed to get the state's confirmation of the allegations in the case." This is crucial for the broader process of legal justice as well. "It does give the cases momentum … cases that have been languishing around for decades take on new meaning and movement," Ms. Doyle argued. Documents like the Diario, the archives, and the U.S. intelligence documents can begin exposing the broader history of the

[10] Romagoza, "Reflections on the Verdict."
[11] Kate Doyle, senior analyst, National Security Archive, interview with the author, January 28, 2010.

violations. As Ms. Doyle stated, "it's a thread we can begin to pull to hopefully unravel the larger truth about what happened."[12]

For the victims these documents can be confirmation, but also can give them information on why their loved ones were targeted. Documents in the Guatemalan police archives explained how and why Fernando García was disappeared. U.S. diplomatic and intelligence documents detailed the massacre of the Jesuits and the subsequent cover-up. Of course, the Diario Militar explained why 183 people were targeted for disappearance. Ms. Méndez pointed out that the IACtHR's opinion in the Diario (*Gudiel*) case "mentions the fact that the one thing that the victims of the military diary have in common is precisely their participation in social movements and that this was the reason why the military intelligence and governments at that time considered them to be a threat to their interests." To her and her fellow petitioners, it was important for the court to recognize the truth about who the disappeared were. "The sentence itself narrates a good part of their story and how they were kidnapped and disappeared," she observed. "Now the families have somewhere in written history their names, who they were and what happened to them."[13]

HUMAN RIGHTS GROUPS

Human rights nongovernmental organizations (NGOs) are absolutely indispensible in moving the process of legal justice. As the case studies I use in this book show, nearly every landmark human rights case is litigated by human rights NGOs – usually more than one. Every case I analyze is an example of local groups working with international groups to pursue legal justice on many levels and fronts. Wendy Méndez, who cofounded HIJOS, recognized the importance of the *Gudiel* case for other human rights activists in the region. "It has much information that will be helpful for other cases in Latin America and the Caribbean." She stressed how helpful groups like the Myrna Mack Foundation and the Berkeley Law School Human Rights Clinic were

---

[12] Ibid.
[13] Méndez, interview with the author, February 14, 2013.

and are for her struggle, and "HIJOS of course played a huge part in helping me with my troubled heart."[14]

EXTRA-TERRITORIAL COURTS

Revealing the truth and proving the truth are essential elements of the process of justice, and extra-territorial courts are frequently the only venue to do so. Kate Doyle described how important it was for Guatemalan victims to testify in Spain. "One of the things that resonated for all of them is the feeling you get when you can really tell someone." "Many of them said they never could have said that in Guatemala – to the authorities, [so] to be able to say that to a judge is a really moving and powerful thing."[15]

In an interview, Ms. Méndez commented that the decision "has brought satisfaction and a level of restoring all the pain and suffering caused by the forced disappearance of our family members." She observed that "all of the family members involved in this case have felt extremely happy with the ruling and have felt like a weight has been taken off of their shoulders." The decision and others like it are important tools for strengthening efforts to overcome impunity at home. Ms. Méndez pointed out that the IACtHR decision requires the Guatemalan government to investigate the disappearances in the Diario together, as one case. This is important, Ms. Méndez explained, because, "in previous years the policy of impunity has been to separate all the cases into different investigating units as a way of scattering the family members in different directions but also as a way of putting obstacles in front of the fact that these crimes were systematic and related to one another." Victims and survivors are set to begin cases in Guatemala, including the recent case against Ríos Montt. These cases are possible, according to Ms. Méndez, "thanks to the continuous effort of the families and survivors but mainly because we finally received the sentence from the Inter-American Court, which helps us to put more political pressure on concrete actions in the justice system."[16]

[14] Ibid.
[15] Doyle, interview with the author, January 28, 2010.
[16] Méndez, interview with the author, February 14, 2013.

The search for justice brought Teófila and Cirila to courtrooms in Florida and Maryland, but what was the justice they sought? As she closed her testimony in the Hurtado case, Teófila told the court what she was seeking, "I would tell [Hurtado] to speak. Who were the ones who told him [to attack my village]? Why did they do this? My mother, the children, they were innocent. I want justice to be done."[17] Cirila told the court why she brought the case in the United States. "For us, it has been very difficult to travel all the way over here to achieve justice," she reflected. "In my town, we have spent our whole lives traumatized in this nightmare since that year when this happened." "And then in order to achieve justice, that's why I'm here, where one can tell the whole truth."[18]

RESTORING DIGNITY

The overarching purpose of the legal process is to restore human dignity to the victims and survivors and prevent future violence. Throughout this book, victims and survivors have expressed this goal. The Inter-American Court recognized the inexorable link between the right to truth and human dignity. It found that when Guatemalan officials denied the truth to the families of the disappeared it attacked their human dignity. The judges pointed out that the "deprivation of the truth about the whereabouts of a victim of forced disappearance is a form of cruel and inhuman treatment for close relatives."[19] After winning her case before the Inter-American Court, Ms. Méndez told me, "An important part of the ruling has been dignifying the fact that the disappeared were teachers, high school students, university leaders, union workers, doctors, engineers, poets and basically people that were building a better society and not the criminals the military have always made them up to be."[20]

---

[17] Transcript of Trial at 44, *Ochoa Lizarbe v. Hurtado*, No. 07–21783-CIV-JORDAN, 2008 U.S. Dist. LEXIS 109517 (S.D. Fla. March 4, 2008), 58.

[18] Ibid. at 94.

[19] *José Miguel Gudiel Álvarez and others v. Guatemala* ("Diario Militar"), No. 116/10, Case No. 12.590, December 21, 2012, para. 301, translated by the author.

[20] Méndez, interview with the author, February 14, 2013.

The Accomarca Massacre cases exposed how those who committed atrocities ignored or rejected the human dignity of their victims. According to former Truth Commission lawyer Eduardo González, "in the mind of the military authorities developing this strategy, there was no difference between the Shining Path and certain sectors of the civilian population. They were just preoccupied with destroying the organization, and for them the organization included the civilians that supported the Shining Path." He explained further that "they did not make any kind of distinction between men of military age, who could be presumably combatants for the insurgents, and women, children, the elderly."[21] The Hurtado and Rondón trials in the United States demonstrated clearly that the Accomarca Massacre and those like it were the direct result of the view that indigenous populations lacked the human worth – the dignity – of those in the military and in government. Mr. González testified, "What happened was the result of disrespect for human life in general, but in particular is a mark of the great shame of Peru, which is racism against the indigenous population." "I think that the treatment that the indigenous populations and the peasant populations received during the war [and] the complete lack of compassion that they experienced after their victimization are a mark of shame that Peru will have for centuries."[22] In addition to the dignity of the victims, this shame must be addressed by the process of legal justice. The U.S. cases, three thousand miles from Peru, were small steps in the process of doing so.

Wendy Méndez has been struggling for truth and justice since she was nine years old. She told me, "It is precisely the restoration of human dignity and the practice of living the principles of 'never again' … that we are working towards." She has lived through the many advances and retreats that are part of the process of legal justice. "It's the process, the history that is lived and written by us that is so important for justice and memory," she observed. Legal justice is a far broader concept than a guilty or not guilty verdict. Each step along the way has an effect on the victims, survivors, and societies from which these violations arise. Ms. Méndez stated, "Because in this process we heal

---

[21] Hurtado Transcript, at 125.
[22] Ibid. at 127.

and become stronger for becoming organized and collectively doing something about what happened." It is a process that is ongoing. As the appeal in the genocide case against former General Ríos Montt progresses, and Hurtado awaits his verdict in Peru, the process is ongoing. In the meantime, as Ms. Méndez told me, "We wash the old suit of my uncle so it's always fresh in the closet, or we dust my mom's old typewriter, we consider all these actions part of the process and we call this a movement." And, "if we are quiet sometimes, it's because we are rearming ourselves with hope."[23]

---

[23] Méndez, interview with the author, February 14, 2013.

INDEX